Ambivalent Childhoods

Speculative Futures and the Psychic Life of the Child

Jacob Breslow

UNIVERSITY OF MINNESOTA PRESS

MINNEAPOLIS

LONDON

Portions of chapter 1 were previously published as "Adolescent Citizenship, or Temporality and the Negation of Black Childhood in Two Eras," *American Quarterly* 71, no. 2 (June 2019): 473–94; copyright 2019 The American Studies Association. Portions of chapter 2 were published as "'There Is Nothing Missing in the Real': Trans Childhood and the Phantasmatic Body," *Transgender Studies Quarterly* 4, no. 3-4 (2017): 431–50; reprinted by permission of Duke University Press.

Published by the University of Minnesota Press
111 Third Avenue South, Suite 290
Minneapolis, MN 55401-2520
http://www.upress.umn.edu

ISBN 978-1-5179-0821-8 (hc)
ISBN 978-1-5179-0822-5 (pb)
Library of Congress record available at
https://lccn.loc.gov/2020058491.

Printed in the United States of America on
acid-free paper

The University of Minnesota is an equal-opportunity
educator and employer.

UMP BmB 2021

Contents

The Wish for Childhood

Four portraits of black children hang on a wall plastered with pink and white polka-dot wallpaper in a gallery whose plush pink carpets and pink ceiling are punctuated by a scattering of multicolored marbled balloons. In one of these portraits, a fourteen-year-old girl, playfully crossing one of her eyes and curling her bottom lip, is surrounded by a highly saturated panoply of glitter, sequins, butterflies, and foliage. An arched array of pink and purple beads encircles her head like a halo as she simultaneously returns and avoids the viewer's gaze. While each of these children are practically subsumed by the vibrant collages that embrace them like saints, her childhood vivacity contrasts her with her more earnest male peers. It draws you to her. As the subject of Ebony G. Patterson's 2016 installation for the Studio Museum in Harlem ... *when they grow up* ... this girl and her magnetism exist within the titular ellipses of Patterson's ebullient and larger-than-life life images. These ellipses, however, are not just filled with glee and exuberance. Their palindromic open-endedness marks both a statement and a question. *When* they grow up becomes a question of *if* they grow up, and Paterson's portraits, which are punctured with holes that reveal the wallpaper underneath and are decorated in a style that evokes the mournful celebration of death in Afro-Caribbean cultures, tread the line between eulogy and a prospective futurity.

Lingering in these ellipses is a wish. A wish that she will grow up, that this portrait will not be her eulogy, and that she'll experience all the joys and pains of childhood. It is a wish, that is, for childhood itself. But what is childhood? Who gets to be a child? Patterson's work, in all its colorful buoyancy, is responding to these very serious questions. Produced in direct riposte to a culture of antiblackness that, as I show throughout *Ambivalent Childhoods*, routinely disavows black childhood, these portraits simultaneously pose this line of inquiry and offer an important response. "We somehow seem to deny these children the same sense of innocence that any other child would be afforded, as if somehow they're different," Patterson says, as she explains the importance of representing black childhoods at this particular time in history, "because of their blackness, they're not allowed the possibility of humanity" (Patterson quoted in Felsenthal 2016). Asserting this young black girl's childhood in abundance, Patterson's portrait is thus not a neutral act of representation.[1] As an affirmation, it is an act of refusal and survival. Patterson's representation of this girl's childhood thus contains within it an awareness of something that I argue is vital to an analysis of childhood in the contemporary United States: There are structures of power whose harmful effects are interrupted by the rearticulation of someone's location in childhood.

As many scholars have documented, the importance of reaffirming childhood has a long history.[2] Robin Bernstein (2011), for example, writes that during the Civil Rights Movement the invocation of black childhood was a key strategy for countering the longstanding violences of white supremacy directed at black children: "When U.S. culture began, at mid-century, to libel black children as unhurt-able and unchildlike, African Americans—both children and adults—began asserting that black children were, of course, children and did, of course, feel pain" (2011, 55).[3] Across various social and political moments within American history, claiming childhood for one's self or for others—as Patterson's work does so beautifully—has been, and continues to be, an essential strategy within social justice movements. The need for this rearticulation is not, however, limited to a rebuttal of the dehumanizing and adultifying of young black girls.[4] While antiblackness has shaped the very contours of childhood from its inception, as I show throughout this book, the need to make this reaffirmation for children is an unfortunate burden that is additionally and unevenly carried by transfeminist, queer, and antideportation projects that work to mitigate the effects of racism, transmisogyny, heteronormativity, and border making. As such, critically engaging with this question of who gets to occupy childhood is of vital importance for children who are girls, trans, queer, undocumented, poor, and of color—children, in other words, who are, and have historically been, precariously understood within the frame of childhood itself.

However, implicit within this necessary assertion is the assumption, or rather the *wish*, that childhood's very confirmation can counter power's subjecting force. In *Ambivalent Childhoods* I argue that this wish—this psychic and political investment in childhood as a straightforwardly productive object—is structured by a twinned fantasy. This fantasy assumes that childhood, in its contemporary political life, is itself separable from the very things we have come to understand as race, gender, sexuality, and nation; and that the persistence and force of racism, transmisogyny, heteronormativity, and the violences of the border are not themselves co-produced with childhood as well. Interrupting these assumptions, Barrie Thorne writes:

> Different types of power—of kings over subjects, slave owners over slaves, and men over women—have been justified by defining the subordinates as "like children," inherently dependent and vulnerable, less competent, incapable of exercising full responsibility, and in need of protection. (1987, 96)

Designating marginalized populations as childlike, Thorne argues, is a tactic by which their position within hierarchical, constraining, and violent structures of power is justified and maintained.[5] Childhood, that is, functions as an exclusionary frame of protection and prioritization limited to privileged and historically contingent groups of young people, *and* as a longstanding means of marking marginalized populations as inferior.[6] Frantz Fanon, for example, describes infantilization as one of the mechanisms through which colonial and racist violence is enacted. Fanon's argument, that infantilization is a central tactic of colonial subjugation, has been elaborated on by scholars uncovering the ways in which childhood has been central to the workings of racism and sexism in a range of global contexts.[7] As Shulamith Firestone (1971) makes clear, childhood must be understood as an expansive, patriarchal power relation that requires overturning for the ways in which it mutually disenfranchises women and children.[8] While the space of childhood is therefore protective for some, enshrining their acts under the banners of innocence or ignorance, and granting them the right to inhabit dependency, or to be a recipient of care, this version of childhood is unevenly distributed. For others, childhood means living within forced dependency, being dismissed, pushed out of the public sphere, and understood as incapable, immature, and in need of discipline. Acknowledging the longstanding link between violence and the uneven and often incoherent distribution of these versions of childhood, then, begs the question of what it means to seek out inclusion within the category of "child." Does reaffirming one's location within childhood interrupt power when childhood itself is ambivalent at best, and deadly at worst?

In *Ambivalent Childhoods* I am analyzing—in critical race, transfeminist, queer, and critical migration studies, and in discursive, political, and cultural productions of race, gender, sexuality, and the border within the contemporary U.S. public sphere—who or what is included within or excluded from childhood. In the process, this book offers new theoretical interpretations of childhood in its particular connections to Black Lives Matter and the murder of Trayvon Martin; trans justice and antitrans discrimination; reproductive justice and the sexually active queer child; and the intergenerational politics of antideportation movements. As a whole, the book interrogates various deployments of childhood across four identity-based sites of contestation over national belonging in the first two decades of the twenty-first century.[9] Importantly, however, as inclusion and exclusion do not align straightforwardly or respectively with social justice or injustice, this book does not put forward an argument for a more universal inclusion of marginalized individuals and populations within the frame of childhood. Nor does it argue that childhood is too tainted an object to be demanded for in the moments it is resoundingly denied to those experiencing intersectional forms of violence and erasure. Rather, while it understands the impulse behind both of these arguments, it prioritizes interrogating the psychic work that the desire for inclusion facilitates, and the political violence that exclusion *and inclusion* allow for. As such, *Ambivalent Childhoods* argues that childhood requires sustained attention as a complex and ambivalent site for negotiating national belonging and contesting the workings of power, and not just for children.

Childhood does not only pertain to young people, and not all young people, infants included, are understood to occupy childhood equally, or ever. Here, I follow a long line of scholars who understand that biological definitions of childhood—childhood as pertaining only to a particular age group—both claim too little and too much about who occupies childhood and what work childhood does.[10] On the one hand, I follow Jo-Ann Wallace's contention that

> the mobilization of the figure of "the child" in response to a perceived set of social problems, regardless of whether children as a specific group are at "real" risk, has "real" effects on our productions of "childhood" and the child-subject, and ultimately on the lives of children. (1995, 297)

Along these lines, I struggle against the impetus to easily separate out the "figure of the child" from the "real" lives of "actual" children.[11] Put another way, I do not assume that "real children" precede "the idea" of childhood. Rather, I argue that the two inform one another in dynamic ways that tend to expel or ensnare various bodies, subjects, and experiences from, or within, the categories of children and childhood. On the other hand, learning from the insights of Erica Meiners (2016), Heaven Crawley (2007), and Ishita Pande (2012), among others, I understand the digits of age to be less evidence of one's location within childhood than the contingent and contested effects of carceral, racist, and colonial power.[12] Age no more determines one's location in or beyond childhood, these scholars make clear, than a racist judge referring a young black boy to adult court, or an immigration officer assuming that an asylum-seeking child, pregnant from rape and lacking an official birth certificate, cannot be age-assessed as a minor because she has a sexual "history" (Crawley 2007, 114).[13] The meanings attached to age, in other words, are not ahistorical nor universal, and the "facts" of age are easily rebuffed by the illogics of racism, sexism, and coloniality. Childhood, that is, is not an objective category. It does more than simply describe someone's belonging to a particular cohort; it carries multiple, contested and ambivalent meanings that have extraordinary implications, particularly for those staking their claim for belonging and justice on the wish for inclusion within it.

Speculative Politics

Embracing the ambivalence of childhood, this book expands upon the questions with which I opened. Interrogating the role of childhood in shaping and challenging the disposability of young black life, the steadfastness of the gender binary, the queer life of children's desires, and the deportability of migrants, *Ambivalent Childhoods* asks: What does childhood *do* and for whom? In what moments? What *else* could childhood do? And what would it take to allow it to do so? These questions are speculative ones. Answering them requires, in other words, a bit of conjecture. A stab in the dark.

There are two definitions of speculative that are central to my project's attempts to reimagine the work that childhood might do.[14] The first defines, and often disregards, the speculative as being engaged in, or based upon, theory or conjecture, rather than knowledge or evidence. However, learning from decades of feminist epistemologists who have called into question what counts as evidence,[15] and in framing childhood not as an empirical fact but as an ambivalent power relation, I reinterpret this definition as forming a theory without knowing in advance what that articulation will bring about in the world. "The speculative," Mark Rifkin writes, "opens the potential for acknowledging a plurality of legitimate, nonidentical truth claims, none of which should be taken as the singular and foundational way that the real is structured" (2019, 8).[16] Here *Ambivalent Childhoods* draws on a range of evidence, from scholarship to testimonials, films, newspapers and online blogs, social media, artwork, federal and local law, interviews, autobiographies, and personal narratives. My resoundingly interdisciplinary approach is necessary, I argue, to track the multiple registers of childhood in its social and psychic life. It is additionally necessary in order to articulate the speculative politics of the book, as cultural productions, aesthetics, cinema, and creative writing practices of various kinds make possible and proximate the alternative worlds that must come into being in order for childhood to have a different social and political life.

Along these lines, more is taking place within Patterson's portraits than a straightforward desire for these children's inclusion within childhood. These are portraits meant to simultaneously evoke what Jacqueline Rose calls the "adult's desire for the child" (1984, 3) and to trouble that very desire. Describing what she calls "the impossible relation between adult and child" (1984, 1) through the language of desire, Rose writes: "Desire [refers] to a form of investment by the adult in the child, and to the demand made by the adult on the child as the effect of that investment, a demand which fixes the child and then holds it in place" (1984, 3–4).

Childhood, in this sense, is not just a time of one's life, nor a description of a series of ontological characteristics like innocence or dependency, it is rather a container for a series of investments. This is something that those of us who have experienced childhood—and are still living it beyond its normative tenure—are intimately aware of. The meanings we attach to our own childhoods not only grant us our own sense of "interiority," as Carolyn Steedman (1995) so beautifully argues, but also become integral to what we understand all childhoods to be, and who a child is or is not. As Rose (1984) argues, childhood is primarily the site of the adult's psychic and discursive self-representation, and thus adults—myself included—use acts of projection and transference that, to varying success, provide themselves with a sense of coherence. Naming the wish that lingers in the ellipses of Patterson's portraits as a wish for childhood, then, I am arguing that it is more than just a hope that this girl will grow up. It is a wish that all the intimate attachments one has to childhood—as an idea and an identification—might have a life that has a future as well. To wish that this girl inhabit childhood is also, in a very real sense, to wish that childhood itself have different contours. It is to wish that childhood becomes a space of care and protection for those who have so resolutely been excluded from the protections of innocence. This is what is so alluring about Patterson's portraits. They represent not childhood itself, but rather the desire for childhood. Yet this wish, Patterson makes clear, is an ambivalent one. Punctured, or wounded, and overflowing their borders, the portraits represent both the excesses of childhood, as well as its fractures. They represent the need for childhood and the impossibility of childhood to ever meet that need. Patterson's portraits are interrogating the very question of what it means to define childhood in a particular way, to fix the child as a static object of desire, as if capturing it in a finite way might resolve the violences that are constitutive of it.[17] Posing this paradox while simultaneously exposing the ruptures and superfluities of childhood, Patterson suggests we speculate about what childhood might be otherwise.

Following Patterson's lead, the speculative politics that I seek to articulate here shares some critical terrain with, but importantly differs from, the prefigurative politics of performativity (Butler 1990), fugitivity (Hartman 2019), anteriority (Campt 2017), and the "not yet here" of queerness (Muñoz 2009). While performativity informs how I read some of the moments in which children, of all ages, engage in the production of new meanings for childhood, my project is not just about fleeting and sustained moments in which individuals or collectives act to resignify childhood. A speculative politics of childhood does not require, in other words, a child-subject to inhabit its enactment. In this sense, it differs from Tina Campt's "anteriority" (2017). Defining anteriority as a black feminist grammar, Campt writes:

> The grammar of black feminist futurity that I propose here is a grammar of possibility that moves beyond a simple definition of the future tense as *what will be* in the future. It moves beyond the future perfect tense of *that which will have happened* prior to a reference point in the future. It strives for the tense of possibility that grammarians refer to as the future real conditional or *that which will have had to happen.* (2017, 17)

For Campt, that is, anteriority is a prefigurative act of living a different future now. Across *Ambivalent Childhoods* I read with Campt, and

I learn from her capacity to articulate futures that must be enacted in the present. But there are also moments across this book in which, while pushing back against the now, I am not as clear about the terms of the future that must become. Here José Esteban Muñoz's formulation of queerness as the longing for the "then and there" of queer futurity (2009, 1) informs my own speculative politics. "Queerness," Muñoz writes, "is a structuring and educated mode of desiring that allows us to see and feel beyond the quagmire of the present" (2009, 1). This desire names the need for the future, and is the very standpoint from within which that future must be imagined, but it does not know the terms of this future in advance. My project shares Muñoz's desire for a then and there, but unlike Muñoz's queerness, its central objects—childhoods and the wishes invested within them—are not inherently utopian. Understanding childhood to be an *ambivalent* object, my speculative approach to childhood seeks to open up the potential for futures in which childhood might find different contours, or none at all.[18]

If there were any doubt that childhood needs new parameters, a cursory look to its histories of violent effects would be in order. And yet, while *Ambivalent Childhoods* is not a historical account of childhood, it both learns from a breadth of scholars producing histories of the child, and takes on the ethical and political call of what Hartman (2008) and Clare Hemmings (2018) call speculative histories. For both Hartman and Hemmings, speculative histories are necessary, particularly for archival research, because the archive is structured by racism and homophobia, and thus any attempts to find black, queer subjects will be mediated by these structures of erasure and violence.[19] In "Venus in Two Acts," Hartman insists that refusing these terms requires producing "speculative arguments" that understand creative approaches to archival research as being a means of "tell[ing] an impossible story [in order to] amplify the impossibility of its telling" (2008, 11). Similarly, Hemmings argues that the creative writing of speculative histories is required to tell a narrative that "eludes the historian's gaze, but which cannot not have been true" (2018, 35). Across the book, I borrow this alternative epistemological approach to evidence and imagination that is central to Hartman's and Hemmings's work. For if the contemporary life of childhood is wholly determined by whiteness, for example, then, as Patterson suggests, alternative modes of representing, desiring, and defining childhood are required. These would be acts of production and refusal that both suggest that childhood must become something anew, and that there are children—black, trans, queer, undocumented—whose "beautiful experiments" with childhood (to again paraphrase Hartman) mark their existence in the face of vast structures that seek to render them impossible. My project, however, is not archival, and thus its speculative readings of childhood are not speculative histories. Indeed, this book sets its sights on the contestations over belonging that are taking place through the child at the start of the twenty-first century. Seeking out a future in which childhood might signify differently, my project, in its analysis of the contemporary moment, emerges from and requires, I argue, a different attitude towards the role of discovery and exposure.

As a way of emphasizing this point, I turn to one of the more powerful accounts of the complex history of childhood's inclusions and exclusions, Toby Rollo's "The Color of Childhood: The Role of the Child/Human Binary in the Production of Anti-Black Racism" (2018). In this article, Rollo argues that "It is common for theorists of race and colonialism to interpret violence against racialized youth as a case of children being treated like adults and excluded from the protective innocence of childhood" (2018, 308). Against this assumption, Rollo asserts that "Black peoples, especially youth, are exposed to violence *precisely because* they are viewed as children" (2018, 308–9, emphasis added). For Rollo, this common misinterpretation—which I am suggesting might more usefully be understood as fantasy than historical ignorance—requires a critical hesitation that only a more carefully delineated history of childhood-as-violence can provide. Rollo writes:

> Without a robust understanding of how childhood grounds modern logics of domination, emancipatory movements will likely reinforce those logics. . . . In a racial order predicated on the designation of childhood as a site of naturalized criminality, violence, and servitude, to which black peoples are principally relegated, not only will appealing

to the category of childhood fail to protect black youth it will reaffirm
an antiquated and pernicious misopedic distinction between human
beings. (2018, 323–24)[20]

As Rollo helpfully elucidates, inclusion within the category of childhood has not guaranteed protection. Indeed, for many, the opposite
was the case. At the same time, more needs to be said about the biopolitical effects of the protective inclusion within childhood, as a
number of historians of childhood have documented how the frame
of childhood came into being in line with various forms of power.[21]
According to Philippe Ariès, author of *Centuries of Childhood* (1962),
childhood initially emerged as a technology by which the bourgeoisie
could invest in, expand, and preserve its well-being and survival.[22] If
we understand this act of "preserving" particular classes of individuals
though childhood as being a biopolitical maneuver, then the "innocence" of childhood is again rendered a construction—rather than
inherent—and its distribution is an act of distinguishing who must
live and who may die.[23]

While Ariès demonstrates that childhood was initially produced
through the intensification of knowledges that set out to mark the
importance of wealthy European boys during the seventeenth and
eighteenth centuries, its function as a modality of power has proliferated in the contemporary moment.[24] As Rebekah Sheldon writes: "the
child [that] exited the nineteenth century as the nexus point coordi-
nating life, species, and reproduction with history, race, and nation . . .
persists into the twentieth century as the subject of biopolitical management" (2016, 3). Here, following Michel Foucault ([1975–76] 1997;
[1977] 1995; [1978] 1990), Jo-Ann Wallace (1995), Karen Smith (2014),
and others, we can think of the ever increasing sets of knowledges
within medical, criminological, and sociological disciplines about
how to raise healthy, successful children—including the biotechni-
cal surveillance of childhood obesity (Butler-Wall 2015), the regimes
of truth about "good" parenting located within what Hartman calls
the "afterlife of slavery" (2007, 6; cf. Spillers 1987), or, as Meiners
(2016) so clearly delineates, the productivity of childhood as "an ar-
tifact" within an ever-expansive carceral regime—as encouraging the

regulating and disciplining of individuals and populations through childhood in order to maximize the life of (some of) the population. These regimes of truth are clearly not just about the effects they have for "actual" children; they are also about the surveillance of racialized, gendered, sexual, and migrant populations and the value placed on them. As such, while I acknowledge the importance and value of this type of critical exposure, much of my work in *Ambivalent Childhoods* embarks on a slightly different trajectory, one that bears a different relation to epistemology.

"What," Eve Kosofsky Sedgwick asks, "does knowledge *do*—the pursuit of it, the having and exposing of it, the receiving again of knowledge of what one already knows?" (2003, 124). Asking this question in her provocative "Paranoid Reading and Reparative Reading; or, You're So Paranoid, You Probably Think This Essay is about You," Sedgwick asks us to consider other questions beyond "Is a particular piece of knowledge true, and how can we know?" (2003, 124). Sedgwick asks these questions of critical theory in the hope that its assumption that exposure is *the* means of interrupting power might be rethought. For what, she asks, is the purpose of exposing state violence when the violence of the state isn't hidden in the first place?

> Why bother exposing the ruses of power in a country where, at any given moment, 40 percent of young black men are enmeshed in the penal system? In the United States and internationally, while there is plenty of hidden violence that requires exposure there is also, and increasingly, an ethos where forms of violence that are hypervisible from the start may be offered as an exemplary spectacle rather than remain to be unveiled as a scandalous secret. (2003, 140)

Along these lines, I wonder what it would mean to call the violences directed at black, trans, queer, and undocumented children a scandalous secret? Can one suggest that the violences directed at these children—mass incarceration, police violence, homelessness, removal from the public sphere, pathologization, and forced separation from their parents, just to name a few—simply need to be exposed in order for them to cease? Would this exposure interrupt the demand for these children to be included within childhood? Or is this demand about something else? Given that the violences of childhood and infantilization have been well established and yet have not altered the force of the demand for childhoods *to be recognized*, I argue that something other than ignorance or knowledge—as a basis for action regarding the normative claims for or against inclusion—is required here. To paraphrase what Sedgwick says about the performativity of knowledge: uncovering more knowledge about childhood's violent history is, it turns out, separable from the question of whether or not a social movement should spend its energies uncovering that history. "For someone to have an unmystified, angry view of large and genuinely systematic oppressions," Sedgwick writes, "does not intrinsically or necessarily enjoin that person to any specific train of epistemological or narrative consequences" (2003, 124). It is in this vein that I consider the demand for inclusion within childhood to be less historical amnesia—as Rollo implies—than to be motivated by a wish. Rather than suggest, in other words, that the demand for inclusion be "corrected" with a proper historical account of childhood's violent histories, I am suggesting that there is something at stake in this wish for childhood that needs to be taken seriously. Motivated by a wish, the demand for childhood might thus be understood as a form of speculative politics, an attempt at bringing about a different series of meanings and effects of childhood without the assurance that they will stick.

The Psychic Life of the Child

Rather than address childhood as an object to be for or against, *Ambivalent Childhoods* defines childhood as a series of ambivalent yet productive investments. Here the second definition of speculative comes to the fore. In the world of finance, a speculative investment is one that involves a high risk of loss. It is undertaken with the prospect of success, but without an established failsafe. *Ambivalent Childhoods* reroutes this definition away from economics and through psychoanalytic understandings of investment as related to desire, object-cathexis, wish fulfillment, and attachment. Doing so, it undertakes forms of analysis and modes of reading that might be considered risky, but it engages them in the hope that these forms of intervention might be worth it. Indeed, my turn to psychoanalysis, and my particular affinity for Freudian psychoanalysis, might itself be considered fraught. Freudian psychoanalysis is not, perhaps, an obvious place to begin to think through a critique of the ways in which childhood works both for and against contemporary social justice movements.[25] As a field that has been rightfully castigated for its racist, misogynist, homophobic, and transphobic frameworks, a careful resistance to psychoanalysis is certainly warranted.[26] In the introduction to their jointly written book *Racial Melancholia, Racial Dissociation* (2019), David Eng and Shinhee Han, for example, argue that psychoanalysis has been slow to think through the social life of power beyond seeing racism as an effect of individual neuroses, phobias, or traumas (2019, 5). They write: "Broadly speaking, both psychoanalytic theorists and clinicians have been slow to examine how histories of race and colonial modernity implicitly frame their field's evolution—its dominant paradigms and theoretical assumptions" (2019, 6). And yet, rather than abandon psychoanalysis, they seek to interrupt the field's elision of race and coloniality as formational both to psychic life and to the clinic, while at the same time arguing that it is crucial to consider the interchange between the psychic and the social. Taking on this challenge, I follow in the footsteps of queer and critical race scholars such as Butler (1997), Ranjana Khanna (2003), Gail Lewis (2014; 2017), Hortense Spillers (1996), Antonio Viego (2007), and others, who insist that one cannot have a full understanding of power without an understanding of power's incorporation into the psyche, *and* that psychoanalytic concepts such as disavowal, projection, melancholia, and loss are absolutely necessary tools for interrogating the social world.

In *The Psychic Life of Power* (1997), Butler argues that any analysis of the social life of power is inadequate without an interrogation of power's psychic life:

> If, following Foucault, we understand power as *forming* the subject as well, as providing the very condition of its existence and the trajectory of its desire, then power is not simply what we oppose but also, in a strong sense, what we depend on for our existence. . . . Thus, if

submission is a condition of subjection, it makes sense to ask: What is the psychic form that power takes? (1997, 2)

Because power takes a psychic form, the proliferative life of power must be understood and analyzed at the level of the psyche, and through a psychoanalytic approach. Following Butler, from whom I take up an affinity for Freud, I argue that the uneven deployment of childhood across various populations must be understood as a form of wish fulfillment, disavowal, and projection of political, subjective, and group traumas and anxieties spurned by the complexities of racial, gendered, sexual, and national belonging. Undertaking what Eng and Han (2000, 669) describe as a depathologized psychoanalytic approach, *Ambivalent Childhoods* foregrounds psychic processes as central to the violent illogics of political violence that have both terrified and, in some ways immobilized, the liberal-progressive wing of American politics for the past several decades.[27] Each of the four central chapters of the book are thus organized not just around a particular social movement or struggle for belonging but also after a corresponding psychoanalytic process and analytic—disavowal, projection, desire, and dream-work, respectively—that I argue helps us reconceptualize the usefulness of childhood and psychoanalysis for enduring the complexities of the ongoing present. Because these reconceptualizations align with ongoing and foundational debates within critical theory—about racial justice, progress, and representation in the face of antiblack state violence; the shared terrain of trans and feminist politics; the critical capacity of "queer" to account for an ever expanding list of sexual politics; and the relationship between citizenship, national belonging, and migration—my analyses across *Ambivalent Childhoods* suggest that the psychic life of power has implications for these political and theoretical projects more broadly.

Embarking on this psychoanalytic exploration of childhood, *Ambivalent Childhoods* argues that childhood needs to be thought about as a set of investments that, in Gayatri Chakravorty Spivak's words, "we cannot not want" (1993, 45). Spivak's quote—initially in response to feminism's relationship to liberalism (1993, 42–46)—has been taken up across many different debates, but I want, for now, to spend a bit more time with the notion of "wanting" that structures her notion of "cannot not." Giving a reading of this wanting, Wendy Brown writes, "Spivak's grammar suggests a condition of constraint in the production of our desire so radical that it perhaps even turns that desire against itself, foreclosing our hopes in a language we can neither escape nor wield on our own behalf" (2000, 230). Indeed, Spivak speaks in a similar grammar across her work. In "Righting Wrongs" (2004), for example, Spivak writes: "Neither [the assumption that it is natural to be angled toward the other, nor the question of responsibility being a begged question] can survive without the other, if it is a just world *that we seem to be obliged to want*" (2004, 537, emphasis added). Here I want to think with Spivak's framing of the ambivalence at the heart of the political together with a psychoanalytic framing of desire, in order to ask, What might this pairing allow for a theorization of childhood? What does it mean to want an object, world, or relationship? And what happens when the wanting is so strong that the demand itself slips from wish to wish-fulfillment?[28] To answer these questions, which structure much of the analysis across the four central chapters, I reframe Spivak's and Brown's questions of wanting and constraint in the production of desire through the psychoanalytic concept of cathexis as theorized by Freud. In so doing, I argue that understanding childhood through the language of cathexis allows for a revisiting of the wish for childhood in productive ways. Thinking about childhood as cathexis, I argue, helps understand why childhood continues to be desired despite the knowledge that it is, and has been, a site of violence for so many.

In "Mourning and Melancholia" ([1917] 1957), Freud describes the relationships one has with objects of love through the language of "object-cathexis." This object-cathexis, he writes, is a "great expense of time and cathectic energy . . . in which the libido is bound to the object" ([1917] 1957, 245). Object-cathexes, as the result of intense investments in libidinal energy, are not merely formed in relation to a particular person (such as a loved one), they are additionally formed by attachments to objects "of a more ideal kind" (245). The cathected object, in other words, is one whose conditions of attachment are structured through an idyllic thing-presentation of the object within the unconscious (256). In *The Ego and the Id* ([1923a] 1961), Freud describes the mother as the infant's primary and original love object, and as the infant's first idealized object-cathexis. In his outlining of the boy's development of his super-ego, Freud writes:

> At a very early age, the little boy develops an object-cathexis for his mother . . . [whereas] the boy deals with his father by identifying himself with him. For a time these two relationships proceed side by side, until the boy's sexual wishes in regard to his mother become more intense and his father is perceived as an obstacle to them. . . . An ambivalent attitude to his father and an object-relation of solely affectionate kind to his mother make up the content of the simple positive Oedipus complex in a boy. ([1923a] 1961, 31–32)[29]

Cathexes, then, are libidinal and psychic investments in objects (both real and phantasmatic) wherein the object's thing-presentation to the unconscious is primarily structured not through identification, but rather through idealization, pure affection (or, alternatively, abhorrence), and, importantly, a refusal (via repression) to consciously acknowledge the object's ambivalence. The object-cathexis is thus structured by a wish that one places within that object: a desire, structured by the id, for a particular version of the object, and what it provides. To approach childhood as a form of cathexis is thus to understand it as an object, real and phantasmatic, whose confines and existence are integral to the psychic attachments and libidinal investments that people place within it. It is to understand that childhood is an object deeply laden with psychic energy and investment whose constitutional ambivalence we've repressed. Indeed, it is precisely because the concept of childhood functions as an object-cathexis that the moments in which it is deployed and demanded expand to include all types of negotiations and contradictions: from using childhood to resolve a conflict with one's own understanding of self, to, as *Ambivalent Childhoods* more specifically grapples with, the use of childhood in resolving anxieties about race, gender, sexuality, and national belonging.

Like the child's mother in Freud's mapping of the Oedipal complex, the cathected object of the child is often flattened, idealized, and

invested in precisely because it provides psychic and material nourishment or sustenance. The wish for childhood responds to historical
and ongoing violences, its reaffirmation is itself a form of political and
psychic nourishment even when the only thing it can provide is wish-
fulfillment. This is because, as Rose argues, the very idea of the child,
one that is premised on childhood being a universal and static thing,
is itself central to how race, gender, and sexuality are experienced
and enacted: "the very idea of speaking to *all* children serves to close
off a set of cultural divisions, divisions in which not only children, but
we ourselves, are necessarily caught. . . . class, culture, and literacy—
divisions which undermine any generalized concept of the child"
(1984, 7). The generalized idea of the child is, Rose makes clear, both
mired in, yet dismissing of, these divisions. Constitutive of the figure
of the child, Lauren Berlant (1997) and James Kincaid (1998) eluci-
date, are a series of absences that allow it to hold a range of projections.
As Berlant writes, the American child becomes an image that is "not
yet bruised by history, not yet caught up in the processes of secular-
ization and sexualization; not yet caught in the confusing and exciting
identity exchanges made possible by mass consumption and ethnic,
racial, and sexual mixing" (1997, 6). For Kincaid, this "not yet" characteristic of childhood is articulated as "flatness," and it is produced
as desirable because, as he writes, "flatness signifies nothing at all and
thus doesn't interfere with our projections" (1998, 17). In this vein, Berlant argues that the vacated figure of the child functions as "a *stand-in*
for a complicated and contradictory set of anxieties and desires about
national identity" (1997, 6). In a political moment where the affective
and material consequences of identity and belonging are experienced
as both deeply traumatic and lifesaving, both unbearable and intimately yearned for in public and private life, it is perhaps no wonder
that childhood, as an object that so easily avows and disavows these
complexities, holds investment as an object that might resolve these
tensions on its own.

In the contemporary political landscape, Freud's elaboration
on the development of object-cathexes is additionally illustrative
for thinking through the workings of social power wherein he understands object-cathexes to be formed not just in relationship to

nourishment but also to prohibition. The cathected object is often cathected in relation to, and intensified in response to, a structuring barrier to the fulfillment of the wish it provides. Mediating his recognition of his mother's inherent relationality, Freud writes, the boy develops both an identification with the father—"You *ought to be* like this (like your father)" ([1923a] 1957, 34)—as well as a separation from the father: "You *may not be* like this (like your father) . . . you may not do all that he does; some things are his prerogative" (34). The father, understood not as the literal father, but as a "dictatorial 'Thou shalt'" (55), operates here as a set of structural conditions under which the Oedipal wish cannot be fulfilled. Theorizing the work of childhood in this context thus means that any analysis of its deployment must locate the wish invested in childhood to be constituted in relationship with, and to be intensified by, the structures—both real and fantasmatic—that oppose it. Here, as I discuss throughout the book, we must understand that part of what motivates contemporary politics are not just positive affects attached to people's sense of justice and belonging but are also various forms of hostilities and traumas that are felt to be spurned by prohibition.

On one hand, then, we can thus understand how and why the child becomes so vital for social justice movements seeking redress and belonging in the face of vast structures of violence and injustice. Childhood, as a stand-in for contestations over national belonging and social justice, gets mobilized with the wish that its professed nourishment—a nourishment whose uneven distribution is known yet repressed—might help us resolve these very tensions. This is particularly the case, it should be said, when the prohibitions being experienced are systemic and interpersonal violences directed at those understood to be children. On the other hand, however, if anything has become clear in the first two decades of the twenty-first century, it is that social justice movements no longer have ownership over the language of prohibition or victimhood.[30] The virulent tone of antitrans politics, the rise in nationalist far-right populisms, and the terms of "postracial" claims to white injury are all, in perverse ways, motivated by fantasies of prohibition. Spurned by fears of social and political abandonment of America's "greatness," as well as anger at the alleged governmental capitulation to "political correctness gone awry," conservative politics has been emboldened. Importantly, of course, these threatening forces need have no material hold: the fantasy that they might, however, is often enough to instigate a heightening of one's object-cathexis. Along these lines, what makes childhood dangerous is not so much its history as a subject position that was, and is, constituted by violence. Rather, childhood is dangerous because the investments cathected within it provide nourishment without discretion. Put differently, childhood is an object of heightened importance within all sides of the political, not just because it figures the future, as Lee Edelman (2004) argues, but also because it operates as a cathected object that, in its capacity to both avow and disavow the pains and pleasures of subjectivity, provides the nourishment of wish-fulfillment in the face of a political landscape that often feels insurmountable.

Childhoods

Across the four main chapters of this book, I work to think through the moments in which childhood becomes a stand-in for, or cathexis of, contestations over race, gender, sexuality, and national belonging. Doing so, I argue that disavowal, projection, desire, and dream-work are not just important processes to unpack within psychoanalysis but are also social modes of relation and tools of analysis that help us understand what childhood does as a cathected object, and for whom. This mode of analysis is not meant to offer a pathologizing diagnosis. Rather, my intention here is to use these tools in a generative sense, to seek out speculative understandings of what these psychoanalytic frameworks might offer for analyses of the mired present. This book, however, is not just interested in the demands that adults make on behalf of the child. It is also interested in thinking through what childhood offers, both politically and psychically, to those understood as children. While I cannot claim to know, or speak for, anyone's psychic life, my speculative reading of childhood and what it offers for the social world seeks to examine what childhood might offer for adults as well as for children. Central to this approach is the recognition that children—however defined—are agentic subjects whose worlds, both social and psychic, need to be taken seriously.[31] This does not mean that I am seeking out "authentic" voices of "real" children (as if this authenticity were possible or desirable).[32] Instead, I am interested in tracing out what childhood does, or what else it might do, for those understood to reside within, or on the precipice of, childhood. Each chapter, then, follows a range of children who want from adults as much as adults want from them.[33] Here the psychic life of the child is not just the adult fantasy of that life but is additionally the demands, investments, pleasures, and ambivalences that children themselves find within the variations of childhoods that they inhabit and contest, even if only for a short while. Across the book, I refer to all the central children by their first names when possible. For some children, like Coy, this is important because doing so validates her chosen name. For other children, like Trayvon, this practice of using a first name is important because it locates him more in the realm of childhood than adulthood. While there is a risk that doing so might come off as informal or disrespectful, especially in the wake of Trayvon's murder, I am following Gayle Salamon's lead, as set out in *The Life and Death of Latisha King* (2018, 23), wherein she argues for the importance of using the names of children—both alive and dead—that they used for themselves.

Chapter 1, "Disavowing Black Childhood: Trayvon Martin, Adolescent Citizenship, and Antiblackness," begins with the tragic murder of Trayvon Martin in February 2012. Taking place just as I was starting this project, his death, as well as the political landscape that emerged in its wake, have profoundly shaped the book. Murdered on his way home from a local store by a vigilante on neighborhood watch, Trayvon received no justice from the courts, nor, subsequently, did his family. His death was deemed justifiable despite nationwide protests and the formation of the Black Lives Matter movement, and George Zimmerman, the man who killed him, walked free. Interrogating the visual and discursive landscape that arose in the aftermath, this chapter pays attention to how racially bifurcated notions of childhood and adolescence were central to the national debate about Trayvon and, by proxy, black citizenship, black belonging, and black critique. It argues that various forms of disavowal—of the ongoing life

of antiblackness, of black childhood, and of Trayvon's humanity—
structure the racial life of the child. Seeking to understand the coming
together of childhood and adolescence within the broader historical
life of antiblackness, this chapter offers the framework of *adolescent
citizenship*. Adolescent citizenship, it argues, is a produced relation
between black citizens and the nation that maintains the state's persistent and insidious paternalism, and additionally interrupts the
adolescent citizen's demand for rights under the guise of the subject's, and the demand's, inappropriate timing. In this sense, it argues
that the incessant representations of Trayvon as a troubled teenager
worked not just to disavow his childhood innocence but additionally
to frame those advocating on his behalf as similarly positioned within
a liminal and juvenile space of citizenship and belonging. Against
this context of antiblack disavowal, the chapter interrogates the
speculative question of what might be required in order to *avow* black
childhood. Pushing back against normative claims to this avowal, it
seeks alternative articulations that refuse to engage in the discourses
of antiblackness.

Chapter 2, "Transphobia as Projection: Trans Childhoods and the
Psychic Brutality of Gender," also centers around a child who was discursively pushed out of childhood, but the hostilities directed toward
this child were grounded in transmisogyny rather than antiblackness.
In December 2012, Coy Mathis, a six-year-old trans girl, was denied
access to the girls' restrooms at her school under the justification that
her "future adult male sex organ" (as her school district's lawyer referred to it) would make the other girls currently using the restroom
feel uncomfortable. This exclusion claimed to be protecting young
girls even as it directed its violences at a young girl. Responding to this
act, this chapter centrally asks how childhood works for and against
a transfeminist politics. Seeking to understand the transmisogyny
directed at Coy as being an effect of the psychic life of gender, this
chapter argues that the violence of sociocultural norms about femininity and the insipid hierarchy that marks girls' bodies as inadequate
is what was being projected onto Coy's body in the district's fantasy of
Coy's adult penis being the source of discomfort. Doing so, the chapter puts Freudian and Lacanian understandings of the penis/phallus

into conversation with trans scholarship, and in an attempt at thinking expansively about the role that projection and childhood play within trans affirmation, a collection of narratives of trans childhood. Analyzing these narratives, this chapter argues that both trans-affirmative and transphobic positions that negotiate the temporality of the trans child do so in nuanced and complex ways that structurally compliment, rather than challenge, each other's terms. Unpacking the work of childhood ambivalence within a number of trans narratives, this chapter resists linear notions of embodiment and instead argues for a transfeminist politics of multiple embodied temporalities that emerge out of the ambiguities, possibilities, and tensions of gendered identification within childhood. Doing so, I conclude by providing a speculative reading of Céline Sciamma's *Tomboy* (2011), a film about a young girl named Laure who introduced herself to a new group of friends as a boy named Mikael. Approaching Laure and Mikael together—understanding these two children as existing simultaneously and in opposition throughout the film—risks negating one at the expense of the other but might also allow for an exploration of, or at least a playfulness with, the gendered attachments and refusals that could be possible for a transfeminist politics of childhood.

Chapter 3, "Desiring the Child: Queerness, Motherhood, and the Analyst," extends *Ambivalent Childhoods'* interrogation of the relationship between the psychic life of the child and contemporary demands for belonging by taking up children whose relationships to life are defined through an all-too-early excessiveness of their desire. It begins with a description of an event I organized in 2009 that brought together a local community in Northern California to celebrate the tenacity of queer and trans youth. At this specific year's event, a hypersexualized provocative dance of a gay twelve-year-old, mixed-race boy caused an ambivalent mix of both intense discomfort and complex identification from the audience. This negotiation between desire, identification, anxiety, and a queer child's performative disruption of a shared queer space functions as the starting point for this chapter's investigation of queer theory's turn to the child and the ambivalent relationship between childhood, queerness, and desire. Under what terms are queer children celebrated, and embraced, this chapter asks, given all their—and perhaps our—ambivalence, complexities, and desires? Exploring this question, the chapter's main focus is on how the "queer child" emerged in queer theory, what psychic investments (in queerness and in childhood) shape its contours, and what the gaps are—particularly in relationship to motherhood, feminist theory, and reproduction—in theorizing it. Specifically, this chapter argues that queer theory's own attachments to the child are productively thrown into disarray by attending to the queer child's own desires. It makes this argument by both exploring queer attachments to antinormativity, and by offering its own—perhaps risky—queer child. Embracing the complexities of a queer, racialized, and reproductive child, this chapter takes Aviva Victor, the central character of Todd Solondz's film *Palindromes* (2004), as its focal child. It uses the film's casting of multiple actors for Aviva as a way into speculating about different terms of belonging for queer, racialized, and reproductive subjects within queer theory and within the sexual politics of the contemporary United States.

The final chapter, "Undocumented Dream-Work: Intergenerational Migrant Aesthetics and the Parricidal Violence of the Border," interrogates the psychic life of the child in the lead up to, and aftermath of, the failure to get the Obama administration to pass the Development, Relief, and Education for Alien Minors (DREAM) Act in 2010. Integral to the discourses surrounding the DREAM Act was the framing of the innocent migrant child: the child brought to the United States through "no fault of their own." The innocence of this child was predicated on what this chapter identifies as parricide: nationalist and anti-migrant state violence contingent on severing the parent–child relationship by naming the child as separable from the parent and insisting that the parent is substitutable with the state. While DREAMers and their allies knew that childhood and parricide were dangerous terms to be relied upon, the deployment of childhood within the DREAMers' rhetoric was pursued nonetheless because childhood operated as a wish fulfillment: the evocation of childhood was assumed to bring about the act's passage almost in and of itself. Sitting with the ambivalence of wish fulfillment in the wake of the act's failure, this chapter moves into psychoanalytic and speculative frameworks by engaging with the oneiric register of the psyche where wishes are most readily manifest. Moving away from the analysis of dreams' conscious life (dreams as aspirations) and toward modes of analyzing the unconscious life of undocumented dreams, the chapter delves into Freud's account of dream-work as a productive mode of thinking for critical migration studies. Working to articulate this speculative conceptualization of dream-work, the chapter links undocumented activism to what I call intergenerational migrant aesthetics. Here it analyzes the work of Carmen Argote, specifically her multimedia installation pieces titled *My Father's Side of Home* (2014). Argote's works' dreamlike quality, I argue, offers a means of articulating an intergenerational migrant aesthetics that might help resist the logics of deportability and parricide at the borderlands.

Finally, the book ends with a brief meditation on loss and decathexis. For if, as I have been arguing across this introduction, it is childhood's productivity as a cathected object that enables it to facilitate a range of competing demands, then enabling childhood to signify otherwise requires thinking carefully about letting go of the fantasmatic notion of childhood that we are so invested in. Doing so, I argue, requires thinking further about loss and the importance of ambivalence. Rather than seek out childhood's end, or declare its irrelevance, I work to suggest that being at a loss with childhood might enable it—and us—to be open to new horizons.

Disavowing Black Childhood

Trayvon Martin, Adolescent Citizenship, and Antiblackness

On the rainy evening of February 26, 2012, a lone child walked through the streets of the Retreat at Twin Lakes, a residential community in Sanford, Florida, whose peach stucco houses look practically identical. Returning home from a local shop, Trayvon Martin, a black seventeen-year-old clad in a hoodie, stood out among the houses. Following Trayvon in his car, George Zimmerman, a twenty-eight-year-old Latino and white man appointed as captain of the local Neighborhood Watch program, called the local police. Speaking to the dispatcher, Zimmerman reported Trayvon's "suspicious" presence and asked for an officer to attend to what he perceived as being a situation:

> Hey we've had some break-ins in my neighborhood, and there's a real suspicious guy, uh, [at] Retreat View Circle, um . . . This guy looks like he's up to no good, or he's on drugs or something. It's raining and he's just walking around, looking about . . . looking at all the houses. (City of Sanford, Florida 2012)

While on the phone, Zimmerman became impatient, eager to not let Trayvon become what he described to the dispatcher as one of "these assholes" that "always get away" (City of Sanford, Florida 2012). When Trayvon ran, spooked by the hovering presence of a trailing vehicle, Zimmerman exited his car and pursued Trayvon by foot. Despite being told that his pursuance was unnecessary, and that an officer was on the way, Zimmerman persisted. Zimmerman thanked the dispatcher, got off the phone, and, a couple minutes later, confronted Trayvon. Screams were heard, a gun was fired, and a child lay face down, lifeless, on the wet grass. When the police arrived at the scene, they pronounced Trayvon dead, took Zimmerman in for questioning, and then released him. It took seven weeks, and an assemblage of protests, and calls for justice by high-profile civil rights activists and Trayvon's family, before Zimmerman was finally arrested and charged with second-degree murder. The trial lasted fifteen days, and on July 14, 2013, Zimmerman was acquitted.

After his murder, Trayvon became a symbol of the institutional racism of the police and the criminal justice system, and of the disproportionate number of fatal shootings of black people by law enforcement. While official statistics are difficult to ascertain, as many organizations do not break down their reports by race, the Bureau of Justice Statistics estimates that between 2003 and 2009 black people were approximately 4.3 times more likely than white people to be killed by police officers (Burch 2011). In just the year following Zimmerman's acquittal, Tanisha Anderson, Michael Brown, Michelle Cusseaux, Eric Garner, Renisha McBride, Gabriella Nevarez, Tamir Rice, and Aura Rosser were among the more widely publicized black people murdered at the hands of the law. In this sense, Trayvon's death is unfortunately far from exceptional. This epidemic of deadly state violence is compounded by the overpolicing of black communities. Not only, then, are black people more likely to be killed by police in arrest-related encounters, they are also more likely to have their livelihoods threatened by interactions with police due to practices such as stop and frisk, broken windows policing, the school to prison pipeline, and the cycle of indebtedness that the criminal justice system perpetuates.[1] Along these lines, the criminal justice system, as a part of the wider prison industrial complex, has historically profiled, arrested, and incarcerated black people in extraordinarily disproportionate numbers.[2] As Michelle Alexander reports, if the current trend of racist incarceration continues, "one in three African American men will serve time in prison," and, in many cities across the United States at the time of Trayvon's murder, "more than half of all young adult black men [were] under correctional control—in prison or jail, on probation or parole" (2012, 9). It is within this context of genocidal carceral politics that Trayvon's murder became a catalyst for widespread, indeed national, condemnation of racist police and vigilante violence, and of the injustice of the prison industrial complex.[3]

In responding to Trayvon's murder, this chapter attends to a number of debates about the visual and narrative representations of black childhood and adolescence, beginning from the initial reporting of his death, to just beyond Zimmerman's acquittal. This chapter, however, cannot possibly do justice to Trayvon's foreshortened life, nor can it bring to justice the person who took that life from him. Knowing that it cannot, I seek instead to interrogate the conditions, like those just mentioned, under which Trayvon's young life was already marked as disposable, and to parse out the ways in which the legitimation and continuation of the systemic violence directed toward black life in the United States operates, in part, through the disavowal of black humanity, black citizenship, and black childhood.[4]

My use of the language of disavowal is purposeful. Disavowal, as a psychic mechanism that is distinct from denial and negation, is a far more complex mechanism that suggests something more serious, dynamic, and troubling. Negation, for Freud ([1925] 1961), is more forgiving than disavowal. It is, he writes, "a way of taking cognizance of what is repressed; indeed it is already a lifting of the repression, though not, of course, an acceptance of what is repressed" ([1925] 1961, 235–36). Disavowal, on the other hand—which Freud introduces in "The Infantile Genital Organization" ([1923b] 1961)—does not so easily lend itself to acceptance. It favors incoherence: a disbelief that is paired with belief of something that is not so. The disavowal of a fact, Freud argues, is defined by a belief that what is not, is. "The contradiction between observation and preconception," he writes, "is glossed over" ([1923b] 1961, 144). In this sense, disavowal, as distinct from negation, does not operate as the starting point of the recognition of something. "Disavowal can lead us further and further away from accepting the reality," Sally Weintrobe writes, arguing that this avoidance has "murderous and suicidal consequences" (2012, 8). What makes disavowal so dangerous, she adds, is that it "can lead to a spiral of minimizing reality with an underlying buildup of anxiety. . . . It involves a destructive attack on the rational mind and is anti-meaning" (2012, 8). Disavowal, she notes, "can arise in individuals or in groups of people, and it can also characterize a culture" (2012, 8). Along these lines, one of my central arguments in this chapter is that under conditions of antiblackness the black child—a subject produced by a dissonant entanglement of the idea of childhood as emblem of futurity and blackness as a different order of the human—becomes the primary site where the dangerous and persistent disavowal of ongoing racism is manifest.[5]

In this vein, my response to Trayvon's murder emerges in conversation with the now expansive and growing scholarship on his foreshortened life.[6] Adding a psychoanalytic critique to this scholarship, I argue that childhood itself is a structure through which Trayvon was already marked as disposable. While there has not yet been other research that has directly made this claim, there has been work which has linked his murder to other black children, and specifically to Emmett Till's.[7] Connecting Emmett's and Trayvon's murders, this scholarship not only situates them in relation to the movements they were catalysts for—the Civil Rights Movement and Black Lives Matter, respectively—but also recognizes that Trayvon's murder was a contemporary instance of the persistent criminalization and dehumanization of black boys, which also marked Emmett as disposable.[8] As Daniel Harawa writes, "The deaths of Emmett Till and Martin . . . reveal one important fact: Black masculinity is still often perceived as threatening and dangerous in the United States" (2014, 57).

Distinguishing itself from this body of work, my analysis in this chapter moves away from thinking about Trayvon just in relation to the violences black boys experience, and it turns to the ways in which childhood itself, as an incoherent structure of ambivalence and belonging through which Emmett and Trayvon were marked as disposable, functions within a continuum of racist and gendered violence to justify Emmett's and Trayvon's murders in particular ways. I argue that the specific work that childhood took on in the wake of Trayvon's murder needs to be interrogated in relation to the particular historical moment in which his death and its aftermaths took place (one separated from Emmett's by almost sixty years). While historical antiblackness and its contemporary life must be understood as contributing to the landscape of violence which disavowed both Trayvon's and Emmett's lives and childhoods, the incoherent evocations and negations of childhood that circulated in relationship to Trayvon must be understood as responding to, and investing in, a different discursive, historical, and affective terrain.

One of the more explicit differences between Emmett's murder and Trayvon's murder is that Emmett's was a catalyst for the Civil Rights Movement, while Trayvon's took place after many claimed the Civil Rights Movement had been a resolute success. Indeed, at the very same time that those protesting Zimmerman's lack of arrest and eventual acquittal were connecting Trayvon's murder to the continuing consequences of slavery and segregation, and to the ongoing effects of mass incarceration and systemic and interpersonal racism, a counternarrative of a "postracial" and "colorblind" America was being entrenched as a national fantasy. This narrative proposes that in the "successful" aftermath of the Civil Rights Movement, race no longer determines one's life chances. In this framing—which, given the statistics above, can only be properly described as a white fantasy and wish fulfillment—anyone claiming that race still matters, or that racism persists, is deemed both racist (for bringing back into being the inherently divisive and "backwards" notion of race), and unpatriotic. At the same time this narrative combines with white fantasies of social and political abandonment—as I argued in the introduction—such that the era of colorblindness also becomes the era of "reverse-racism" and political correctness gone awry.[9] Precisely at the moment that white people fantasize that their racial privilege is slipping, childhood jumps in as a cathected racial object—as a marker of and investment in whiteness—such that the wish fulfillment of the postracial becomes mapped onto the disavowal of Trayvon's childhood, and onto the discursive production of his location in a particular frame of "adolescent." I turn to this particular moment, not because it is an exceptional incident of deadly violence directed at a black child, but rather because I am interested in how his location in childhood and/ or adolescence was evoked and denied. I argue that the inconsistent positioning of his childhood was a way of negotiating the impossibility of holding together the fantasies of postracial unity and reverse racism amidst the persistence of deadly antiblack violence. Borrowing from Lauren Berlant's notion of "infantile citizenship" (1997), in the latter half of this chapter I offer the frame of *adolescent citizenship* to describe the coupling of the postracial and the persistence of antiblack state violence, of which Trayvon's murder is just a part.

Constructing an Image

In the immediate aftermath of Trayvon's murder, Tracy Martin and Sybrina Fulton (Trayvon's parents) provided the media with a photograph of him as a smiling young teenager to accompany their demand that Zimmerman be arrested. Along with this initial image of a happy, youthful Trayvon in a red Hollister T-shirt, photos of him holding his baby brother, as well as one of him as a baby himself, were used to accompany news coverage and various articles. These photographs were both illustrative and purposeful; they gave a face to the person who was murdered, and they painted an image of young boy whose childish innocence demanded that justice be done in his name. As part of their demand, Trayvon's parents started a petition, which received over two million signatures, calling for the Florida attorney general to persecute; they organized "Million Hoodie Marches" in New York, Pennsylvania, and Florida; and, in recognition of their activism, President Obama addressed Trayvon's murder in a White House press conference, saying that if he had a son, "he'd look like Trayvon" (Office of the Press Secretary 2013). This activism, however, was met with vehement resistance, much of which—perhaps incited by Obama's signaling of the role of appearance—played out within visual culture. Contesting the images of Trayvon that his parents were using, arguing that they portrayed him as an innocent child and less capable of instigating a violent altercation with Zimmerman, bloggers, news sites, online commentators, and Zimmerman's own legal defense team challenged this "youthful" representation. Many responses to these photographs offered their own representations of Trayvon and Zimmerman, ones that they argued provided a more honest (and consistently older) image.[10] These images, and the stories they told, became the most followed news item for weeks (Pew Research 2012b), and the intensity of Zimmerman's, and his supporters' investment in representing Trayvon's age "accurately" grew increasingly vociferous after the Florida police released Zimmerman's 911 calls from the night of Trayvon's murder (Pew Research 2012a). In the midst of this, the representation and framing of Trayvon became an overburdened site in which childhood was cathected as an object of investment, and its disavowal was central to his defaming.[11]

The debates about Trayvon's imaging were structured through disavowal, mired in what Weintrobe calls the "stuck terrain of delusion," where "unreality and irrationality are not only more likely to prevail, but may, indeed, escalate" (2012, 36). This becomes clear in assessing the visual field, as the images used to represent him often pushed at the limits of intelligibility. Speaking to this, Jonathan Capehart, an opinion writer for the *Washington Post,* wrote an article documenting a number of complaints he received from readers about an image of Trayvon he used on an earlier article about the murder. Capehart's readers, he wrote, decried this "youthful image" as a misrepresentation:

> Many folks took issue with the picture I used yesterday and again today—that of a smiling, fresh-faced Trayvon wearing a red T-shirt from Hollister . . . Some think he's as young as 11 years old or as old as 14 in that snapshot. Martin family attorney Benjamin Crump told me this afternoon that the slain teenager was 16 when that photo was taken in August 2011 [six months before he was murdered]. (Capehart 2013)

One of the readers who took issue with this image sent him an email with an "updated" image attached, asking: "Why didn't you show the up-to-date picture of Trayvon Martin as below instead of the one where he is much younger? . . . I don't take either side because I just don't know all the facts, but what I do know is you can't beat honest reporting" (Capehart 2013).

This reader, Capehart reports, sent him a "more accurate" photograph of Trayvon that actually turned out not to be of him. Attached instead was an image of Game (Jayceon Terrell Taylor), a rapper who was thirty-two years old at the time of Trayvon's murder. The insidiousness of sending this particular image, Capehart notes, becomes palpable when we consider that Trayvon, who was seventeen years old at the time of his murder, will never live to be as old as the man, Game, whom this commenter mistook him to be.

How should we read this commentator's elision of Trayvon's body? Rather than simply disregard their sharing of Game's image as a mistake, I argue that we need to take it as evidence of a collective disavowal of black childhood. For indeed, this reader's insistence that Game's body was Trayvon's was not isolated. As *PolitiFact* reported, Game's image was claimed to be Trayvon's in a chain email (Sanders 2012), and news sites from *Business Insider* and *Good Morning America* similarly "mistook" Trayvon's body (Chittum 2012a, 2012b). Along with this image of Game, other images of young black men circulated online. In their circulation, two interconnected lines of mediated disavowal emerged. The first focused specifically on Trayvon's age in the photos being distributed, and insisted—as Capehart's reader did— that only an "up-to-date photo" of him should represent him. The second relied on and reproduced gendered and racialized frames of deviance to implicate Trayvon in a range of criminalized activities, in the hopes that this association would discredit him.

Seeking to defame Trayvon along these lines of antiblack disavowal, conservative news blog *The Daily Caller* obtained Trayvon's social media profiles (despite their being deactivated by his family after his death) and published photos of his that they argued painted a more accurate picture of him (Martosko 2012). These images (which, presumably, were only the ones chosen by the blog, rather than the extent of Trayvon's collection) show him "with gold dental grill and making obscene gestures to the camera" (Guttman 2012). The *Daily Caller* additionally published a selection of Trayvon's tweets, along with images taken from his phone (released by Zimmerman's defense team) of marijuana plants, and a gun. Soon after, memes were produced from digital manipulations of these images and they were published online across blogs and social media. Composite images comparing the media's "biased" portrayal of Trayvon (as youthful and innocent) to more "accurate" ones went viral. These composite images not only decried Trayvon's innocence, they also challenged the use of Zimmerman's mug shot to represent him. The use of the mug shot, many argued, framed Zimmerman as guilty before his trial, and was thus a "perversion" of the American justice system. One composite image paired two versions of Trayvon's and Zimmerman's image, one pairing sitting above the other. On top were Zimmerman's mug shot and the image of Trayvon wearing a Hollister T-shirt, accompanied by text: "Don't believe in the 'Media Narrative?' Then why are you shown this . . . (5–7 years old)." Below, an image of Zimmerman in a business suit sat opposite an image of Trayvon, shirtless, sagging, and flipping off the camera, and captioned with: "Instead of this (current)." Challenging a perceived bias in media reporting that was, in this image creator's mind, too soft on Trayvon and too criminalizing of Zimmerman, this meme sought to unveil the truth about Trayvon's character in order to criminalize him and to decry the political correctness of the mainstream media. Other images like these with similar captions that pointed out the "dated" nature of the images used in mainstream media and the more recent production of the uncovered images proliferated online.

And yet this shirtless image of Trayvon, along with a number of others, were not, however, actually images of him. These images passed as representations of him even though they were other black boys (and men) because the depicted performances of black masculinity mapped onto the assumptions of who Trayvon was or could be. The pervasive publishing of these virulent images must not be dismissed as online trolling, not just because trolling has its own material consequences and signifying chains, but also because they were taken to be legitimate representations of Trayvon by a number of mainstream news outlets. An article in the *Business Insider*, for example, used this image and another one which was also not of him. Eventually *Business Insider* removed the image, revealing that they initially sourced it from a white-supremacist online forum. Explaining their use, and removal, of these two images, they wrote:

> There are images circulating online that are supposedly other pictures of Trayvon Martin. We saw one on Stormfront a racist message board.

It was embedded with another picture purporting to be Trayvon that the *Miami New Times* points out is not Trayvon Martin. One conservative website has already apologized for publishing it. (We originally published the entire image found on Stormfront, which included two photos, but we took the second down after finding out it wasn't Trayvon Martin). And now there is also question as to whether the other image is of Trayvon. We have now removed both. (Dougherty 2012)

In this retraction, which is explicitly *not* an apology, *Business Insider* justified not just their removal of these images but also their initial posting of them. Here the "mistake" that required correction was apparently not their practice of sourcing material from white supremacist websites but, rather, their misrecognition. And still this misrecognition, they clarify, was not really (or not only) theirs: their justification for profiling is that this practice is shared.

The collapsing of these bodies into the same signifying image—as if all of them occupy the same adult body—explicitly uses racial difference and the "fact" of the black body to both claim a representation of a particular body (Trayvon's) and to mark this body as expansively replaceable under the sign of blackness. This act of using an image to encode a narrative of deviance onto a racialized body follows a longer history of subject production through the technology of photography. As Tina Campt writes, photographs are "one of the most accessible objects through which complicated processes of projection, desire, and identification come into view" (2012, 23). Photographs, Campt argues, have been and continue to be "forces in the deployment of the racialized index" (2012, 33). This indexing, Campt writes, "produce[s] subjects to be seen, read, touched, and consumed as available and abjected flesh objects and commodities, rather than as individual bodies, agents, or actors" (2012, 33). Aligned with the political project of the racial index (in which hierarchal racial difference is made truthful through its imaging) yet explicitly refusing the "precise" nature of the photograph to document embodied specificity, these photographs abstracted black masculinity as the grounds upon which Trayvon was consumed and framed. This "framing" of the image works across both meanings of this word—Trayvon was simultaneously contained by the image, and "his" image was presented as false evidence against him. Speaking to the register of the visual that allowed these other boys and men to replace, or stand in for, Trayvon's body, Mimi Thi Nguyen (2015) argues that they must not be simply understood as "misrecognitions." For Nguyen it is "resemblance, not recognition" which informs the "preemptive rationale that pervades our political moment" (2015, 805). Resemblance, Nguyen argues, more accurately describes the current regime of policing and security, which conceives of threat as an "absolute potential" that is carried within particular bodies and signs and is imagined as signifying a "violence [that] is realizable at any moment" (805). In this context, the other bodies that replaced or resembled Trayvon's constituted what Sara Ahmed (2006) might call the "background" of Trayvon's framing. Under conditions of antiblackness, then, the criminalized codes of black masculinity that circulated between these other racialized and gendered bodies thus conflated the slip between resembling Trayvon and representing him. As such, this slip must be understood not as an exceptional mistake or momentary lapse of judgment. Rather, it must be understood as evidence for the pervasive disavowal of black childhood. Here I argue that it is precisely this disavowal makes it so deadly for black children like Trayvon.

Childhood, like the visual field, is not neutral to the question of race; indeed it is also a racial logic, and a forceful episteme. And while a certain space within the debates about Trayvon's imaging opened up to allow Trayvon's innocence to rest on depictions of him as a child (which I return to later in the chapter), the racial life of childhood as it met with the psychic structure of disavowal rendered this an impossibility. "Disavowal," Stuart Hall writes, "is not an uncommon historical phenomenon, especially in matters of race" (2017, 96). It enables a society's "collective psyche," Hall argues, to "invest so much energy in maintaining racial dominance and at the same time [to] categorically deny the efficacy of race" (96). Disavowal, that is, is not just saying no: it is a saying yes to something that plainly is not. Here, to paraphrase Hall, black childhood is collectively and categorically refused by antiblackness, at the same time as a wealth of psychic energy is invested in maintaining antiblackness through the evidencing of Trayvon's adolescence.

We can see this explicitly in an argument made by Zimmerman's defense team. The following narrative, which again responds to the image of Trayvon in the Hollister shirt, explicitly contests the image's representation of him as an innocent child:

> On the surface, it seems like a ridiculous pursuit to note the difference between these photographs, but here is the important distinction: it is lunacy to think that the "fresh-faced" boy in the red T-shirt could successfully physically assault George Zimmerman—which is George's claim, and it is no stretch to believe that the young man [Martin] pictured in the 7–11 security footage [taken the night of Martin's murder] could. (George Zimmerman Legal Case 2013)

The rhetorical shift here from innocent "boy" to culpable "young man" happens exactly as Trayvon's representation shifts from a "smiling, fresh-faced Martin wearing a red T-shirt from Hollister, the mass clothier of adolescence" (Capehart 2013) to "more recent" photos of him being taller, older, and defiant (George Zimmerman Legal Case 2013). The jump from boy to man, Zimmerman's lawyers argue, extends the plausibility that Trayvon attacked Zimmerman and thus that Zimmerman's actions were done in self-defense. His image as a young man thus not only founds this plausibility, but, because of its production within and as a history of the optics of blackness, it becomes the evidence through which the violence Trayvon experienced was justified and, in the moment, required.

But what do we make of the pairing of these images by Zimmerman's defense team? How do these two images sit together? This younger photo, we remember from Benjamin Crump's description of it (as cited in Capehart), was taken merely six months prior to the security camera footage. Trayvon, in other words, is effectively the same age in both images. It is thus precisely because these images mark *no age distinction* that the entire question of Trayvon's age becomes both meaningless and exactly the point. Both Trayvons—separated by mere months—are preemptively "read, touched, and consumed" (Campt 2012, 33) through the optics of antiblackness. And yet only one image tenuously—and we must say "tenuously" because it was this body, too, that Zimmerman registered as suspicious—locates Trayvon in innocent childhood.[12] The other, while also a representation of Trayvon as a child, is unintelligible within that signifying space. This contradictory and ambivalent reading of Trayvon as a boy *and* man might make for an interesting challenge to Zimmerman's capacity to assess Trayvon's age, let alone his suspiciousness on the night of his murder. What becomes clear in this contested visual field, however, is not that precise age verification matters. For if the collective psyche is structured through a disavowal of black childhood, then, to paraphrase Freud, no attention is paid to the difference between fact and comprehension.[13] What is being contested in the visual field is not Trayvon's age but rather what Trayvon's age signifies. Childhood is deployed and disavowed here precisely because it does something. For Trayvon's family, and for those advocating that justice be done in his name, childhood is both an acknowledgment of Trayvon's innocence and a way of registering a devastating personal loss. For those defending Zimmerman, on the other hand, childhood must be disavowed because to acknowledge it would be to acknowledge Trayvon's innocence, and the role that Zimmerman's racism played within the encounter. These images of an "older" Trayvon, then, become evidence less of his age and more of the need to simultaneously deny the deadliness of contemporary antiblackness while investing so strongly in the maintenance of whiteness.

Narratives of a Troubled Teen

The contested visual terrain was supplemented by discursive and narrative constructions that actively disavowed Trayvon's childhood. The representation and framing of Trayvon became an overburdened site in which race and childhood gave one another meaning. One of the ways in which Zimmerman's case attempted to gain legitimacy was by claiming that he responded in self-defense to an aggressive and intoxicated teenager. Repeatedly, in these accounts, Trayvon is referred to in racist and gendered language that uses the frame of "teen" to establish a liminal space between childhood and adulthood that nevertheless indicates a departure from the innocent space of childhood. The racialized and gendered portrayal of Trayvon as a teenager who engaged in criminal and problematic behaviors centers around the "exposing" of his life history. Having a history that can be exposed, as Kathryn Bond Stockton (2009) argues, is grounds itself to no longer be considered a child. This is so, Stockton argues, because childhood is constructed as "the specter of who we were when there was nothing yet behind us," and, as such, antithetical to childhood are "sex, aggression, secrets, closets, or any sense of what police call 'a past'" (2009, 30). Proving that Trayvon had a past was thus vital to proving that he was no longer a child. However, in looking over the material that was presented as evidence of Trayvon having a past, it becomes clear that not just "any" past signifies an end to one's childhood. To have a past that properly lifts one out of childhood is to have a past that is already produced through racist and gendered discourses. Stockton's language of having "what police call a past" is crucial here as it points to the role of criminalization, institutional racism, and white property ownership in shaping what type of past is marked. For Trayvon, these were discourses that implicated him in a specific futurity—or, more precisely, a history that justified the negation of his futurity. Trayvon's past worthy of exposure, then, was his complicated history with school and his alleged affinity for objects that carried the racial markers of blackness—a grill, a bag with marijuana residue in it, a gun—not, on the other hand, his time spent in a nonprofit program that introduces young people to aviation.[14] As such, the material from which his past is produced includes primarily Trayvon's previous suspensions from school, as well as his self-representation on social media sites. Although Zimmerman had no knowledge of Trayvon's identity, let alone his history with suspension, this history played a central role in the portrayal of Trayvon within the media and the national imagination as someone who was more than likely to have acted violently in response to being confronted.

In reporting on one of the gatherings of people in Sanford to protest the lack of Zimmerman's arrest, the *Miami Herald* presented this lengthy depiction:

As thousands of people gathered here to demand an arrest in the Trayvon Martin case, a more complicated portrait began to emerge of a teenager whose problems at school ranged from getting spotted defacing lockers to getting caught with a marijuana baggie and women's jewelry. The Miami Gardens teen who has become a national symbol of racial injustice was suspended three times, and had a spotty school record that his family's attorneys say is irrelevant . . . In October, a school police investigator saw Trayvon mark up a door with "W.T.F"—an acronym for "what the f—." The officer said he found . . . women's jewelry and a screwdriver that he described as a "burglary tool." . . . Word of the incident came as the family's lawyer acknowledged that the boy was suspended in February for getting caught with an empty bag with traces of marijuana, which he called "irrelevant." (Robles 2012)

Rather than begin with a description of the protest that thousands attended, the *Miami Herald* opened its reporting with a damning account of Trayvon's past. In their repeating of the argument that these details are "irrelevant," it becomes clear that they not only believe these "facts" to *be* relevant but that they are also suspicious of Trayvon's family for questioning them. This "complicated" portrayal of Trayvon as a "troubled teenager" is also explicit in reporting by CNN:

"I am Trayvon Martin" has become the catchphrase for protesters expressing solidarity with the slain Florida teenager and outrage over his killing. . . . But who really was Trayvon Martin? There is plenty of speculation, including some bloggers who point to his recent school suspensions—including for drug residue in his backpack—and images of him sporting tattoos and what appeared to be a gold tooth grill as possible evidence of a troubled teen. (Segal 2012)

Like the reporting in the *Miami Herald,* this article opens with a questioning of Trayvon's innocence and a removal of him from childhood. This questioning of Trayvon's life was a reiterated trope, and was explicitly evoked in the headlines of such news features as: "Multiple suspensions paint complicated portrait of Trayvon Martin" (Robles 2012), "Trayvon Martin: Typical Teen or Troublemaker?" (Alcindor 2012), and "Trayvon Martin was suspended three times from school"

(MSNBC 2012). These insistences on making Trayvon's life a question ("Who really was Trayvon Martin?") point to the fact that Trayvon's childhood, and his innocence, were always already in question.

Trayvon is not alone in having a past here, as the terms under which his life were questioned are part of a longer history of anti-blackness. By centering on particular criminalized acts—graffiti, marijuana possession, and theft—these narratives tied Trayvon to a historical discourse that has defined deviance, poverty, and criminality as inherent to black culture and black masculinity.[15] In this discourse—which Maxine Baca Zinn (1989) calls the "cultural deficiency model"—deviance is located within racialized, classed, and gendered values and behaviors.[16] The criminalization of blackness that is part and parcel of this sociological model has been used to disavow black childhood across a number of flashpoints in America's history of antiblackness: from slavery and the antebellum era—as I've argued elsewhere (J. Breslow 2019)—to Daniel Patrick Moynihan's infamous *The Negro Family: The Case for National Action* (1965), to the postracial era.[17] While one could thus unpack a series of antecedents for the disavowal of black childhood, I turn to the rhetorical fear-mongering that most directly preceded Trayvon's murder. In the mid-1990s the US government fabricated the War on Drugs, a hyperintensification of the criminalizing of blackness that brought into being policies that escalated the incarceration of black youth. The discursive and material ramifications of the War on Drugs set much of the stage upon which Trayvon was profiled and his past was criminalized.

One of the instigators for the War on Drugs was a 1995 editorial for the *Weekly Standard* written by John Dilulio, a Harvard professor. Citing an alleged "soaring" increase in crimes committed by black youth from the 1970s to the mid-1990s, one that exceeded (but was apparently made all the more troubling by) the "spike in the young [black] male population," Dilulio introduced the term "super-predators" into public discourse. Dilulio wrote:

> On the horizon . . . are tens of thousands of severely morally impov-
> erished juvenile super-predators . . . for as long as their youthful

energies hold out, they will do what comes "naturally": murder, rape, rob, assault, burglarize, deal deadly drugs, and get high. . . . We're not just talking about teenagers. . . . We're talking about boys whose voices have yet to change. We're talking about elementary school young- sters who pack guns instead of lunches. We're talking about kids who have absolutely no respect for human life and no sense of the future. (Dilulio 1995)

This quote is nothing if not explicit in its laying out of what I am call- ing the disavowal of black childhood. Dilulio moves swiftly between describing these "natural murders" as juveniles, youth, teenagers, boys, elementary school youngsters, kids, and prepubescent boys. Black childhood here is rendered simultaneously ever expansive *and incompatible with childhood.* Dilulio's emphasis on the youthfulness of these "superpredators" actually functions, that is, to remove these children from childhood: "The buzz of impulsive violence, the vacant stares and smiles, and the remorseless eyes were at once too frighten- ing and too depressing (my God, these are children!)" (Dilulio 1995). Here Dilulio's shock emphasizes the implausibility of his recogni- tion and registers at once that these are, *and are not,* children that he is describing. This being-yet-not-being must be understood, I argue, as a form of structural disavowal that comes to define black child- hood under conditions of antiblackness. As Ann Ferguson argues, "A discourse that positions masculinity as 'naturally' naughty is re- framed for African American boys around racialized representations of gendered subjects. They come to stand as if already adult, bearers of adult fates inscribed within a racial order" (2001, 96). This racial order, I argue, marks blackness as another register of the human, one which rejects the perception that black children are indeed children. The narratives about Trayvon's past that consistently name him as a "troubled teen" thus directly evoke the racist discourse of cultural deficiency, as well as the construction of black masculinity as deviant and criminal, in order to both justify their assumptions of Trayvon's guilt and to remove him from the space of childhood.

While the use of childhood in these narrative and visual depictions of Trayvon as a "troubled teen" clearly emerges out of a continued investment in the reification of the discourse of deviance as located in black communities and particularly in black masculinity, something else seems to be at stake here. Inherent in these descriptions of Trayvon's past is a tone that establishes the necessity of their revelation with a sense of frustration, elation, and righteousness. What is revealed, I ask, in the affect that structures these disavowals of Trayvon's childhood? Particularly in a moment where, as I argue below, minor and major progress toward racial justice has been experienced by many white Americans as an injurious personal attack, attending to the affective register of these negotiations shows that what is at stake in Trayvon's location far surpasses its implication for Trayvon or Zimmerman. The feelings of righteousness and anger that are enunciated in the demands that Trayvon's past be revealed and that his age be represented "accurately" demonstrate that feelings of victimization and loss located in whiteness hinge on the results of such proclamations.

To give an initial sense of the affective weight that childhood carries in this context, I present a reader comment on an article for the *Huffington Post,* since deleted:

> You are so right. . . . [The mass media] have him [Zimmerman] guilty already[.] They of all people should know the way the law works. . . . They [the mass media, as well as Martin's mother] are all pot stirrers and should wait for the outcome of this trial. [T]here is no doubt in my mind that Trayvon could have been the aggressor. Also they should stop showing his picture when he was 5 or 6 . . . Let[']s remind people that he was suspended from school for drugs, burglary tools[,] having women[']s jewelry and tardiness. This teen is no angel . . . (galfrmjerz3 2012)

In this narrative, as within the others I have cited, Zimmerman's profiling, shooting, and killing of Trayvon is reasonable, if not justifiable, because of Trayvon's previous and unrelated actions. Possession in these narratives, namely the possession of marijuana and stolen goods, and specifically "women's jewelry" (something a teenage boy would never possess without suspiciously acquiring), marks Trayvon as an already established criminal. By reporting these possessions as relevant to the night Trayvon was profiled, chased, and executed on his way home, these narratives work to legitimate his death by firmly locating him within the frame of troubled adolescent and not innocent child. All of these examples work to push Trayvon outside of childhood in slightly different ways, but what they share is an underlying legitimating discourse about race and gender as tied to deviance and criminality that has a longer history.

Unpacking the affective register of this comment, a layer of meaning and investment emerges beyond the discursive linking of Trayvon's past to his alleged guilt. Something else is at stake here that is cathected by Trayvon's location within childhood: a sense that the commentator, and the wider public, has been deceived; a sense that the media's framing of Trayvon as a child is duplicitous and unethical; and a sense that the premise of "equality under the law" and a fair trial is being overthrown in the name of "race." The tone of the comment thus points to a feeling that Trayvon's representation in the media has provoked for this commentator. While there is much to say, and to challenge, about this quote, I want to take this comment seriously as an indication of the political work that adolescence—as a specific racialized disavowal of childhood—does within the postracial moment. Here the phrasing of "this teen is no angel" cannot be understood as purely beholden to the commenter. This reiterated phrase was so central to depictions of Trayvon that it appeared in a feature article for the *New York Times*—"But Trayvon was a teenager, not an angel" (Barry et al. 2011)—and it was so proliferative that it was the second most popular search suggestion for Google after the phrase "Trayvon Martin was" (Noble 2014). In this particular usage, the commenter's palpable racist anger is clearly being cathected by Trayvon's portrayal as a child. The images of Trayvon as a young child are thus framed by this reader comment as manipulative and as sharing an incendiary distortion that its author argues is inherent to those supporting Trayvon.

Putting this comment into the context of a wider array of similar ones, like the following indictment from a blog entry that is even more explicit in its declaration of outrage, we can begin to build a picture of a national feeling, or what I am calling adolescent citizenship:

> At the time of the shooting, the media and Martin's family, abetted by race hustlers Jesse Jackson and Al Sharpton, portrayed Zimmerman as a trigger-happy racist, with the *New York Times* describing him as a white Hispanic, an unusual term the paper never uses. A congresswoman portrayed it thusly: Martin was [a] "sweet young boy hunted down like a dog." It turned out that Martin was anything but sweet, despite the media's repeatedly showing photographs of him that led readers and viewers to believe he was only 12 or 13 years old when he was shot. (Kirkwood 2012)

As the affect in this language makes clear, what is at stake in proving Trayvon's guilt and his placement in adolescence hinges on this author's (clearly incensed) feelings about racial belonging. What is revealed in the affect that structures these reiterations of Trayvon's adolescence, I argue, is the link between the disavowal of black childhood and the negation of black citizenship. Central to both of these accounts is the connecting—through vitriolic affect—of Trayvon's location within a troubling adolescence to a defamation of those advocating for him: his parents, civil rights activists, protestors, politicians. The similarity between these two comments' affects is important, and it is indicative, I argue, of a larger structure of feeling that constitutes what has been called the postracial or colorblind moment.

Defining the postracial moment is tricky, as the term itself can be understood to emerge from a future-oriented politics that aspires to a day in which race carries less weight for socioeconomic realities.[18] But it can also describe an assumed reality in which racial tensions and inequalities are deemed to be irrelevant already. Outlining this latter understanding of a postracial America, Lawrence Bobo writes:

> post-racialism has the most in common with the well-rehearsed rhetoric of color blindness. To wit, American society, or at least a large and steadily growing fraction of it, has genuinely moved beyond race—so much so that we as a nation are now ready to transcend the disabling racial divisions of the past. (2011, 14)

Fueling this notion that the United States has transcended "previous" racial tensions and inequalities is a social, political, and legal discourse that marks its difference from the racism of the past by refusing to use overtly racist language while still actively disavowing ongoing and persistent inequity. As Lisa Marie Cacho asserts:

> No longer imbued with open racial overtones, law and policy—as sites where the fictional becomes real—employ a "color-blind" liberal discourse, which functions to mask the implicit, yet just as consequential, racialized "nature" of legal apparatuses. This "color-blind" ideology operates to disavow systemic racism, defining racism as aberrant actions of individuals while simultaneously, turning a "color-blind" eye to institutionalized and systematic racism. (2000, 405)

Precisely because it disavows systemic racism and locates racism instead in the individual psyche, the discourse of colorblindness situates itself as the ethical imperative for a post-civil rights era. Indeed, although many civil rights leaders advocate for race-conscious policies like affirmative action, or racially-targeted housing, mentoring, and fellowship programs, many Americans, as Rogers Smith, Desmond King, and Philip Klinkner point out, believe that these policies are "unjust—even a form of reverse racism" (2011, 125). Ironically, they write, this split understanding of the ethics of racial justice after the Civil Rights Movement has meant that "both advocates of color-blind policies and proponents of race-conscious policies present themselves as the true heirs to the antisegregation civil rights movement. Both criticize their opponents for betraying its aims" (2011, 125). This assumption of rightful ethical inheritance has meant that advocates of colorblind policies frame their politics in affective terms of both righteousness and anger. Here again the psychic structure of disavowal comes to the fore. As Weintrobe argues, disavowal goes hand in hand with narcissistic arrogance and entitlement. For Weintrobe disavowal involves the "the more stuck terrain[s]" of psychic life such as "a delusion of being special—indeed, god-like," or an unchecked arrogance (2012, 36). Weintrobe elaborates: "With arrogance, a destructively narcissistic part of the psyche has gained the upper hand in a power struggle with the part that feels wedded to reality. A sense of narcissistic entitlement to be immune to emotional difficulties has triumphed over a lively entitlement to a relationship with reality" (2012, 38).

This arrogance intensifies through a combination of, on one hand, "the waning salience of what some have portrayed as a 'black victimology' narrative" (Bobo 2011, 13), and, on the other, resistance to the disavowed yet persistent "mechanisms for skewing opportunities and life chances along racial lines" (Cacho 2000, 392–393).[19] Combined, these competing framings of the social solidify into what Cacho has identified as "an ideology of white injury depicting European Americans as 'victims' of efforts to remedy racial discrimination" (2000, 393). In the reader comment and the blog post excerpt cited above, this discourse can be seen explicitly. Disavowing the systematic structures and histories that marked Trayvon's body, both of these authors responded in defensive and self-righteous ways to what they perceived to be an unethical introduction of race—sometimes termed "playing the race card"—into a moment that should be free of it.[20] These "white victims," and the white injury discourse more generally, thus produce, and are a product of, a fantasy of racial relations that imagines that "minorities (especially blacks) are the ones responsible for whatever 'race problem' we have in this country" (Bonilla-Silva 2006, 1). This affective reorientation of suffering illuminates the psychic life of colorblind racial politics, but it also suggests something further. Because injured white affects, particularly those which emerge in relationship to Trayvon's murder, are tied to notions of temporality and progress that are cathected by childhood, they suture the state to a (fantasmatic) race-neutral present, while containing black people themselves in a backward, or out-of-time, relation to it.

ADOLESCENT CITIZENSHIP

What is taking place within the above accounts of Trayvon is a reiterated attempt by the authors to have the final say over how, and where, Trayvon exists within time. How old Trayvon is understood to be; whether or not he should have had a future; how and if he should be represented; and what images and narratives of his past should be used: all are temporal negotiations. In this sense, these accounts resonate with Eduardo Bonilla-Silva's analysis of the importance of temporal positionings to white people's fantasies of the postracial. In his interviews, one of the temporal demands white people place on black communities and those advocating for race-conscious politics is to "get with the times." Bonilla-Silva writes:

> Most whites believe that if blacks and other minorities would just stop thinking about the past, work hard, and complain less (particularly about racial discrimination), then Americans of all hues could "all get along." . . . In case after case, . . . respondents vented anger about what they interpreted as blacks' whining ("I didn't own any slaves and I do not understand why they keep asking for things when slavery ended 200 *God-damned* years ago!") . . . The story lines then serve whites as legitimate conduits for expressing anger, animosity, and resentment toward racial minorities. (2006, 1, 98)

In this quotation, the relationship between affect and the refusal to acknowledge ongoing racism by white people is clearly structured through a negotiation of temporality. White anger is directed at black people for not conforming to a particular framing of history and the present. The way that anger functions within this quote mirrors the accounts of Trayvon's childhood given above: the demand that Trayvon's childhood is over and needs to be gotten over works akin to the claim that slavery has ended and needs to be properly placed in the past. Both indicate that negotiating competing understandings of temporality becomes vital to how racism is acknowledged, and by whom.

These narratives position the white people who deploy them as temporally located in a present into which, they imagine, black people have not yet emerged. As such, this claim of black "whining," or what might be understood as the assumed temporal dislocation of black critique, functions as an infantilizing interpellation through which the whining subject is situated as both childish and out of time. Here the demand of "getting with the times" can thus be understood as functioning like a demand to "grow up." One could argue that this derision of black critique as "whining" is therefore straightforwardly an infantilizing discourse, positioning Trayvon and his supporters as what Berlant (1997) would call "infantile citizens." And here Berlant analyzes infantilization in relation to citizenship and the creation of what she calls the "intimate public sphere" (1997, 4). Berlant writes about the figures, fetishes, and effigies—like the figure of the child, or the image of the fetus—that "condense, displace, and stand in for arguments about who 'the people' are, what they can bear, and when, if ever" (1997, 66–67). The "image of the citizen as a minor, female, youthful victim," Berlant writes, justifies and produces a state whose "adult citizens, especially adult men" are primarily mobilized around civil protection and the regulation of sexuality (1997, 67). While infantile citizens, through their innocent naiveté of the workings of power, have the potential to "unsettle, expose, and reframe the machinery of national life" (1997, 29), their figuration as the "ideal type of patriotic personhood in America" (1997, 21) rests precisely on their location within a naïve "patriotic childhood" and not an adult citizenship position that is mired in the "travesty" that "everyday life can make of national promises for justice" (1997, 29). The infantile citizen, whom Berlant argues is "tacitly white" (1997, 6), is a subject positioning that requires protecting because its paired innocence and patriotic utopianism stakes a claim on a future that both maintains the structural position of those currently in power and demands a resurgence of uncritical nationalism.

The appropriateness of infantilization to wholly describe what is taking place in relation to Trayvon and the postracial falters, however, when it is analyzed in relationship to the landscape of representation that sought to characterize Trayvon not as a child but instead as an adolescent. Trayvon, that is, does not easily fit within the figure of the child or the image of the fetus. As I have argued, Trayvon's location within childhood has been explicitly and feverishly disavowed. And yet the discourses used to vindicate Zimmerman and criminalize Trayvon still position Trayvon and his supporters within a temporality that is not yet coeval with the present. While the contestations over Trayvon's age did clearly disavow his location in childhood, they still placed him in a juvenile, rather than adult, subject position.

While the fantasmatic relations that adulthood has to childhood are often, as Berlant notes, ones of paternalism, care, and protection (with all the insidiousness that these relations have for colonized, enslaved, and infantilized subjects), these relations can become messy and difficult in adolescence. As Stanley Cohen writes, adolescence was historically produced within the discourse of moral panic, as a dangerous space of "limbo" that is "characterized by conflict, uncertainty, defiance and deviance" (1972, 151).[21] Indeed, in adolescence the relation of dependency can become a central site of conflict, as parents and teenagers grapple with how much independence and autonomy teenagers can have, and what rights and privileges they are afforded. Adolescence, therefore, becomes a negotiated period of the child's *progression into their future adulthood,* but it is still one that is negotiated, for many, through a power dynamic that carries over from childhood. What becomes important then, along with situating the vitriol directed at those, like the mass media, who, R. Cort Kirkwood argued, worked "deceptively" to depict Trayvon as a child, is unpacking the specific placement of Trayvon into adolescence rather than adulthood. By marking him as an adolescent rather than a child or an adult, those defending Zimmerman (and those accounts questioning Trayvon's grieveability) also interpellated those advocating for justice in Trayvon's name into relational tropes that posited them as *precociously demanding*—on behalf of Trayvon—to be recognized as adult subjects.

This is the central condition of adolescent citizenship: a subject positioning that negates the subject's demands for recognition and equality on the grounds that they have yet to deserve full citizenship rights. Unlike infantile citizenship, which defines citizenship by and for "fetuses, children, real and imaginary migrants—persons that, paradoxically, cannot act yet as citizens" (Berlant 1997, 5), adolescent citizenship describes subjects who can act as citizens but whose acts of citizenship are derided and negated for being out of temporal sync with a fantasy of the nation's present. While infantile citizenship produces mixed and ambivalent relations of paternalism and care, adolescent citizenship negates the demand of recognition or justice by demarcating the subject as immature (and thus unworthy of the right), and by figuring the demand itself as out of sync (and thus precocious, if not alternatively anachronistic). Adolescent citizenship, then, is the produced relation between some citizens and the nation that both maintains the nation's paternalism and additionally interrupts the adolescent citizen's demand for rights and recognition under the guise of the subject's and the demand's inappropriate timing.

The troubled teen discourse thus functions on a few different levels. In a straightforward sense, it became a way of refuting Trayvon's innocence through a disavowal of his location in childhood. Beyond this register of subject positioning, however, this disavowal additionally marked black critique as itself a temporal dislocation, and thus as evidence for the claim that black people were not yet ready to occupy a paternal relationship to the nation. Mapped to the fantasies of differently situated subjects of historical and contemporary racial relations, the placement of Trayvon into adolescence by those whose structural grip on America was presumed to be under threat (those experiencing white injury), can be read as an attempt to reestablish the authority of whiteness in a postracial moment confronted by a national spectacle of black death. We can see the extrapolation of this framing from Trayvon to those that supported him in a number of places. In the *Miami Herald* article that I began with, for example, Trayvon's becoming a "national symbol of racial injustice" is connected directly, in the very same sentence, with his "spotty school record," making this link a way of both discrediting Trayvon and connecting his alleged deviance to those demanding justice. The implication of the *Miami Herald* article is that if, as the speculations assert, Trayvon was a troublesome teenager, then those gathered in his support might also be supporting of, or indifferent to, his complicated past. The protestors—as well as, I would argue, their concerns about racial injustice—thus become as "complicated" and as problematic to support as Trayvon himself. In this vein, under the disavowal of racism in the postracial era, the very demand that black people be recognized as full citizens is what justifies their location outside the frames of intelligibility the postracial state relies on. As such, we can understand this belittling discourse of adolescence in relation to Trayvon in the face of the demands that he be recognized both as an innocent child victim and as a valid subject and citizen of

America, as being indicative of a postracial desire to reaffirm the partial subjectivity of black people in the face of the alleged success of the Civil Rights Movement.

Avowal Is Not a Flavor of the Rainbow

Thus far I have documented and analyzed the visual and narrative ways in which Trayvon's childhood was disavowed and his location within a "troubled" adolescence was emphasized. These narratives of Trayvon's adolescence, however, did not go without fierce challenge. As already noted, his death instigated widespread protests and the Black Lives Matter movement, and thus the critiques of racist violence and the demands for justice for Trayvon cannot be reduced to a singular response. That said, I am interested in one of the lines of defense that emerged, one which specifically sought to counter the disavowal of Trayvon's childhood through the evocation of candy.

Interestingly, one of the main ways that an attempt was made to avow Trayvon's childhood was through a proliferation of references to the fact that he had bought a pack of Skittles on the night he was murdered. Indeed, Skittles was ever present in various responses to Trayvon's death. In the *New York Times,* for example, this account was given:

> At Spelman College, the historically black women's liberal arts school in Atlanta, the student government is buying Skittles in bulk and reselling them for 50 cents a bag to raise money for the family of Trayvon Martin. . . . The candy has been piled into makeshift memorials, crammed into the pockets of thousands of people who have shown up at rallies in his name and sent to the Sanford Police Department to protest the lack of an arrest in the case. (Severson 2012)

Along with these uses of Skittles, the candy was taped over protestors' mouths at public gatherings, attached to signs calling for Zimmerman's arrest, presented as evidence during the trial, and superimposed over viral images of Trayvon online. It was also evoked in personal terms by those who attended rallies in support for Trayvon and his family. Skittles thus took on a lot of work in the visual and narrative landscape in the wake of the murder—functioning as a primary signifier of Trayvon's childhood, and thus his innocence.

Skittles, however, like most other aspects of the case, played a dual role: they were simultaneously evidentiary and fantasmatic. They stood in for and evoked forms of racialized subject production that are under constant negotiation and tension. As such, their role in the evening of Trayvon's murder and in the responses to it were ambivalent. While the candy was used to connect him to the realm of childhood, its precise relationship to him was complex. One of these challenges is about who the Skittles were for. We can see this, for example, in the following two narratives about the night of Trayvon's murder, both of which present us with two children and a childish object:

> The family of a 17-year-old African-American boy shot to death last month in his gated Florida community by a white Neighborhood Watch captain wants to see the captain arrested, the family's lawyer said on Wednesday. Trayvon Martin was shot dead after he took a break from watching NBA All-Star game television coverage to walk 10 minutes to a convenience store to buy snacks including Skittles candy requested by his 13-year-old brother, Chad, the family's lawyer Ben Crump said. (Liston 2012)

> His [Trayvon's] killer, George Zimmerman, saw the teenager on the street and called the police to report he looked "like he's up to no good." At the time Trayvon was walking home from the nearby 7–11 carrying a bottle of Arizona iced tea and a bag of Skittles for his younger stepbrother, leaving many people to guess that the main thing he was doing that made him look "no good" was . . . walking while Black. (M. W. Edelman 2012)

These accounts of the evening (the first from *Reuters* and the second from Marian Wright Edelman, the president of the Children's Defense Fund) suggest that Trayvon was purchasing the Skittles for his younger brother. Other narratives of the evening, such as within an article from the *New York Times* (Kovaleski 2012), mentioned both Trayvon's younger brother (whose age also changes depending on the report) and Skittles, but not who desired them. The Skittles and Trayvon's younger brother were both simply present, and their presence was important. These narratives, I argue, worked to entrench Trayvon's connection to childhood by placing him into proximity to another child's body and to a childish object. And yet Trayvon's younger brother only persisted in some narratives of the evening. The candy, however, took on an affective and highly politicized role in the galvanizing of support for Trayvon and the demand that Zimmerman be arrested.[22] In many iterations that paralleled those above, the inclusion of Skittles into the story was used repeatedly to stand in for, or avow, Trayvon's childhood. His stated possession of Skittles begged the repeatedly asked question of what possible mal intent someone could have had whose journey out into a rainy and dark evening was motivated by a desire for candy.

This argument, and its explicit and implicit racialization, was made clear in an article in *The Guardian:*

> Whether or not you believe George Zimmerman, the neighbourhood-watch co-ordinator who says he shot Martin in self-defense, these [the items Trayvon Martin had with him at the time of his death: his cellphone, a cigarette lighter, earphones, a can of Arizona watermelon fruit juice cocktail, $40, and a bag of Skittles] don't sound like instruments of burglary. Indeed, the Skittles especially, with their bright playground colours and "Taste the Rainbow" slogan, have become a symbol of Martin's innocence. He may have been suspended from school at the time, and had traces of cannabis in his blood, but when you look behind the appearance of a menacing black teenager, those Skittles say, you find the child inside. (Benedictus 2013)

Skittles thus takes on a figurative life that shifts from something that Trayvon had placed in his pockets, to something that comes to act as an intermediary for Trayvon himself. In stark contrast to the ways in which his body (or the bodies assumed to be his) were used to place him in a gendered and racialized space of deviant adolescence, the packet of Skittles challenges, albeit tenuously, his "appearance as a menacing black teenager" and claims him as a child. The striking visualization of this replacement in the protests which demanded justice for him—the repeated images of Skittles packets covering, burying, and accompanying images of Trayvon and his supporters—created a collective demand that the childhood innocence that the candy evoked would speak back to the histories of criminalization that had encapsulated him as a "really suspicious" young black person.

But what are the terms of this avowal? If, as I have been arguing, the conditions of historical and contemporary antiblackness disavow black children's location within childhood, we should attend to why *this* embodiment rather than any other, was able, at least at this particular moment, to assert Trayvon's innocence. As Erica Meiners argues, we need to be cautious about the terms upon which affirmation of childhood are made:

> Claiming nonwhite youth as children or juveniles does not allow for a critical exploration of the conception of innocence: who benefits, who does not, and why. Nor does widening the category of who might have access to childhood (and therefore possibly innocence) unpack the underlying nexus of other associations tied to childhood. (2016, 62)

In calling the use of the Skittles into question, I do of course recognize that what William David Hart (2013) called the "execution" of an unarmed young black boy absolutely must be decried and challenged. As such, while I insist upon Trayvon's innocence, I locate my critique within the activism and scholarship of black, queer, trans, and feminist abolitionists.[23] As these scholars have argued, innocence itself is a racial logic, one that is unevenly distributed. With the evidence of Trayvon's innocence so heavily wrapped up in the rightful claim that he was "just a child"—as evidenced by his possession of Skittles—the very frame of childhood must be understood as structured by the same racial logics and deployments that are bound to innocence.

The use of the Skittles packet simultaneously evokes the innocence of children—an innocence that is coded along and as whiteness—and transfers that innocence to Trayvon's body, decrying the horror of Zimmerman's violent murder of a (now) innocent child.[24] For the candy—being brightly colored and pure sugar—symbolized childhood and innocence in a way that his own body could not. Within a discursive terrain that assumes black guilt, Trayvon, without the Skittles, would have simply been a suspicious black boy in a neighborhood where he was not recognized. He would not have had something to signify his innocence, and the only thing that would have been available to make sense of his death would have been Zimmerman's word and Trayvon's past—a history whose narration I have already shown to be laden with racist and gendered discourses of criminality. Furthermore, the claim of innocence that is transferred to Trayvon through Skittles would not work if that object, like the gold tooth grill, implicated him in histories of the skin that further criminalize black men and cast them out of childhood. While it was his blackness that initially made him a suspect to Zimmerman, the claim of injury—the claim of racial profiling—can seemingly only be made through the intelligibility of the injury done to his childhood innocence as figured by Skittles. This is deeply concerning, for it implies that optimistic calls for racial justice that use Skittles in Trayvon's name are predicated on forms of racial intelligibility—scripted through and as childhood—that reify the deviance of black masculinity and the innocence of whiteness.

#IfTheyGunnedMeDown

What does it mean to need Trayvon to be a child in order for him to be innocent? What does it mean, as well, to need him to be innocent at all in order to deplore his murder? Are the conditions of empathy and sorrow so neatly aligned with the conflation of childhood and innocence that childhood itself—rather than Trayvon's mere fact of being alive, and certainly, it seems, rather than his black life—must structure our critique of his death? By way of answering these questions, and drawing this chapter to a close, I turn to a speculative archive of representation that emerged in the aftermath of another loss of young black life.

On August 9, 2014, thirteen months after Zimmerman was acquitted, Mike Brown, an eighteen-year-old black male, was shot dead by Darren Wilson, a white police officer in the Ferguson Police Department. The next day, C. J. Lawrence introduced the hashtag #IfTheyGunnedMeDown on Twitter, tweeting: "Yes, let's do that: Which photo does the media use if the police shoot me down?

#IfTheyGunnedMeDown" (Lawrence 2014). Along with this text, Lawrence posted two images sutured together: one of him giving a speech at his college graduation (at which a highly amused President Bill Clinton laughs at something Lawrence has said), and another of him gesturing to the camera and holding a bottle of alcohol. Directly challenging the postmortem representation in the media of black people after their murders by the police, Lawrence's hashtag quickly went viral, and over 180,000 reiterations of the tweet were posted in the following three days. These posts became part of a digital archive collection through the social media site Tumblr.[25] Some of these sutured images were posted simply with the hashtag, while others were accompanied by personal narratives and rebuttals like the ones below:

But seriously . . . #IfTheyGunnedMeDown which picture would they use? I already know the answer to that, they'd do anything to portray me as a criminal even if I was so innocent I didn't see the bullet coming. This is white America and the police are making sure they do their part to keep it that way. (@vicariouslylivingx)

Would they paint me as a kid who had trouble in school? Who was struggling with mental illness and was probably unstable and probably running the streets at all hours of the night? Or would they paint me as a kid who was loved in school by teachers? A kid who had trouble, but did their best? A kid with lots of friends and family? I think we know. (@gentlemanlypansexual)

When Trayvon Martin and Jordan Davis were killed, various outlets used the most thuggish pictures they could find of those young men. So, I ask you all, #IfTheyGunnedMeDown, which picture would the media use of me? I think I already know the answer. #RIPMichael-Brown (@benny-thejet)

They wouldn't show the smiling girl who graduated abroad at one of the best schools in the country. The media would portray me as a hard and mean-looking girl who was asking for it. They wouldn't honor the life I had lived, but rather, justify the reason I was dead. (@mariefatale)

"Trayvon Martin," Hart writes, "was dead before his deadly encounter with George Zimmerman. His execution . . . was a post-mortem event; a ratification after the fact of the facts of black male being-in-America" (2013, 91). As I have argued throughout this chapter, one of the ways in which Trayvon's body was marked as already dead, and his deadly encounter—his execution—was justified, was through the racial logics imparted by the disavowal of black childhood. Childhood, as a historically negotiated racial technology that distributes exclusion, negation, enslavement, and incarceration to black communities, worked directly in the political aftermath of Trayvon's murder to mark him as deserving his death. It also, I have argued, became a dense transfer point of innocence and whiteness through which Trayvon's own innocence could be established, but at the cost of replacing and negating his particular body. While we will never know whether or not Trayvon anticipated his own premature death, nor can we assume what stories and images he would have used himself if he had contributed to the #IfTheyGunnedMeDown campaign, we might ask what political work these images do in relationship to the representational field that emerged in the aftermath of his murder.

Writing about this campaign, Campt analyzes these images through a black feminist politics of fugitivity and refusal:

> Refusing to wait passively for a future posited as highly likely or inevitable for black urban youth, the sitters [in the #IfTheyGunned-MeDown campaign] actively anticipate their premature deaths through these photos. In doing so, they enact anterior practices of fugitivity through their refusal to be silenced by the probability of a future violent death they confront on a daily basis. Through these images they fashion a futurity they project beyond their own demise. (2017, 109)

This refusal, coupled with the intentional suturing of apparently "opposed" (and oppositional) imagery, is central to my own reading of these images.[26] For in the suturing of these images, the future imagined and demanded by them is created as a speculative space in which both images exist simultaneously. These young people's repeated references to their own future death, and their invocations of "we already know," suggest that they are all too aware of the collective and categorical disavowal of black childhood. Knowing that using a "positive" image to counter a "negative" one buys into the logics of antiblack disavowal, these paired images seek to articulate a speculative politics of black childhood. Refusing the histories of signification that have violently criminalized black youth, the #IfTheyGunnedMeDown campaign insisted that alternative forms of avowal be found within *both* of these images, rendering them exculpatory of, as well as irrelevant to, their subjects' prospective grievability.

In the digital melding of imagery, the posting of two images as one, these images demand that they be seen and read together. As representations of these subjects' pasts and futures, these seemingly "opposed" images, and the foreshadowed postmortem narratives they tell, cannot not be read as belonging to the same person.[27] As Campt notes, it is not simply that these images and narratives project a future beyond these people's potential—or inevitable—deaths; rather, their suturing acts as a "fundamental renunciation of the terms imposed upon black subjects that reduce black life to always already suspect by refusing to accept or deny these terms [possibility or negation] as their truth" (2017, 109–13).

The speculative holding together of possibility and negation, the renouncement of the postmortem representation of preemptive black death through a demand that the complexities of the contradictory pasts that these images speak to and reject, thus becomes an act of refusing the simplistic and violent reading of childhood—and its disavowal—upon these subjects. While Trayvon did not have the opportunity to decide how his young life would be represented and accounted for, thinking with the speculative political work of the #IfTheyGunnedMeDown campaign, we might work to acknowledge, center, and avow all of Trayvon's nuances and demand that they, more so than simply his "innocence," place him squarely within childhood. And yet the politics of rearticulation that emerged within the #IfTheyGunnedMeDown campaign were not just confined to childhood; these images and narratives demand that we urgently understand the present to be mired in an antiblackness that itself needs to be publicly avowed in order for it to end.

Transphobia as Projection

Trans Childhoods and the Psychic Brutality of Gender

Speaking to the media in February 2013, Kathryn Mathis, a middle-aged white woman living in Colorado with her husband and their five children, defended her and her husband's decision to file a discrimination complaint on behalf of Coy, their six-year-old daughter:

> We were very confused because everything was going so well, and they had been so accepting, and all of a sudden it changed and it was very confusing and very upsetting because we knew that, by doing that, she was going to go back to being unhappy. It was going to set her up for a lot of bad things. (Payne and Fantz 2013)

The confusing incident that shook the Mathis family was a decision, made in December 2012 by their daughter's school district, that Coy could no longer use the girls' restrooms:

> We got a call one evening, it was the principal and he said he wanted to set up a meeting with us to discuss options for Coy's future use of the restroom.... It came out that Coy was no longer going to be able to use the girl's restroom and they were going to require her to be using the boy's restroom or the staff bathroom or the bathroom for the sick children. (Whitelocks and Greig 2013)

This decision was made because the district believed that it was no longer appropriate for Coy, a trans girl, to share the space of the restroom with the other girls. Fearing for their child's safety, and upset that the school district was abruptly curtailing their support of Coy's gender identity, the Mathis family took her out of school and filed a discrimination complaint.

In a response letter by W. Kelly Dude, the school's attorney, he justified the district's stance by putting into question Coy's location in childhood, her sexed embodiment, and her gender identity. Dude, who excuses his use of male pronouns for Coy as "not [an] attempt to be disrespectful, but because I am referring to male genitals" (Dude 2012), made the following statement:

> The District's decision took into account not only Coy but other students in the building, their parents, and the future impact a boy with male genitals using a girls' bathroom would have as Coy grew older.... However, I'm certain you can appreciate that as Coy grows older and his male genitals develop along with the rest of his body, at least some parents and students are likely to become uncomfortable with his continued use of the girls' restroom. (Dude 2012)

On the premise of Coy's potential (and fantasmatic) future male genitalia and the discomfort they would allegedly create, the school district argued that it would be inappropriate for her to use the girls' restrooms.[1] What does it mean, this chapter asks, to regulate access to a space based on the future possibility of "male genitals"?[2] What does it mean, particularly in this case, when the possibility itself of adult male genitalia is both fantasmatic—hormone and surgical interventions for trans girls shift the temporality and necessity of obtaining "future" male genitals—as well as foreshadowed. Coy, at the time of being excluded from the girls' restrooms was six years old, most likely a long way off from obtaining this fantasmatic adult male penis. As this exclusion both directed its violence at a child, and simultaneously and transphobically projected that child into adulthood, this chapter centrally asks how childhood works for and against a transfeminist politics.[3] In answering this question, this chapter begins with and keeps returning to Coy, as it thinks through the role childhood plays in trans narratives of self-discovery and transition; in the psychic life of gendered attainment; and in the possibilities of imagining collective solidarity between a feminist tomboy girlhood and a trans boyhood.

The questions I ask in this chapter in relationship to Coy, and the research that I undertook to write it, emerged out of a particular moment in which Coy's challenge to her school was the most public case in which trans bathroom access was being debated.[4] Since writing this chapter, Coy's case has been won, but the question of trans people's access to public facilities—particularly in schools—that align with their gender identity (rather than the sex listed on their birth certificate) has become a seething national debate with particularly violent rhetoric and consequences.[5] Indeed, it is not just trans access to public spaces that is up for debate in the current political climate. As a leaked memo from the Department of Health and Human Services in 2018 made clear, the Trump administration was seeking to define trans people out of existence. Defining gender as determined "on a biological basis that is clear, grounded in science, objective and administrable" (Green et al. 2018), the agency, as reported by the *New York Times*, would render sex as "immutable biological traits identifiable by or before birth" (Green et al. 2018). On more local levels, trans people, and particularly trans women of color, are facing increased instances of violence, despite, or perhaps because of—as the editors of *Trap Door* (Gossett et al. 2017) suggest—the visibility of trans people in the wake of the so-called trans tipping point (Steinmetz 2014).[6] Alongside increased awareness of trans children in particular comes a subsequent series of campaigns to remove trans people from public and private spaces.[7] These include North Carolina's infamous, and now repealed, Public Facilities, Privacy and Security Act (General Assembly of North Carolina 2016), and the Texas Privacy Bill (Texas Senate 2016), both of which, Gayle Salamon writes, "state explicitly that they are about the safety of girls and women and are intended to protect them from sexual harassment and assault" (2018, 163). In these campaigns—which conveniently ignore the fact that trans inclusive bathroom policies do not, of course, seek to legalize sexual assault or rape, and the fact that the sex segregation of bathrooms does not in any way act as an effective barrier to an individual's forced or unnoticed entry into the "wrong" space—childhood operates along the now familiar lines of sexual and racial innocence and victimhood.[8]

In this way, the laws that emerged to exclude trans people from public facilities over the last decade are extensions of the logic behind Coy's exclusion from the girls' restroom: the safety and comfort of the girls who are imagined to rightly occupy the restroom operates as justification for the prohibiting of an assumed-to-be adult trans person's entrance. In the Colorado district's exclusion of Coy, however, the trans person being excluded was herself also a child. Seeking a way around the paradox of "protecting the child" while simultaneously directing violence at a child, in the very justification for Coy's exclusion, Coy was lifted out of the space of childhood and projected into the body of an older male. The district, as cited above, argued that Coy must use other facilities because of "the future impact a boy with male genitals using a girls' bathroom would have as Coy grew older" (Dude 2012). In this rhetoric, then, Coy was also understood to be an adult male. In the terms of this argument, the district relied on complicated and contradictory logics and deployments of gender, sexual difference, and childhood, which I argue are important to work through in order to think critically about the wider connections between transfeminism and childhood.[9]

Specifically, the district claimed that a six-year-old girl could be understood to be already possessing (through its ghostly foreshadowed presence) a future adult male penis, and yet, at the same time, it made a very different claim. For a moment, that is, Coy was recognized as (or, according to the district, misrecognized as) inhabiting the same subject position as the other girls at the school. Because of this (mis)recognition, she was able to use the girls' restrooms without issue. Explaining their previous leniency in relation to Coy's gender, the district argued that it was the essential androgyny of childhood that allowed Coy to use the girls' restrooms prior to their intervention: "The reason it has not been 'an issue' to date is that fellow students and even the other teachers in the building are not aware that Coy is a male and at his young age, he may appear to be a female" (Dude 2012). This reasoning—based on the premise of an understandable yet "inaccurate" collective (mis)reading of the child's body—emphasized the fluidity of a six-year-old's gendered embodiment, rendered Coy's sexual anatomy temporarily inconsequential and allowed her to coexist with the other girls for a time. In other words, the temporary (mis) reading of Coy as girl negated the very need to know whether or not she had a penis. As such, in the district's argument that Coy's body had "not yet" or "only just" become problematically located in the girl's restroom—a suggestion that is explicitly made in the district's declaration of her body *eventually* causing trauma—her temporary access was thus only excused because as a child she, like the rest of the girls, was not yet understood to be inhabiting a properly sexed body.[10] Coy's location in a particular position within childhood meant that she oscillated between these two discourses, one that understood her body as an adult male's, and one that could not distinguish her body from other girls' bodies. While the district asserted that the issue had to be reexamined because Coy's enrollment in the first grade meant she would be more likely to use shared restrooms rather than single-occupancy ones, it was precisely this jump between her passing as a girl due to her "young age" and her being unable to pass due to fantasies of her "growing older" that the district decided she needed to use alternative facilities.

In this chapter I use this oscillation of Coy's positioning as a springboard to ask after the investments at work in the fantasy that sexual difference and bodily inhabitation are simultaneously inconsequential during childhood and always under threat. What does this fantasy mean, I ask, particularly when the gendering of boyhood and girlhood is so intense? What does this fantasy allow for when trans people themselves evoke this particular duality of the child's positioning within and before sexual difference as a justificatory device through which trans narratives of self-discovery and transition can be legitimated? Alternatively, what role does the temporary dismissal of sexual difference and sexual anatomy in childhood play in the psychic life of the gender binary, and what demands—of femininity and of girls in particular—does it allow for in the violence (and pleasure) of cisgender attainment? Understanding the transphobia that excluded Coy from the restroom and was justified through a narrative of her as an adult male as being an effect of the psychic life of gender, this chapter turns, initially, to two different types of texts. In the first section I work with trans narratives of childhood found in autobiographies, biographies, published interviews, and testimonials. In the following section I read Freud's and Lacan's analyses of the role of the penis/phallus as they structure gendered achievement. I argue that the language of projection helps us make light of the school district's decision to exclude Coy and needs to be understood as a structure of transphobia more widely. The final section turns to the film *Tomboy* (Sciamma 2011), and it explores the speculative question of how one might read a gendered self upon its central character—sometimes known as Laure, sometimes known as Mikael. Across these three explorations of gender and childhood—trans narratives of gendered identity, psychoanalytic understandings of transmisogyny, and the transfeminist possibilities of Laure/Mikael—this chapter seeks out a speculative transfeminist politics of articulation that might intervene in the ways in which childhood makes possible transphobic and misogynist projects.

Narratives of Trans Childhood

While the conventions of gendered normativity generally take as given and natural a cisgender person's gender identity, this same acceptance is not so routinely granted to trans people, and trans children in particular are subject to pervasive disbelief. As Jules Gill-Peterson writes in the preface to *Histories of the Transgender Child*:

> Subject to radical skepticism and verification in the best instances and to being dismissed as unreal or brainwashed in the worst, trans children's consistent experience in this country is to be excluded from having a voice, from having a say in the public battle over whether they should find themselves allowed to be, as if such determinations are not procedurally genocidal in their holding open the door to a world where trans life would be violently extinguished from growing in the first place. (2018, vii)

One of the central discourses that fuels this genocidal skepticism is that trans children are too young to know their true gender, and that therefore any action they take to realize their gender will not only harm them bute will also be regretted later. Against this a counter-discourse has emerged which reiterates trans children's gendered precocity. Trans children, as I show through my analysis of the following narratives, are defended by their parents and by those telling their stories through positioning them as having advanced knowledge of gender. This investment in claiming trans precocity, however, is speculative. It carries immense risk but also potentially reorients childhood in unexpected ways. These speculative narratives have vast implications for trans children and childhood more generally, because they rely on, *and expose the ambivalence of,* terms that align childhood with normative temporalities of sexual difference.

The Mathis family's legal battle with Coy's school district to allow her to use the girl's restrooms was propelled to national recognition when a feature article about Coy was published in *Rolling Stone.* The article, "About a Girl: Coy Mathis' Fight to Change Gender" (Erdely 2013), which uses male pronouns for Coy up until she is described as having been officially diagnosed with gender identity disorder at age four, gives credence to Coy's desire to transition and to use the girl's restrooms through a narration of her early childhood. The article begins with a highly gendered anecdote of eighteen-month-old Coy:

> When Coy Mathis was a year and a half old, he loved nothing more than playing dress-up. He didn't show much interest in the fireman costume or the knight outfit, but would rummage through the toy box to grab the princess dress with the flowery headpiece. His mother, Kathryn, would text photos to her husband of their plump-cheeked blond boy twirling in a pair of pink-and-purple butterfly wings or wearing a frilly tutu. (Erdely 2013)

While Coy's parents are recounted as lovingly accepting this dress-up play even as they brushed off the retrospectively obvious (at least to *Rolling Stone*) implications of it, diminishing it as merely the "cute" play of a toddler, this moment is narrated as the introduction to Coy's story precisely for the ways in which it secures as natural and given Coy's girlhood. Anything but "merely play," *Rolling Stone* asserts, this moment establishes the inherent nature of Coy's identity as evidenced by her desire for princess dresses and flowery headpieces during her toddler years.

When narrated through what Elspeth Probyn (1995) calls the "event"—or what Carolyn Steedman (1992) calls the "form"—of childhood, the claims to one's rightful or honest inhabitation of gender are understood to gain further legitimacy. Event, form, interiority, and self-explanation—all of these are central to trans narratives, both because the "self" that they help explain is one that, in a context of widespread transphobia, requires defending, and because having a coherent or intelligible gender is so central to understandings of the self. As Jay Prosser argues, one of the key political motivations of transsexual autobiographies is the use of this crafting of interiority via narrative in order to take ownership of one's gendered self: transsexual autobiographies are the putting into writing of "the transsexual as authorial subject" (1998, 9).[11] Transsexual autobiographies, then, are a response to the fact that providing a narrative—telling a particular type of story about gender identity, something that is often required in order to receive hormones, name changes, or any other support for transitioning—is what Prosser calls "the linchpin of the transsexual diagnosis" (1998, 113). In this light, Prosser argues, "it is not simply in the clinician's office but in the very conception of transsexual subjectivity that autobiography subtends (supports and makes possible) transsexuality" (1998, 115). For Prosser, Probyn, and Steedman, the writing of memory—and particularly childhood memories—is a complicated act, one that raises questions of temporality, history, evidence, and subjectivity.[12]

While Prosser writes about narratives that include moments within childhood, his attention is not drawn to childhood in particular but rather to how childhood is called upon to interact with other narrative devices. Recounting, for example, a moment from Mario Martino's *Emergence: A Transsexual Autobiography* (1977) where Martino thinks back to a time in his childhood in which he stood in front of a mirror and transformed his female body with prosthetics to give himself a penis, Prosser argues that it is the device of the mirror and its doubling back of the gaze that "coheres this young girl with the [adult] male subject writing" (1998, 102). "The childhood mirror scene," Prosser writes, "functions simultaneously as autobiographical and as transsexual prolepsis, foretelling and naturalizing this plot of sex change, suggesting that, in the imaginary (the mirror) the penis has been there all along" (1998, 102). While Prosser privileges the mirror as a narrative device, one that he adeptly traces through numerous transsexual autobiographies, I am interested in how childhood, more so than the mirror, is understood to so easily take on the roles of fore-telling and naturalizing for gender.[13] For Prosser, then, narrating the childhood mirror scene—from the vantage point of the adult—as evidence of Martino having had fantasies of trans embodiment all along, allows for the production of a linearity, a sexed and gendered coherence across time, precisely because it mirrors narrative form. For me, however, doing so posits this coherent gendered selfhood as stemming not from narrative structures generally, but from the specific form of childhood as narrative.

In the following excerpt, taken from one of Andrew Solomon's interviews in *Far from the Tree* (2012), the father of Scott, a trans man, thinks back to a moment in Scott's early childhood when he first asserted a desire for masculinity:

> Gender irregularities were plentiful in Scott's early life. "As a little girl, Anne-Marie [Scott's assigned name at birth] had this beautiful curly blonde hair," Scott's father, Morris, said. "One morning we got up and Anne-Marie, who was eighteen months old, was in her older brother Ben's room, and Ben, maybe five, had cut off all her hair. Ben got in trouble, but later I wondered if Anne-Marie somehow asked for it." (Solomon 2012, 637)

This narration uses Scott's desire for having short hair in early childhood as a sign that his gender identity is not only stable (concordant with his adult gender identity) but also natural. Narrating Scott as "somehow" asking for a haircut is a way of positioning him as desiring maleness and masculinity before being able to articulate, in language, this desire. Placing his desire for masculinity, short hair, and perhaps to also be like his brother, before his capacity for speech is a tactic of locating his desire before cultural influences and even before con-struction. It is a way of using the framing of childhood as existing prior to (or on the edge of) sociality to validate Scott's claim—or the claim made on Scott's behalf—to gendered selfhood despite the "re-ality" of the sexed body. Mapped along the understanding that sees the child's ability to speak as one of the markers of the child's emer-gence into sociality, precocious gendered performativities in early childhood—like this speculative narration of Scott persuading his brother to cut his hair—take on the signification of precultural natu-ralization for trans gendered selfhood.

Another way that this placing of trans identity before language is articulated in these narratives is through stating that the child's own first use of language was to correct their repeated misgendering by their parents. Asserting that this correction is the first thing trans chil-dren articulate, the identification with a gender is located before the child could speak.[14] In the following three narratives about trans chil-dren, it is this very telos that gets used:

> From the moment he could speak, Jazz made it clear he wanted to wear a dress. At only 15 months, he would unsnap his onesies to make it look like a dress. When his parents praised Jazz as a "good boy," he would correct them, saying he was a good girl. (Goldberg and Adriano 2007)[15]

> When I asked Hillary [Ryland's mom] when she knew Ryland was transgender, she said there were a lot of signs. Ryland would scream "I'm a boy" as soon as he started speaking, and showed an aversion to anything feminine, said Hillary. (K. Wallace 2015)[16]

> As a parent of a young transgender child, I encounter [disbelief] on a daily basis. My child is five years old, was born anatomically male, and has identified strongly and unvaryingly as female from the moment she could speak. (Gendermom 2013)[17]

All three of these narratives (and these are just a selection of the many others like them) use the same phrasing—"from the moment [he/she] could speak"—to give credence to these children's innate and prelinguistic claim to their gender identity. In so doing they position childhood *as well as gender* as existing before linguistic capacity, and as before—precisely by being against—the influences of culture.

Across these narratives, the knowledge of one's own gender identity precedes, or is formed simultaneously with, what Judith Butler calls the "founding interpellation" of gender that takes place in the medical declaration "it's a boy/girl" (1993a, 7). For Butler, unpacking this interpellation is important because it allows for the recognition that gendering takes place prior to—or through the same structures as—the sexing of the body, and that therefore both sex and gender are available for radical contestation and possibilities. But the temporality of this being "brought into the domain of language," even as it requires a "matrix of gender relations [to be] prior to the emergence of the 'human'" (1993a, 7), can also produce a subjective before-space wherein the child's *own* founding interpellation of a shift from an assigned gender to a self-identified one renaturalizes gender identity through the pregendered space of childhood. Co-constituting meaning for one another, both childhood and gender are mutually produced as before and outside of language, culture, and discourse in these narratives. The solidification of gendered subjectivity thus moves from the moment of being interpellated by others as inhabiting a particular sexed body at birth (and the repeated reiterations of this interpellation) to naming one's gender for one's self—through a trans child's initial speech act or, in Scott's case, through performatively enacting gendered desires and embodiments prior to the ability to speak.[18]

These claims to children's natural identification with gender often refer back to a time in which children are also understood to be before sexual maturation. In another interview in *Far from the Tree* where this temporal positioning of the sexed body plays out, Solomon speaks to a trans man named Tony. In Tony's narration of his childhood, he remembers bursting into tears at five years old after his mother scolded him for taking his shirt off to play football with (and like) his brothers:

At five, Anne [Tony's assigned name at birth] and her twin, Michelle, were playing football with their brothers, Frank and Felix, and Anne

took her shirt off. Her mother said, "Girls don't take their shirts off."
Anne began to cry and said she was a boy. (Solomon 2012, 616)

This memory, along with others, is produced as gendered self-knowledge even before sexual or genital knowledge. Tony relates his story in his interview:

> Three early behaviors are often taken as indicators of fixed identity: what underwear the child selects; what swimsuits the child prefers; and how the child urinates. "I remember trying to stand up and pee as a little kid," Tony said. "I never wore girl underwear or bathing suits. I didn't even know that people had intercourse, but I knew that my gender was male." (Solomon 2012, 616)

Here, narrating himself as not knowing about sexuality places Tony within a space of childhood that exists before sexual desire and sexual maturation. Interestingly, it is his very location in this space of childhood innocence where sexual difference (along with sexual desire) has not yet taken hold of the body that reifies his claim to his maleness. Knowing he is a boy and desiring to perform masculine behaviors before he had been introduced to the sex practices of others—or even to his own sexual body—Tony reifies the innateness of gender identity. At the same time he dislodges the "inherent" connection between sexual anatomy and gender identity or expression. This deployment of childhood as being *before* sexuality, sexual maturation, or genital embodiment tends to both posit children's gendered performativities as natural and inherent as well as negate children's complex gendered experiences: imagining children as being before sexual difference requires them to also be before the pains, joys, and relations that having a sexed body engenders. It also demands that the complexities and failings of the binary gendered system be ignored or overstated. In this light, how might we read Tony's desire to place himself within naturalized hegemonic masculinity through his narrations of childhood when his bursting into tears might be read as either the act of a childish tantrum (an act which seemingly sees no gendered limitations) or as the (dis)allowed expressions and experiences of femininity, emotionality, or failure inherent within hegemonic masculinity?[19] In other words, the use of childhood innocence to reify gender identity in this way both establishes a strong claim to gendered selfhood, and exposes the ambivalences of the very grounds upon which that gender's coherence is put to use. My intention in stressing this point is not to open it up for grounds upon which to refute Tony's claim to maleness. On the contrary, I am suggesting that Tony's enactment *of maleness* opens up what maleness and masculinity might signify, and how they could be lived.

Another narrative that places the child's desire for gender before genital embodiment, and thus marks the ambivalence of gender, occurs through stories in which trans children articulate an imagined developmental telos of genital maturation that unfortunately does not take place. In Cortez's *Sexile* (2004), an explicit and beautifully illustrated graphic biography of Adela, a trans woman who fled Cuba for the United States, one version of this fantasmatic development is articulated. Adela recalls being a child and thinking: "I couldn't wait to grow up because I knew that when I turned 10 my dick would fall off my pussy would grow and finally I'd become a complete girl" (Cortez 2004, 6). This understanding of genital development demonstrates a creative reimagining of the body that allows trans children to use their partial awareness of puberty and genital becoming to find hope in their body's wished for ability to intervene. As a narrative structure, this imaginative story again uses the culturally imposed ignorance of sexuality in children—an ignorance fabled to be natural—as a naturalizing narrative frame. Here, Adela's gender identity is thus located within a pre-cultural, unadulterated space of self-awareness. And yet, as with Tony's story, the use of a narrative device that cannot quite live up to the work it is required to do raises some interesting questions. For it is not that Adela is sexually innocent, as the narrative deployment of childhood might require her to be. Speaking about her own childhood sexuality, Adela recalls:

I was fascinated by farm sex. Cow sex. Chicken Sex. Insect Sex. . . . Oh my god, I was the most horniest little kid. I used to fuck this one banana tree. I carved a little round hole in the trunk and child, I hit it hard! ... The tree [eventually] got boring and I graduated to humans. I used farm temptations to get sex. ... Nine years old and I was pimping a goat to get laid! (Cortez 2004, 6–7)

In this context, the naturalization of Adela's gender in childhood is not produced through her being prior to sexuality, but rather through her having not yet been socialized into a particular type of appropriate (or adult) sexual knowledge. Adela's use of childhood ignorance thus puts her gender identity into a moment of sexual development when sexuality is understood to be unorganized: a pre-Oedipal messy desire, rather than a distinct orientation. In this hyper-sexual, unorganized and "ignorant" space, Adela and her childhood fantasy of trans puberty locates her transness as having no relation to a cultural imposition.

Adela is not the only trans child to fantasize about the body's capacity to enact its own transness.[20] And yet, when the body does not intervene in its own trans becoming, sometimes the child does. Here, narratives of trans children's intervening in their bodies are exceptional for the ways in which they acknowledge "precocious" trans agency within childhood. In an interview with Sarah, the mother of a young trans girl named Danann, for example, she relates a story in which her daughter's precocious self-awareness led to Danann taking her body into her own hands:

[At the age of four] Danann began insisting she was a girl. ... One morning we were getting ready to go to church, and Danann said she didn't want to go. I asked why, and he said, "I don't think God is that great. He made a mistake when he made me," and pointed to his penis. ... Just a few weeks later I walked into the kitchen, and Danann had taken scissors and was getting ready to cut off his penis. (Edwards-Stout 2012)

A similar distressing scenario is relayed in a newspaper article for the *Metro* by Kerry, the mother of a girl named Danni:

Kerry McFadyen, from Scotland, has let her child, Daniel, live as Danni, after she realised she was more interested in dolls than footballs. The

32-year-old knew that Danni, who is now six-years-old, should have
been her daughter when she caught her with a pair of scissors. Kerry explained how she found Danni in the bathroom with a pair of scissors
"above his bits." She said: "I tried to be calm and asked him what he was
doing, and he told me he was about to cut off his willy so he could be a
girl." (Mann 2015)

In these narratives, trans children's refusing of their sexed bodies—an attempt at chopping off a penis, or creating a narrative
of development that understands genitalia as swapping at
puberty—troubles the understanding that children are before genital awareness. Because of this, the use of these narratives raises
interesting and critical questions about the assumptions of children's
embodied knowledge of sex and gender. And yet, the cultural cur-
rency of this assumption of children's genital ignorance means that
when trans children articulate an awareness of mistaken genital presence, they are seen as preemptively aware of sexual difference. Being
defined as exceptional, this "precocity" shuts down what could otherwise have been opened up as the implications of these narratives
for children. Instead, trans children's precocious awareness places
them—and them alone—into an ambivalent relationship to gender. In response to Sarah's narration of Danann's declaration of trans
identity at age four, for example, the interviewer (Kergan) and Sarah
share this dialog:

[Kergan]: What a profound thing to come out of a four-year-old's
mouth!
[Sarah]: Exactly. Who has that kind of self-awareness at that age?
(Edwards-Stout 2012)

Here it is precisely because Dannan's awareness is cast as precocious
that she is deemed as both exceptional to the normative telos of childhood development and as experiencing a natural gendered and sexed
relationship to her body and her selfhood.
    While this telos works—through its production of the exceptional
trans child—to justify and naturalize the trans identities of children,

it has repercussions for children of all gender identities. As Claudia Castañeda argues:

> For a child to claim a transgender status (or for an adult to claim transgender status for a child) is difficult because the child is always already seen as incomplete, as not yet fully formed; its gender is not fully mature, and the child is also seen as not fully capable of knowing its own gender. (2014, 59)

Castañeda's argument that the child's "gender is not fully mature" is not her own but is rather made in reference to the claims made by people who seek to invalidate trans kids' desires for self-determination. On one hand, then, the understanding that the child's gendered self is not yet fully formed gets used to delegitimize trans desires, and, on the other hand, when a trans child asserts an awareness of their body—one which appears out of sync, too aware, perhaps—their gender identity is understood to supersede the "given" fact of their body (their sex) and to naturalize their claim to a gender. In this sense the ambivalent positioning of childhood as prior to and formed by various types of knowledge of sexual difference allows childhood to both naturalize gender identity and to delegitimize trans desire as childish. In a framework in which trans children are not deemed mature enough to know their gender and are too young to be appropriately aware of their sex, the trans child only needs to state an awareness of the genitalia they have to be understood as having a precocious or asynchronous gendered development. As I have argued throughout this exploration of a few forms of trans narratives of childhood, this ambivalence of childhood both founds and troubles the effectiveness through which childhood coheres trans selfhood. This ambivalence also took place in the narratives about Coy.

COY'S PRECOCITY

Coy's feature article in *Rolling Stone* relays a now familiar anecdote of Coy's "precocious" genital awareness that begins with a questioning of Coy's sexuality:

[Kathryn Mathis] told no one of her suspicion about Coy [being gay]—it felt creepily premature to speculate about the sexuality of a kid still in diapers. Then one night in January 2010, Kathryn was tucking him in for bed under his pink quilt, and Coy, then three, seemed upset. "What's wrong?" she asked. Coy, his head resting against his kitty-cat-print pillow, hugged his pink stuffed pony with the glittery mane that he'd gotten for Christmas and said nothing, his mouth bent in a tight frown. "Tell me," Kathryn urged. Coy's chin began to quiver.

"When am I going to get my girl parts?" he asked softly.

"What do you mean?"

"When are we going to go to the doctor to have me fixed?" Coy asked, tears now spilling down his cheeks. "To get my girl parts?" (Erdely 2013)

Like the other narratives I have relayed above, in this account, Coy's gender identity becomes all the more justified, naturalized, and necessary to establish in her daily life, precisely through her awareness of her genitalia (and their mismatch with her gender) at a moment in time when to even speculate about her sexuality is deemed "creepily premature." This narrative of Coy's knowingness as the impetus for her transition uses the device of childhood to cohere a gendered selfhood to her, but it does so by reifying this understanding of childhood (childhood as genital ignorance) through Coy's shocking break of it.

As such, while Coy's troubling of the understanding that defines childhood through a lack of embodied knowledge justifies her rightful occupation of the girls' restrooms and of femininity and femaleness (at least for a sympathetic reader), its effectiveness in doing so maintains the space of childhood as that which is defined by its ignorance. Coy is thus produced as a girl both through her location within childhood, and through her narrativized break from it, and it is this break that was also used against her by her school district. Indeed, in the school district's logic, it was Coy's assertion that she was a girl—and thus her acknowledgement that her body included incorrect and unwanted genitalia at a time in which children (and particularly girls) are not supposed to have an understanding of their anatomy—that produced the concern around her presence and interpellated her into the realm of male adolescence. For the district, Coy's awareness of her genitalia, and the rupture it caused in relationship to her own location in childhood—and even her own body—was understood as potentially threatening to the other children; the district assumed a contagiousness of this genital awareness that they used as justification to keep her out of the very space that her narrativized precocious knowledge sought to naturalize her inclusion within. Coy was thus explicitly excluded from the girl's restrooms because she disrupted the normative timing of the movement from early childhood to adolescence: at six years old her bodily awareness cast aside her actual body, being understood as so asynchronous to childhood itself that the district understood her as already having mature, adult, male genitalia.

Narrative itself played a central role in this temporal and subjective positioning. As I argued above, trans lives and trans narratives are intimately intertwined. As Prosser writes: "transsexuality is always narrative work, a transformation of the body that requires the remolding of the life into a particular narrative shape" (1998, 4). Therefore, what trans narratives expose, Prosser argues, is a collective desire for coherence and bodily integrity such that "transition does not shift the subject away from the embodiment of sexual difference but more fully into it" (1998, 6).[21] Prosser thus contends that before critiquing trans autobiographies "for conforming to a specific gendered plot," one that establishes one's self and one's gender as coherent and linear, "we need to grasp the ways in which the genre of autobiography is conformist and unilinear" (1998, 115).[22] Autobiographical narratives, Prosser writes, function precisely by taking the randomness of life events and endowing them with "chronology, succession, progression—even causation" (1998, 116). The work that trans narratives do thus specifically asserts a trans person's "claim to already (truly) be" the gender they identify with (1998, 119). Because the narratives that Prosser is reading are ones written by adults about their current gender identity—and thus their returns to childhood are a reading back onto childhood of their coherent gendered selves—the linearity of them is retrospective: it builds a coherence that begins in adulthood and reads that self back into the past.[23]

However, in many of the narratives that I have been working with here—and certainly for Coy—the subject at stake is a child, and thus their constructions of coherence, linearity, chronology, and causation jut them into an adulthood that has not yet come to be. Relying on narrative structures that implant the child subject "more fully into" sexual difference, and define them as "already (truly) being" an adult future self, thus create the conditions under which a transphobic re-reading also functions, precisely because they emerge out of the ambivalent (and fantasmatic) space of childhood. Put simply, for those advocating on Coy's behalf, this narrative entrenchment in a future sexual difference, and this linear production of a future self that has always been, relied on childhood as narrative to stake the rightful claim that Coy must be recognized as a girl.[24] For those advocating against her, however, those same structures of entrenchment and "already currently being" a particular gendered and sexed self, functioned as the device through which her fantasmatic adult male body could already be read onto her. Because childhood as narrative functions so ambivalently in this context—often by virtue of disregarding the ambivalence of childhood itself—it needs to be approached carefully in advocating for trans children like Coy.

The Psychic Brutality of Gender

Trans affirmative narratives are not the only places where the ambivalence of childhood gendering requires further attending to. Indeed, one of the key facets of transphobia, I argue, emerges from a refusal to grapple with the constitutive ambivalence of gender itself. Here, moving away from narratives and toward the psychic life of gender, I work to think through the implications of ambivalence for trans children like Coy. As I noted at the opening of this chapter, Coy's school district argued that her future male genitalia would transform the space of the girls' restroom into one of discomfort. "As his male genitals develop along with the rest of his body," Dude declared, "students are likely to *become uncomfortable* with his continued use of the girls' restroom" (Dude 2012, emphasis added). This fantasmatic narrative, one that revels in a perverse desire for its own fulfillment, seems to understand the space of the girls' restroom as currently being comfortable because it is understood to be a place of shared girlhood. The district thus assumes an imaginary of mutual recognition within sex (between girls) that posits similarly sexed bodies as not being sites upon which the ambivalence of gendered recognition and identification are read. Against the school district's claim that Coy would introduce an otherwise absent discomfort into the same-sex space of the girls' restroom, psychoanalysis might suggest that gendered recognition and psychosexual development—particularly in relation to girls and femininity—is anything but comfortable. While *comfort* is not, of course, a psychoanalytic term, we can see in Freud's discussion in "Femininity," for example, that the process of psychosexual development through which "a woman develops out of a child with a bisexual disposition" ([1933] 1964, 116) is one that is born out of relationships between women (between mother and child) involving hostility, hate, reproach, and ambivalence. Freudian psychoanalysis, then, is helpful here in relationship to Coy not only because it questions the presence and source of discomfort within allegedly same-sex spaces but also because it does not assume as natural nor necessary the link between femininity and female embodiment.

Indeed, for Freud, as well as for the early feminist psychoanalysts like Karen Horney ([1926] 1967) and Helene Deutsch (1946), the ability to explain psychosexual development is not just a question that needs to be asked after; it is also most complex in regard to femininity. Horney, for instance, who challenged Freud's phallocentrism and the wider discipline's androcentrism ([1926] 1967, 54), argued that one of the key stages in the Oedipus complex for women—the girl's turning away from her mother, or what she called the girl's "flight from womanhood" (64)—is not a natural or given process but is, rather, "reinforced and supported by the actual disadvantage under which women labor in social life" (69). Making a similar argument from a different disciplinary position, Gayle Rubin argues that what is commonly understood as a "normal" disposition might best be understood as a form of gendered violence: "The creation of 'femininity' in women in the course of socialization is *an act of psychic brutality.* . . . Freud's essays on femininity [are] descriptions of how a group is prepared psychologically, at a tender age, to live with its oppression"

(1975, 196, emphasis added). In arguing, from a sociopolitical perspective, that normative gendering is not a fact of biology but instead a process of integrating misogyny into the psyche, Rubin asserts that it is not a girl's potential failure to achieve normative femininity that should be of concern (as it is within at least a normative reading of Freud). Rather, Rubin contends, concern should be placed in the conditions under which the *desired* outcome is produced, precisely because it is produced as desired (and as natural) despite only being achieved through an act of psychic brutality.

Along these lines, Elizabeth Grosz argues that "patriarchy requires that female sexual organs be regarded more as the absence or lack of male organs than in any autonomous terms," and as such, "for the others in the child's social world, the child's female body is lacking" (1994, 59). This inscription of misogyny onto the female body, Karin Martin (1996) suggests, begins in early childhood and is enacted through norms that discourage girls from learning about (or being taught about) their own bodies.[25] In other words, there are intense disciplinary norms (which are highly policed in early childhood) that construct the female body as having, as Freud would say "inferior" genitalia or as having genitalia defined through "lack." In this sense, the idea that the girls' restroom is a space of comfort might be understood as a disavowal of the violence of normative gendering, as it seeks to name the communality of that gendered experience as having nothing to do with anxiety or resentment. This analysis in and of itself might be productively understood as a trans-affirmative position, for in its universal questioning of the attainment of masculinity or femininity, psychoanalysis dislodges the uneven burden placed on trans subjects to defend, justify, and assume a particular body and identity. Within this framing of psychoanalysis, that is, all gendered positions—cis, trans, and otherwise—must be explained in a framework that includes, but is not reducible to, the body.

But more needs to be said about how this disavowal functioned in relationship to the threat Coy's fantasmatic body posed to this space from within psychoanalytic, rather than sociopolitical, explanations. In a particular biologically determinist reading of Freud's outlining of the Oedipus complex—a reading that many challenge and that I shall also challenge—the girl begins her move from polymorphous sexuality to "normal" femininity only after acknowledging real physical anatomy (Freud [1933] 1964, 124–125): the presence or absence of the penis comes to signify for the child either their own masculinity and authority (in boys) or their own inferiority and femininity (in girls). This understanding of the Oedipus complex fits within, indeed structures, a straightforward reading of the transphobic exclusion of Coy. It is precisely, in other words, the district's biologically determinist reading of sex, as well as its disavowal of the psychic brutality of psychosexual development, that, on the surface, justifies Coy's exclusion.

We can see this taking place in Dude's statement, wherein it was the assumption of the visual recognition of Coy's "male genitals" (Dude 2012) by the other girls in the same-sex space of the restroom that was produced as the precise act by which the girls would recognize their own inferiority, and their discomfort would arise. This is explicit in the fourteen-page decision by the court. Steven Chavez, the director of the Colorado Civil Rights Division and author of the decision (which sided with Coy), had to argue against the district's contention that if Coy were allowed to use the girls' restroom on the basis of gender identity it would set a harmful precedent:

> The Respondent [the school district] also proffers "what-if" scenarios, such as a request coming from "a male high school student with a lower voice, chest hair and with more physically mature sex organs who claims to be transgender and demands to use the girls' restroom after having used the boy's restrooms for several years." (S. Chavez 2013, 8–9)

The link between the projection of Coy into an older male body—"as Coy grows older and his male genitals develop along with the rest of his body" (Dude 2012)—and this phantasmatic figure of the older, hairy, and sexually mature man is more than simply evidence of the district's creative gendered imaginary. In this narrative, the school district locates the site of gendered violence and vulnerability as taking place in the meeting of opposite sexed (and aged) bodies; reproducing the biologically determinist Freudian narrative almost directly, the school district lifted Coy out of childhood and into a postpubescent male body, eliciting the Oedipal moment of genital recognition between the girl and her father. In locating Coy's body as being the phantasmatic penis that produces this discomfort, the district overemphasizes the act of perception, assuming that it—rather than the meanings already assigned to the perceived organ (to which I next turn)—is the source of discomfort.

As Jacqueline Rose argues, this biological reading of Freud and, I am arguing, its use within the exclusionary logic of the Fountain–Fort Carson School District "systematically [fall] into a trap" (1982, 28). This reading is problematic, Rose writes, because it fails to recognize that "the concept of the phallus in Freud's account of human sexuality was part of his awareness of the problematic, if not impossible, nature of sexual identity itself" (28). Central to this misreading, Rose argues, is the failure to grasp that the process that Freud describes for achieving femininity is a process formed through a patriarchal society that itself delineates and produces the "fact" of sexual difference. Here sexual difference, in Rose's account, is not exactly the sexual difference of Luce Irigaray (1993), Rosi Braidotti (1994), or Drucilla Cornell (1994)—for whom sexual difference is "both an epistemological approach and a creative process" (Foster 1999, 435). While Rose shares with them an analysis of symbolic relations, she understands sexual difference to be a structure of constriction (rather than creative liberation) by which the incredible range of gendered possibilities, performativities, and subjectivities that could come into being—and indeed can even be imagined—are limited into fewer and fewer options (Rose and Malabou 2016).

As such, sexual difference, for Rose, is distinct from anatomical difference, even, and precisely, as the latter comes to figure the former. Anatomical difference (mistakenly understood as naturally binary), Rose writes, "becomes the sole representative of what [sexual] difference is allowed to be" (1982, 42). If we take Rose's point about the figuring of sexual difference by anatomical difference, then the assumed effects of seeing, and being affected by, the anatomical body can be understood as the consequences of a misrecognition. The body one sees, in other words, is the body produced through language, desire, fantasy, and identification. The girl in the Oedipal triangle thus begins the process of becoming feminine not in the very moment she sees the genitalia of her mother and father but, rather, in the moment she comes to identify with her body's *signification*. As Rose writes:

> Freud gave the moment when boy and girl child saw that they were different the status of a trauma in which the girl is seen to be lacking (the objections often start here). But something can only be *seen* to be missing according to a pre-existing hierarchy of values ("there is nothing missing in the real"). What counts is not the perception [of the penis] but its already assigned meaning [the phallus]—the moment therefore belongs in the symbolic. (1982, 42)

For Jacques Lacan, that is, anatomy is not at all central to the process of psychosexual development (what he calls "sexuation"); rather, the symbolic meanings that are ascribed to anatomy are. He writes: "[The] facts reveal a relation of the subject to the phallus that is established without regard to the anatomical difference of the sexes" ([1958] 1977, 576). Lacan thus shifts Freud's language from the penis to the phallus and argues for a reading of Freud's Oedipus complex along the lines of the symbolic rather than the anatomic (indeed, he argues that such an anatomic reading of Freud is an inaccurate one). For Lacan it is not whether or not one has a penis but whether one represents, within the structure of desire, what it means to "have" or "be" the phallus (582). The phallus, for Lacan, is thus a signifier—indeed *the* privileged signifier—by which sexual difference is introduced. It is not, Lacan writes, "an object (part-, internal, good, bad, etc.). . . . Still less is it the organ—penis or clitoris—that it symbolizes" (579). Rather, the phallus is a signifier whose function is to designate meaning and to position one within sexual difference through one's relationship to it. "Clinical experience has shown," Lacan writes, not that "the subject learns [of its location within the structure of desire by] whether or not he has a real phallus, but in the sense that he learns that the mother does not have it" (579). Put another way, the girl child does, in a material sense, not have a penis; and yet, while this not-having is a real absence, the Real, for Lacan, cannot be lacking—the vagina does not lack a penis—and as such it is only when the girl perceives the penis as being absent (as not being where it "should" be) that she reads her body as lacking in relationship to the phallus and thus the symbolic. The fantasy of being deprived of an object that she never had and is not missing is thus not just the initiating division for the girl, it is also the catalyst by which she comes to notice anatomical difference itself. It is therefore the slip between the phantasmatic body (phallus) and the anatomical body (penis) that begins this process.[26]

This shift from penis to phallus is important. It reiterates my analysis of Coy's exclusion because it insists that it is not the presence or absence of a penis that is at issue but, rather, the meaning assigned to the phallus. Being thus related to the symbolic, rather than the anatomical, the question of where gendered violence comes from absolves Coy from the equation and instead points to the hierarchal values ascribed to bodies within the symbolic. Indeed, it is precisely because Coy's actual presence is not the source nor catalyst for the other girls' relationship to the phallus that the school had to produce Coy as the figure of the older, hairy male that she was not and would never be. To justify removing her from the girls' restroom required removing her from childhood. She had to be framed as already having the phallus.

Lacan's move from the penis to the phallus helps unpack the ways in which childhood, embodiment, and temporality co-constitute one another in this moment. Here I follow the insightful work of Patricia Gherovici, a Lacanian psychoanalyst whose book *Please Select Your Gender* (2010) proposes a rethinking of sexual difference and advocates for a depathologization of transness within psychoanalysis. For Gherovici, who draws upon Morel (2000b), sexual difference must be understood in relationship to time. "We need to stress both the temporal and spatial aspects of the word *difference*" (2010, 195), Gherovici writes. Drawing upon the French verb *différer*, which suggests both to differ and to defer, Gherovici advocates for the concept of difference to be understood within its double meaning—"[the] temporal (to postpone, to delay) and the nonidentical" (195). In this light, the first temporal register of sexuation, Gherovici writes, takes place "in the reality of anatomy, that is, in a mythically 'natural' difference" (193). The second, she argues, is the subsequent temporal register of sexual difference "and it is here that 'anatomy' is interpreted according to values of difference brought about by the signifier" (193). Put simply, Gherovici argues:

> Children notice anatomical differences *only after the symbolic event* brought about by the threat of castration. Anatomy, with its chromosomes, gametes, and genitalia, becomes *then* part of a mythical Real that acquires signification on this second stage, when the values of the sex assigned at birth are structured and a sexual positioning is assumed. (106, emphasis added)

In a way, the Fountain–Fort Carson School District proposed this very mapping of sexuation as a temporal concept. As I argued above, it thrust Coy into adulthood at the very moment that she acknowledged her anatomy, thus framing her "precocity" as a temporal and ontological break from childhood. But it also produced a narrative justification for its earlier leniency in relation to Coy's gender, which used a different entanglement of sexuation and temporality. The district, as cited above, argued that they had been caught unaware:

> The reason [Coy's presence in the girl's restrooms] has not been "an issue" to date is that fellow students and even the other teachers in the building are not aware that Coy is a male and at his young age, he may appear to be a female. (Dude 2012)

For the district, childhood is defined by being prior to the threat of castration, such that anatomical differences are real but are not yet part of the mythical Real. The district's slippage between sexual and anatomical difference thus only extended to the limits of childhood. When read as a child, she, like the rest of the girls, inhabited a space within the district's framing of psychosexual development prior to sexual difference (prior to the threat of castration)—in which anatomical difference was present but not yet perceived or perceivable. For a moment, that is, all the girls, including Coy, were understood within the realm of the Real where nothing is missing. For the district, to be a child is to be unaware of anatomical difference, to be prior to the threat of castration and the Real's acquisition of signification. In this sense, the district's previous support for Coy was thus premised not on whether she had a penis but on whether she was a child. In their reversal of the decision to support Coy, the district corrected their supposedly mistaken (mis)reading of her gender by correcting their reading of her age. Coy became "a male high school student" (S. Chavez 2013, 8), and she had "grow[n] older [and] develop[ed]" (Dude 2012). Coy was thus not only projected into a phantasmatic phallic body. She was also projected into adulthood.

PROJECTION

So far I have been arguing that the district "projected" Coy into adulthood, but I have not located this language of projection within an analysis that grounds it as a psychic defense mechanism. Coy's projection into adulthood has been framed here as akin to a *portending* of her "future self," but this act might be additionally understood through a projection of another kind. For Freud, projection is a defense mechanism that seeks to protect the ego from identifying with "unpleasurable" aspects of itself. Writing on projection initially in regards to paranoia, Freud ([1911] 1958) elucidates the concept with example of a man's paranoia borne out of what we might now identify as his own internalized homophobia. Because there is "no other way" for the unconscious of a man to express love for another man, Freud writes, the proposition "*I* (a man) *love* him (a man)" transforms through projection into, first: "I do not *love* him—I *hate* him," and then: "*He* hates (persecutes) *me*, which will justify me in hating him" ([1911] 1958, 63). Here, as Freud notes, "an internal perception is suppressed, and, instead, its content, after undergoing a certain degree of distortion, enters consciousness in the form of an external perception" (66). Projection, in other words, is the unconscious act of the ego's splitting off a part of itself which it finds unpleasurable, projecting it off into the world, or onto another object, and experiencing that object as the *source* of hostility. Here the "projection" of Coy into adulthood might thus be understood as the outcome of a psychic projection, a defense mechanism against an identification with the violence of sociocultural norms about femininity and the insipid hierarchy that marks the female body as inadequate. Suppressed, and in undergoing some distortion, these "unpleasurable" aspects of girlhood are projected onto Coy's body in the district's fantasy of Coy's penis being the source of discomfort.

As a way of further unpacking the role of projection in what I am calling the psychic brutality of cisgender attainment, and of locating these "unpleasurable" aspects of girlhood as constitutive of gender on a structural, rather than individualized and pathological level, I turn to Butler's "Melancholy Gender / Refused Identification" (1997). In this chapter of *The Psychic Life of Power*, Butler engages with Freud's outlining of the Oedipus complex to argue that the assumption of femininity and masculinity "proceed through the accomplishment of an always tenuous heterosexuality" (1997, 135), and through a disavowal that one ever sustained homosexual attachments. Butler's argument is not that everyone is secretly queer, but rather that cultural homophobia can partially be understood as an extension of the prohibitions on desire that structure normative gender itself. Here I want to supplement Butler's account of the role that repudiated *attachments* play in the formation of gender by adding an account of repudiated *identifications*. Tracing out the melancholic formation of femininity, Butler writes:

> Gender is acquired at least in part through the repudiation of homosexual attachments; the girl becomes a girl through being subject to a prohibition which bars the mother as an object of desire and installs that barred object as a part of the ego, indeed, as a melancholic identification. . . . If one is a girl to the extent that one does not want a girl, then wanting a girl will bring being a girl into question; within this matrix, homosexual desire thus panics gender. (1997, 136)

This repudiation of homosexual attachments that Butler describes is also structured by a repudiation of what might be understood as "trans" identifications such that the girl becomes a girl through a simultaneous prohibition that bars the father as a subject of gendered identification. Sex, as Butler argued in *Gender Trouble* (1990), already signifies gender (or the gender to be) such that what it means to be properly gendered, or to have "accomplished" gender, is to have one's gender correspond to one's sex in ways that are culturally intelligible. Femininity and masculinity thus proceed through the accomplishment of an always tenuous cisgender episteme, one in which sex must always correspond to gender in order for it not to be failed. This produces what Butler calls a "foreclosure of possibility" (1997, 135) in regard to intimacy, desire, and passion that is foundational to heterosexuality (as both a lived desire and as a structuring element of the political). It also, in regard to identification, forecloses the possibilities for avowing trans life and sets up psychic and social mechanisms to discipline cisgender-gendering that falls beyond the realm of the heterosexual matrix. To continue paraphrasing Butler: if one is a girl to the extent that one does not want to become a man, then engendering, or identifying with masculinity will bring being a girl into question. What is disavowed within this episteme is that cis—as an allegedly intelligible, coherent, and "natural" position prior to power—only exists as such because of its routine and constitutive subordination of trans as distinctly open to "trans" identifications. Structured by tentative and failing prohibitions of both desire and identification, the achievement of cisgender-gendering (one premised on the simultaneous foundation of whiteness) does not allow adequate space for the ambivalence of gender, nor acknowledgement of persistent yet disavowed "trans" positionalities that are also constitutive of gender itself.[27] As a mechanism against the potential recognition of the fleeting and lifelong moments of gendered identification that panic cisgender subjectivity, gendered ambivalence becomes split from the ego and projected onto the avowedly trans subject—the one who outwardly acknowledges and embraces the complex role of desire and identification within gendered attainment.

This analysis of transphobia as projection has implications for children well beyond Coy, and its implications demand that sitting with the ambivalences of gender and childhood should be central to a transfeminist politics. This is particularly so in a contemporary moment wherein trans and feminist are routinely positioned against one another. Despite the fact that transfeminism has a long genealogy, contemporary debates have framed trans rights as a threat to women and girls (always understood as cis) and to feminism. Here, attending to projection helps differently intervene in this debate, as it posits that transphobia is not just a symptom of misinformation, or a lack of understanding, but also of a collective psyche mired in the brutality of misogyny. Because the psychic brutality of cisgender attainment often becomes too much for the ego to bear, and because the ambivalences one has about the psychic life of gender cannot be grappled with in a cultural moment that is so highly invested in cisgender heteronormativity, this distress is projected onto the trans subject, registering *her* genital presence—or her mere existence—as the source of this brutality, rather than our collective identifications with a gendered system that is harmful at worst, and ambivalent at best. Transphobic projection not only directs hostility at trans subjects while experiencing trans people themselves as hostile, it does so while maintaining—through a refusal to acknowledge and grapple with the constitutive ambivalences of gender—the violences of normative gendering.

Playing with Laure and Mikael

Not wanting to overemphasize the psychic brutality of gender as the node of solidarity through which a transfeminist politics emerges and is most useful, I turn now to a speculative pairing of trans and feminist children in order to explore a transfeminism that revels in performativity, refusal, and pleasure. To do so, I turn to Mikael, the main character in Sciamma's *Tomboy* (2011).[28] Or, do I do so by turning to Laure? Granted, Mikael and Laure are the same person, and they are cast by the same actor (Zoé Héran). But which one of them—the girl, Laure, that the film closes with, or the boy, Mikael, that Laure becomes (has always been?) in the transitory space of summer, between moving to a new town and beginning a new school year—is the proper subject of the film?

Tomboy is Sciamma's second full-length feature, after her debut film *Water Lilies* (2007). Receiving numerous awards at international LGBT film festivals, the film, which was shot over twenty days with a small budget, tells the story of Laure, a ten-year-old French girl who moves to a new neighborhood and attempts to make new friends and attract the affection of her neighbor Lisa (Jeanne Disson) by presenting herself as a boy named Mikael. Most of Sciamma's feature films—including *Girlhood* (2014)—tell intimate tales of the bonds of identification and desire between young girls, but *Tomboy* centers around her youngest characters and is most explicitly about the performativity, and ambiguity, of gender in childhood. The film—in which, Darren Waldron argues, the camera "functions like an anonymous child observer who scrutinizes Laure's behavior and its reception" (2013, 65)—is set in a small world where the intimacies of the young characters' desires are mirrored by the natural and picturesque scenes in which they find one another, play, share glances, and bask in the risk and pleasure of opening up to one another.[29] The film portrays this risk and pleasure as central to childhood through the main character's gendered becoming. Approaching Laure and Mikael together, thinking about these two ten-year-old children who exist simultaneously and in opposition throughout the film, allows for, I argue, a speculative exploration of, or at least a momentary playfulness with, the gendered attachments and refusals that take place through childhood that have troubled this chapter so far.

Mirroring the narratives of trans childhood that I have worked through, Mikael presents his future self with memories of childhood that might sediment his future (and current) gender identity: alone in his room, Mikael carefully, though not precisely, cuts in half his old one-piece swimsuit. Trying on the makeshift briefs, he stands in front of his reflection and realizes that something is missing. Biting a nail, he stands unconvinced as he brushes his dangling arm against his slightly protruding hip. In the other room his sister is assembling a puzzle that she cannot seem to get right: the pieces, despite her forceful pounding, do not seem to fit. Mikael joins her, bringing out a box of toys and a few small tubs of modeling clay. Rolling the clay between his hands, he slowly crafts and sizes up his forest green prosthesis. Satisfied with its weight and shape, he returns to his room, stands in front of the mirror, and drops the clay into his swimsuit. The clay, he decides, makes a perfect bulge. Turning, again, side to side, he smiles. The scene cuts, and we next see Mikael swimming in the lake with the other laughing children.

Throughout the film, Mikael presents himself with himself in a number of mirror scenes like this, and he molds (and models) his own prosthetic clay penis to develop a bodily schema of a boyhood that will be and currently is. Placing his penis in his homemade swimming briefs, he might be read as allowing for a future narrative that would place his adult post-op penis, as Prosser would argue, as having "been there all along" (1998, 102). The film, too, might be read as similarly using childhood to produce and naturalize Mikael's trans identity. The tropes of summer, new beginnings, and play, all function within the film as metaphors for transition and for childhood itself. Indeed, the film revels in transitional spaces and moments. It opens with Mikael perched upon his father's lap in a car, as they engage in the particular intergenerational masculine father-son pedagogical bonding act of teaching one's son to drive. The space of childhood as naturalized transience becomes a scene upon which Mikael's transition is experienced. No longer Laure, and not having been her even from the opening shot, Mikael may never have been her in the first place. His negotiation of his male embodiment presents not a subversion of the regulation of femininity—as it might be understood through a tomboy lens—but rather a desire for masculine gendered coherence that can only be (at least somewhat) safely expressed within the time-space of childhood. Indeed, it is precisely the androgyny of this space that allows Mikael to be himself without being questioned by his family too much. Knowing that they will accept (at least for a while) his androgynous masculine gender presentation because it might be read as childish play, Mikael is deeply invested in the mutual coherences of gender and childhood that I have been troubling throughout this chapter.

Turning to Laure, I might read this film as a girl's desire for, and creative embodied production of, a feminist subversion of the male dominated space of childhood. The world that Laure lives in, a French suburb filled with lush forests and fields, is an affluent childhood space that is explicitly regulated along gendered lines. The children of the neighborhood exist within a landscape that allows free roaming movement, play, wrestling, and flirtation; and yet, these activities are deeply gender-segregated. Girls stand aside as the boys play; they are the spectators while the boys take up space. All of girls, that is, except for Laure, who joins the boys as a (tom)boy.[30] And yet, is Laure's becoming a (tom)boy an entrenchment of this gendered divide, or a subversion of it? Does it require that we recognize Laure as partaking in what Owain Jones describes as a "quasi-male identity" that reinforces "the always problematic admission of female gender within childhood" (1999, 118)?[31] Challenging and reversing this argument, I want to also suggest that Laure uses her body to refuse that very distinction and to trouble the assumptions made within feminist scholarship about the gendered critiques tomboys engage in. Importantly, Laure's ability to trouble gender in this way is dependent on her existing within a particular child body. We watch as she decides this for herself: Laure stands facing the mirror in her bathroom at home. Tentatively feeling her chest under her tank top, she hesitates, and then removes the top, standing in front of herself shirtless. Viewing her from behind, with the camera lingering over her shoulder, we see her examining her reflection in the mirror. She takes her time touching her skin, inspecting her arms for signs of musculature. Sighing, she does not speak. Shifting back and forth she presents her profiles, left and right, to herself and to us. Her young chest has not quite yet begun to develop. She might still be able to get away with being shirtless in a group without giving herself away. The boys go shirtless while they play, and she wonders if she might risk joining them. She looks at herself, folds her arms, sighs again, and then spits. Smiling as her saliva hits the sink, she finds pleasure in her ability to persuade herself.

In the film, it is Laure's predeveloped chest that allows her to remove her top, not just in the private space of her bathroom but also in the public landscape of the soccer field and the open air of the lake. It is Laure's current yet temporary embodiment of the presexed androgyny of childhood that gives her body access, and yet she still stands there in a girl's body. Her naked flat chest is (mis)read by others as a boy's, but it is still hers. In this instance, Laure does not embody quasi-male childhood, nor does she simply imply, as Waldron argues, that the "outward signs of masculinity [swaggering, spitting, playing football, and fighting] have no innate grounding in boys" (2013, 67). Rather, Laure flaunts a body that is (mis)recognized by the other children as a male child's, thus shifting the site of the embodied sign of sexual difference from her genitalia to her chest.[32] If her flat chest is what allows her to access male childhood spaces, might we need to rearticulate the relationship of gendered bodies and the meanings they carry in the moment of childhood (mis)recognition and say that maleness, rather than being understood as the genital presence by which female embodiment is produced as an absence, is actually a childish embodied lack of female definition? Temporarily embodying maleness as childhood femaleness, Laure (re)presents maleness back onto itself as a childish lack that she, as a girl, has the ability to move in and out of. Holding onto the moments left before her body might betray this movement—before school begins, her body starts to change, and the seasons with it—Laure strategically uses (and reverses) the contradictory frameworks of childhood and sex to negotiate her own feminist self-determination for them.

Laure's gendered representation has important connotations, not just for her but also for the other girls in her social space. At the very end of the film, after her she has been forced by her mother to come out as a girl to her friend Lisa, the two girls stand together next to a tree, and Lisa asks Laure to tell her the truth about her name.[33] Cautiously, as the camera moves in for a close up shot of Laure's face, keeping Lisa out of frame, Laure tells Lisa that her name is Laure, not Mikael, and, after a short inhalation of breath, and a couple of nervous glances, Laure catches Lisa's eye. Something in Lisa's off-camera glance resonates with her, and her caution turns to a smile, and then a smirk. This smirk, I argue, might be read as a playful recognition between Laure and Lisa that "Mikael" was not just an identity Laure exploited to get to Lisa (or to leave Lisa on the sidelines), but rather was a cunning refusal of the values and assumptions that stick to their female bodies.[34] This mutual recognition thus functions as a generous re-reading of the pleasure they both had (for indeed they did both find pleasure) in what they can now remember as the summer they created the possibility for intimacy amidst the space opened up by the boys' inability to read gender as anything other than anatomical difference.[35] What emphasizing this shared recognition between Laure and Lisa makes clear, in other words, is that analyses that castigate

tomboys (and tomboyhood) for sitting too closely with heteronormativity and normative gender roles cannot quite hold when the tomboy
is understood not as simply an individual, nor even just a girl among
boys, but is rather a girl formed through her intimate and political relationships with other girls.[36] Indeed, Laure flirts with, plays with, and
confides in Lisa; and she bonds with, resists, and teaches her younger
sister Jeanne (Malonn Lévana). These connections—Laure's, Lisa's,
and Jeanne's—are important. By focusing on Laure's expansive relations, by insisting that the multiple ways of inhabiting and resisting
girlhood must be read within and through these intimate connections, a more generous reading of Laure's political project emerges. All
three of these girls, then, share risk and pleasure in Laure's gendered
play, and the shared smirk between Laure and Lisa reminds us of the
feminist potentials that childhood makes possible.

There is more that could be said about the various moments of
gendered play, regulation, and sexual difference within the film, but
I want to conclude by way of taking up a speculative and reparative
reading of Laure and Mikael. As I've argued, both of these children
present us with various readings of the ways in which particular
gendered forms of intelligibility are given meaning and resonance
through the child. Indeed, this openness in terms of reading and audience identification was one of Sciamma's aims for the film:

> I wanted to keep all the hypotheses open when I was building the
> character. Not to avoid answers, but to make it more complex and ac-
> curate. . . . I made it with several layers, so that a transsexual person can
> say "that was my childhood" and so that an heterosexual woman can
> also say it. (Sciamma, quoted in Bendix 2011)

In Sciamma's opening up of the audience's identification with Laure/
Mikael, it is childhood itself, as a narrative form and trope of return—
"that was my childhood"—that allows for this multiple reading.
Perhaps, then, instead of taking Laure/Mikael up as confined subjects
and separate political projects, we might work to understand their
mutuality and struggle against the reading of them as part-objects.[37]
Here, inspired by Eve Sedgwick's (2003) reading of Melanie Klein's

work on manic depressive states ([1935] 1986; [1940] 1986; [1946] 1986), I first read Laure and Mikael through Klein's object relations in order to think further about ambivalence, and then I work to weave Coy back into this reparative reading of childhood gender.[38]

In her analysis of the connection between the development of the infantile ego and the conditions of mania, melancholia, depression, and paranoia, Klein argues for a theory of object relations in which the objects that nourish the infant (the mother, the breast), are split into two: the good and bad mother, the good and bad breast. The splitting of these objects, Klein argues, has consequences that manifest themselves differently, albeit relatedly, in depression and paranoia. In her work, Klein frames depression and paranoia as two defensive positions which emerge from different relationships to this splitting of whole objects into part objects. On one hand, the depressive position is productive of, and the result of, an anxiety that the good object will be destroyed as it is embraced. Its relationship to the part object (the good mother, the good breast) is: If I love them I might lose them, so I must not love them (or myself). My love for them is harmful to them, because they are only good, and it is my love which will destroy them. On the other hand, the anxiety that characterizes the paranoid position responds to the fear of incorporating the bad object: If I love them, they'll destroy me. I must not let them in, for they are a dangerous object, and I must protect myself from the harm they might cause. Importantly, Klein's theory of good and bad objects relies on the knowledge that these objects are part-objects: "the loved object is at the same time the hated one" ([1935] 1986, 141). These good and bad objects, in other words, are actually different infantile responses to the same object: the mother. "The object-world of the child in the first two or three months of its life," Klein writes, "could be described as consisting of hostile and persecuting, or else of gratifying parts and portions of the real world" (141).

While this framing of the mother (and the world) as split part-objects constitutes the initial months of the infant's psychic life, over time this view of the world gives way, and the child "perceives more and more of the whole person of the mother" (141). This process takes place through, and in relationship to, ambivalence. Klein writes:

Ambivalence, carried out in a splitting of the imagos enables the small child to gain more trust and belief in its real objects and thus in its internalized ones—to love them more and to carry out in an increasing degree its phantasies of restoration on the loved object.... This goes on until love for the real and the internalized objects and trust in them are well established. Then ambivalence, which is partly a safeguard against one's own hate and against the hated and terrifying objects, will in normal development again diminish in varying degrees. (143–44)

Ambivalence, in other words, is both a defense mechanism protecting against one's defensive positions, as well as a means of repairing one's object relations. It both splits the objects and is required for their repair.

In this light, ambivalence becomes important for our analysis of Mikael and Laure as well. Understanding them as part-objects suggests that the positions we take towards them—paranoid, depressive, or reparative—depends both on what nourishment these subjects provide us and on whether or not we can recognize that Mikael and Laure are whole objects: both on their own and as one. Describing Laure and Mikael as part-objects suggests as well that the (political) positions we take toward them—including one that requires eschewing Mikael and all the modes of "trans" life he figures, in order to avow Laure and whom she figures—depends on what nourishment they provide us, and what anxieties they provoke. Making this argument is not to claim that feminism or transness are constituted by depressive or paranoid positions (respectively or otherwise), but rather it is to suggest that pitting one against the other, as if transness is the bad object and feminist the good, is to misrecognize these politics as separate whole objects, rather than part-objects of the same whole. It is also to suggest that, as I have been arguing across this chapter, ambivalence founds our politics toward gender and childhood and can be the means through which restoration takes place. Theorizing Laure and Mikael as part-objects, and particularly as objects to be read from within a reparative transfeminist politics of childhood, is a way of embracing an "oscillatory" reading (as Sedgwick describes it), one in which Laure and Mikael need not be wholly separated. Laure and

Mikael variously present simultaneous speculative readings of the same situation that offer not competing versions of what the scene might definitively mean, but rather various interpretations of how the scene is multiply experienced. As I have worked to demonstrate throughout this chapter, yet have continuously struggled with and against, gender and childhood confer and disentangle one another. Yet even in this phrasing "gender and childhood" the two are separated by an "and" that splits yet states their coproduction.[39] Laure and Mikael, gender and childhood, trans and feminist, the act of pairing is predicated on a splitting that is both present and refused at every turn. Reading with Laure and Mikael, attending to their ambivalence, and taking them up from within a reparative position, requires embracing "the essential and fundamental elements of the feelings we call love" (Klein [1935] 1986, 125) as we advocate for ways of living that make both of their lives possible.

With this reparative mode in mind, I want to conclude by way of thinking through where and how Coy may fit into this scene. On one hand, I have already argued that centering Laure's (tom)boy refusals and reconfigurations of sexed embodiment might also be of use for those defending Coy, in as much as it may push back on the phallic logics of inclusion and exclusion within girlhood. On the other hand, I have argued that those who would argue that avowing Mikael does violence to Laure are evoking a narrow version of gender, premised on paranoia rather than reparation. But what a reparative reading of Laure and Mikael also suggests is that if we can sit with this ambivalence, rather than project the unpleasant "parts" of it off onto those subjects who come to figure the source of that displeasure, then we might be able to allow that ambivalence to begin the work of repair. Ambivalence, as a mode through which we understand and grapple with our bodies and their psychosocial formations, is thus necessary for our continued advocacy for girls like Coy, even as it challenges us to articulate such affirmations in ways that complicate what it is we think we mean by gender.

3

Desiring the Child

Queerness, Motherhood, and the Analyst

Eight years have gone by since I first came out, and I am twenty-two. I am sitting at the back of a dark auditorium in the midst of the swelter-ing heat of the California summer, sweating as stationary fans attempt to make up for the lack of air conditioning, and I am hoping that it will go well. It is why, after all, all two hundred of us are here in the first place. To support courageous queer kids like the next performer, an out, twelve-year-old, mixed-raced boy whose lesbian mothers have been fierce advocates for him in the face of harsh bullying (what else could a celebration of the tenacity of queer youth want?). As the lights go down and the music begins to boom, my heart races—and then, appearing from behind a rainbow flag, a small kid with spiked, gelled hair and a slight frame, wearing a shirt proclaiming G-A-Y in large block letters and a huge smile on his face, commands attention at cen-ter stage and begins break dancing to the beat. What a sight! To have been able, at twelve, to not only be out but to be twirling a pride flag around my head and my body to the beat of music and the applause of a full house! The crowd erupts, cheering him on with shouts and praise. They know, as I do, that this performance is a product of all our years of hard work, of creating not just a livable life for young queer kids but also a present—this moment!—where they are celebrated.

And then it happens. His dance betrays us. As his movements tran-sition from those that mimic break-dancers to those that mimic sex acts, repeating the easily citational gesticulations of pelvic thrusts (citations of sex acts, it seems to me, probably not yet accessible from a personal lexicon—but perhaps that is beside the point), the cheers become a murmur. In the moment of those thrusts, the room itself is pushed into a collective affect of discomfort and anxiety, completely unsure of what to make of this performance before us. I, on the other hand, find myself caught up in exhilarating waves of memory, identification, and desire: a wish. A wish that I could have been this boy (or that this boy could have been me), a hope that this boy will have and will be all that I desire for him, and a desire for him himself. To be next to him and, maybe, to dance with him. A memory emerges of a past self—myself at twelve: reclusive and closeted—that I longingly place into this moment. A fantasy of two gay children dancing on stage as if there was no one else but us. Time slows down. I am this boy and this boy is mine. I am my childhood self again (although this version of me is different—I'm more outgoing, more like the me I wish I could have been), and we are two kids dancing together.

My fantasy breaks momentarily (as with all fantasies, I'll return to it again and again) as I scan the audience. They look panicked. The applause has died down. Caught between a desire to support this kid and an anxiety about celebrating, let alone witnessing, something akin to a child's sexuality, the reactions to this moment are swift and harsh. At the end of the night I, as the organizer of the event, find myself in trouble. The performance was "too much," I was told. It was "inappropriate," and "uncomfortable." I realize at that moment—or (allow me the fantasy), I like to believe that it was this moment, as if my realization happened amidst a backdrop of stage lighting and collective queer celebration and panic—that our embrace of queer children rests on unstable and ambivalent grounds. That to celebrate queer kids is to applaud them in their bravery of declaring publicly their orientations, but not to witness, or acknowledge, that they, too, might have desires of their own. In our embrace of queer kids, the kids themselves, in all of their mechanical thrusts and unpolished movements, disappear. In their absence a narrative—one that has been persistently used to define and constrain both queers and children— seeps in. In the years following this event, I have continued to return, not just to my fantasy of it, but also to the questions that linger in my attempt to grapple with the evening in all its complexity.

This is where this chapter's work began: with questions that followed this child's performance. How to accommodate his young, queer, unruly, dancing, mixed-race body into queer activism? How to address the investments cathected in and refused by his body? And how to understand the disarray his performance produced? Seeking out answers to these questions, I turned to queer theory at a time when the child was a dense site of engagement and debate, as Lee Edelman's polemic *No Future* (2004) was met with playful resistance by Kathryn Bond Stockton's *The Queer Child* (2009). I turned to theory both because it sustained me and because it was impossible then, as now, to have public conversations about the tensions and ambivalences that childhood sexuality produce within activist spaces, or the public space more generally.[1] Alongside this impossibility, queer theory opened up a space for carefully thinking through the complexities of the queer child. Indeed, writing on childhood within queer theory has proliferated immensely in the years since Edelman argued that queerness is antithetical to the figure of the child and the heteronormative reproductive futurity that it signifies. Perhaps as an attempt to mitigate, if not wholly refute this opposition, the argument made by Edelman's detractors—that queers and children are, or can be, one and the same—has since been taken up as the presiding position for queers to take.[2] This position can be found most directly stated in Steven Bruhm and Natasha Hurley's edited collection *Curiouser* (2004a), Hannah Dyer's *The Queer Aesthetics of Childhood* (2020), Jack Halberstam's *Gaga Feminism* (2012), and Stockton's *The Queer Child* (2009). It has also been articulated in journal articles and special issues, such as the 2010 special issue on childhood and feminist theory in *Feminist Theory* (Burman and Stacey 2010a), the 2011 special issue of *Lambda Nordica* (Vänskä 2011a), the special issue of *Women's Studies Quarterly* (Chinn and Duane 2015), and "The Child Now," the special issue in GLQ edited by Jules Gill-Peterson, Rebekah Sheldon, and Stockton (2016), in which the queer child emerged anew within a series of transnational, legal, paradoxical, and settler colonial contexts. This captivating body of theory, detailed throughout this chapter, has in many ways invigorated the field of queer theory and the arena of queer politics. As with the crowd's reaction to the boy's performance, however, there are particularities to this body of work that often require seeing a specific child in order for the child within its frame to extend, grow sideways, be radical, and be queer.

Or at least that's my reading of it. For the story that I tell in the first half of this chapter about queer theory and the child is, I'll admit, a response to my own grappling with the failures of *my* investments in the queer child—and perhaps queer theory—to live up to the demands I've made of it. Here I build on the conclusion of the previous chapter and learn from Robyn Wiegman's *Object Lessons* (2012), recognizing that perhaps my disappointments with queer theory and the queer child are products of my fantasy that either of these objects might make good on the wishes I have invested in them. As Wiegman argues, "Formed by affection, attachment, identification, disavowal, refusal, aspiration, intention, want, or need, our objects of study are bound to duty, invested with the fantastic expectation that they will fulfill all our dependent needs" (2012, 318).[3] Beginning with my memory of this child's performance, this chapter seeks to extend the reach of what this body of theory might do as it embraces the queer child.[4] In conversation with queer theory on the child, queer feminist critique, and, as we shall see, mothers and children of varying kinds, this chapter asks for a different type of politics to coalesce around, in, and with the queer child. Centrally, then, what this chapter is asking is: How does a queer project support queer kids? But lingering in this question, and made striking in the moment of this boy's unruly movements, is another provocation: How can a queer project support the queer child who refuses, betrays, and interrupts queer theory's own lines of identification and desire? Upon what grounds is a queer child identified, desired, or secured in the first place? And how might attending to desire itself, as a central dynamic of queerness and queer children, productively throw the queer child (in theory) into disarray?

The queer child, inasmuch as this subject and figuration can be defined, facilitates queer interventions and world building projects, but it also aligns with, complicates, and subverts these very investments. What, then, do we (and I include myself within this "we") do with the queer child whose movements betray us? Or perhaps, I wonder, is this the wrong question? Perhaps it needs to be asked the other way around: What does queer theory do with its investments when they betray the queer child? I ask these questions of support and betrayal in the face of a queer theoretical project that has come under multiple strain for its aim, orientation, and object (cf. Wiegman and E. A. Wilson 2015). In asking how a queer project might support the queer child who refuses it, I am thus asking how queer theory might support and define a (queer) child when queer theory itself is so deeply entrenched in a *fort da* relationship with the very questions of identity, definition, coherence, and refusal themselves.[5] My suspicion, one which I grapple with in this chapter through a close reading of a few different registers and subfields of queer theory, and through a reading of a film that flirts with the issue of desiring children, is that what the child most provocatively offers queer theory is a troubled relationship with some of queer theory's most animating questions.

To put it simply, my argument is that there is a wish within queer theory for the queer child to be the queer subject par excellence, which will refuse reproductivity and heteronormativity. The child becomes a site for this wish, I argue, because it is precisely the subject that has been so vehemently used against queers to render queers nonnormative, nonreproductive, criminal, deviant, and subjugated. It also becomes the site for this wish because queer theorists, I imagine, *lived* childhoods that were nothing like the queer childhood of the boy whose dance opened this chapter. Precisely because queer childhoods were, and still are, so intensely hostile and inhospitable for most queer adults, the idea—or fantasy—of the queerness of childhood and the "queer child" has become a dense site of wish fulfillment. The (queer) child thus becomes a hyperproductive object for queer theory. It is sexual (despite being told not to be), it is queer (despite all attempts at enforcing heterosexuality on children), and, in being queer and sexual, it is against normativity and the family (despite being produced by one). In this sense the queer child is formed by affection, attachment, identification, disavowal, and refusal; it is produced through the wish that it will fulfill all our dependent needs. But the child—and no less the queer child—cannot be owned by the wishes queer theorists have invested in it. As Wiegman writes, "We no more own our objects of study than we possess the ideas we use to authorize them" (2012,

318). We are unable to own the (queer) child, because, as Wiegman argues, "our objects of study, like all objects, have wishes of their own" (2012, 318).

What, then, are the wishes of the (queer) child? While it would be remiss of me to claim to fully know these wishes, this chapter focuses on one (queer) child, and her singular wish: the wish for a child of her own. Embracing the act of making strange that is constitutive of queer critique, my intervention into queer theory's desire for children finds its resolve in a (queer) child who also desires children. Her desire, I argue, complicates our own, even if these desires are, on the surface, the same. Making this embrace of a peculiar queer child, this chapter undertakes two moves. First, I argue that the production of the queer child within queer theory is itself a desire for childhood, one which emerges within the larger disciplinary framing of Queer Studies (as Wiegman titles it) which requires queer critique to be antinormative. While I am of course partial to the critiques made within antinormative queer theory, I remain unconvinced by the convergence of the queer child with antinormativity, as well as within the refutation of this negation as outlined within queer proliferations of the child. Second, I seek to twist the formulation of "desiring children" by taking it seriously. I seek, that is, to establish the queerness of a child who, like queer theorists, invests so heavily in what a child might bring her.[6]

Queer Theory's Desire for the Queer Child

Arguably, the first enunciation of the queer child comes from Sedgwick, in her article "How to Bring Your Kids up Gay" (1991). Sedgwick documents some of the extensive efforts that are undertaken to maintain what she calls the "open season on gay kids" (1991, 18). This open season, Sedgwick writes, is fueled by an "annihilating homophobic, gynephobic, and pedophobic hatred" (21), a hatred sustaining a wish "endemic in the culture . . . that gay people *not exist*" (23). Enforcing this wish are "institutions whose programmatic undertaking is to prevent the development of gay people" and whose "scope . . . is unimaginably large" (23). These institutions, "the state, the military, education, law, penal institutions, the church, medicine, and mass culture," Sedgwick writes, enforce this wish "all but unquestioningly, and with little hesitation at even the recourse to invasive violence" (23).

Sedgwick's focus on gay and proto-gay kids comes about through her critique of a shift toward ego psychology in the 1980s that defined a "healthy homosexual" as "one who (a) is already grown up, and (b) acts masculine" (1991, 19). In this context, the proto-gay child, rather than the gay adult, becomes the site of intervention because they are made visible through different types of knowledge (gender rather than sexuality), and because they are implicated in different structures of blame and accountability (socialization, the family, mother and father figures, and education). Because the markers of proto-gay children are produced through discourses of homosexuals' failed assumption into normative masculinity and femininity, attempts to make proto-gay children straight (and thus gay adults not exist) get targeted toward gender-nonconforming children. For Sedgwick, then, the proto-gay child is the "gender-nonconforming child," the "effeminate" or "sissy" boy or the girl who asserts "that she actually is anatomically male." Being "proto," for Sedgwick, is less about a child's process of coming into sexual self-determination as a "queer" adult but rather about the structures through which the gender binary is entrenched, and masculinity and homophobia are secured as sites and techniques of power. Here we can begin to see one of the initial demands made of the queer (proto-gay) child. Sedgwick's desires for this child emerges in response to a competing demand. The articulation of the proto-gay child, that is, comes about as a direct counter to the endemic targeting of queer, gender-nonconforming children and the queer adults they will potentially eventually become.

In this sense, the queer (or proto-gay) child is the subject who, as I noted above, most troubles the sexual and gendered norms which have so thoroughly plagued queer communities. For Bruhm and Hurley, the queer child is thus the child who most explicitly refuses the "dominant narrative" about children and childhood. This narrative, they write, states both that "children are (and should stay) innocent of sexual desires and intentions," and that, "at the same time, however, children are also officially, tacitly, assumed to be heterosexual" (2004b, ix). Within this narrative, they argue, romantic attachments between boys and girls are seen as precursor for an eventually mature heterosexuality, while homosexual affinities are disregarded merely as play, as a phase that one will outgrow. Referencing Stockton's early work on the gay child, Bruhm and Hurley argue that this dominant narrative makes it such that homosexuality in childhood is something "that will not *be,* but will only *have been*" (2004b, xix). And yet, they write, the production of the sexually innocent heterosexual child within narrative has its inherent queer cracks. "In telling stories about children and sex," Bruhm and Hurley argue, "our culture's storytellers have long gestured to the stories that ought not feature children: stories that make children 'queer' in a number of distinct ways and therefore are rarely told" (2004b, x). Inherent to the stories that we do want to feature children, and those that we do tell to and about children, something queer is still happening: "The very effort to flatten the narrative of the child into a story of innocence has some queer effects . . . in this sense the figure of the child is not the anti-queer at all. Its queerness inheres instead in innocence run amok" (2004b, xiv).

Here we can see the queer child's queerness being detailed, so that to "queer" the child means resisting the ways in which, as Ellis Hanson writes, the "sexual behavior and [the] sexual knowledge [of children] are subjected to an unusually intense normalizing surveillance, discipline, and repression of the sort familiar to any oppressed sexual minority" (2004, 110). The queer child thus refuses the naming of homosexuality as a "phase" and revels in the childhood sexualities that are understood as problematic and perverse. This notion of queer children's sexual alterity is articulated in Michael Moon's *A Small Boy and Others* (1998). Moon describes queerness as typified by a "daring and risky weirdness, dramatic uncanniness, erotic offcenteredness, and unapologetic perversity" (1998, 4), and he traces out the many ways in which pleasure and perversion in childhood are central to producing a queer analysis of children and childhoods. Additionally, for Kevin Ohi, at stake in queer theory's recognition of children's queerness is the possibility for "thwarting" the "comforting self-recognitions" about the adult self and its "sexual normativity" (2004, 82). For Ohi, queering the innocence of the child is thus a means through which the "murderous disregard for proto-gay, proto-pedophilic, proto-masochistic, proto-voyeuristic lives" can be interrupted (2004, 82). As such, for Bruhm and Hurley the queerness of the child is established specifically in relation to its sexual alterity and its peculiarity:

> the figure of the queer child is . . . the child who displays interest in sex generally, in same-sex erotic attachments, or in cross-generational attachments. . . . The essays in this volume . . . tease out the range of possibilities for child sexuality. [They] look to the dominant heteronarrative to see how normalizing language itself both produces and resists queer stories of childhood sexual desire. . . . In short, this collection suggests that the children who populate the stories our culture tells about them are, in fact, *curiouser* than they've been given credit for. (2004b, x, xiv)

Clearly, then, across these framings of the queer child, the queering that "queer" does to the child encompasses resisting the child's alleged asexuality and heterosexuality; allowing for the child's pleasures, desires, and perversities; and thwarting the normative frames of sexuality and identity that have constrained the child and the queer.

The other site of resistance through which the queer child emerged is in relation to the normative act of growing up. As Stockton argues, "There are ways of growing that are not growing up" (2009, 11).[7] Growing sideways, rather than up, Stockton writes, "suggests that the width of a person's experiences or ideas, their motives or their motions, may pertain at any age, brining 'adults' and 'children' into lateral contact of surprising sorts" (2009, 11). In this text Stockton uses the model of the ghostly gay child—a child "lingering in the vicinity of the word gay, having a ghostly, terrifying, complicated, energizing, chosen, forced, or future connection to this world" (2009, 2)—to argue not just that every child is queer but also that childhood is the "queerest of categories" (Stockton 2016, 507). Through Stockton's work, growing sideways is articulated along a number of creative and fascinating lines. Of central importance to my argument here is her explanation of the forms of lateral relation—between children, dogs, pedophiles, and money—that wholly subvert the traditional family and its demands for normative, upward growth.

While I cannot flatten out Stockton's interventions into a single argument—her work's breadth and creativity renders any attempt to do so futile—I want to stick with this specific intervention into the family that the queer child poses. For this intervention is not beholden to Stockton. The refusing of the family is common to a range of queer texts. But the queer refusal of the family finds new footing and new complexities in the production of the queer child. The norms of the family and reproductive futurity are (in ways that Wiegman and E. A. Wilson would find unsurprising) consistently if not prescriptively resisted by the queer child. Effectively and specifically queered by the queer child, queer theory tells us, are the "inevitable" role of motherhood for little girls (Bruhm and Hurley 2004b, xi); the demand to grow up, get a "real job," and get married (Kent 2004, 179); the discourse of "pro-reproductivity" that reduces women "to their childbearing and maternal capacities" (Downing 2011, 60); and even an emergent "hetero-parental tolerance" of gay and queer children that incorporates them into the family without changing the family structure itself, nor heterosexuality (J. Jacobs 2014). The queer child refuses this growing up, "delays" it, as Stockton argues, and in "growing sideways" builds alternative relations, futures, and possibilities for living an intimate life.[8]

In this particular articulation of the queer child, however, a few questions arise. To begin with, as I have suggested above and as I will return to via my own queer child, the prescriptive negativity towards reproductive futurity is premised on an analysis of reproduction that is rather limited. While many have chastised Edelman for his argument that queer theory should be against the child—because childhood as a structure actively punishes and renders incoherent queer and trans children of color (Muñoz 2009)—ironically, those who argue *for* the queer child on these more inclusive and intersectional frames of the child do not take a similarly expansive view of reproduction and motherhood. What does it mean for rejection of the family to be axiomatic for the queer child when the family, along with the child, has its own heterogeneity? As Patricia Hill Collins writes, "Given the power of family as ideological construction and principle of social organization, Black nationalist, feminist, and other political

movements in the United States dedicated to challenging social inequality might consider . . . reclaiming the language of family for
democratic ends" (1998, 78).

Embracing black feminist critiques of the rejection of family,
motherhood, and reproduction might also mean interrogating the
work that the queer child does for queer theory's relationship to feminism (a mother of another kind). For the relationship that the queer
child's articulation has to feminism is often ambivalent within this
scholarship. On one hand, gender—as a structure through which
the queer child is marked—has been central to the articulation of
the queer child since its emergence in Sedgwick's "How to Bring
Your Kids Up Gay." In the analyses that subsequently prioritize gender, same-gendered affiliations within childhood (Kent 2004), and
children's embodiment of gendered play and rebellion (Halberstam
2004), are also integrated into an analysis of children's queerness.
The question of gender has also been important to the queer child,
as the very notion of children's sexual innocence is, as Kilby (2010)
and Vänskä (2011b) point out, gendered such that girlhood is already
constructed through a hypersexualized virginity. As such, queer theory *has* analyzed gender as a structure through which the queer child
comes into being. On the other hand, however, the actual scholarly
endeavor of feminism, wherein it is referenced in queer approaches to
the child, has been consistently framed as a barrier to the types of sexual liberation that queer theory advocates for the child.

In the introduction to *Curiouser,* for example, feminism is a haunting absence, named only in the moments it—via the requisite citation
of Andrea Dworkin's and Catharine MacKinnon's "certain branch of
radical lesbian feminism in the 1980s" (Bruhm and Hurley 2004b,
xxii)—is mapped along and as a conservative (Reaganite) policing
of the child's sexuality. The citations of Gayle Rubin, Pat Califia, and
Kate Millett, however, despite also being feminists (lesbians! in the
1980s!), are only named in the introduction's mapping of the genealogy of queer critique on the child as "writers on child sexuality"
(Bruhm and Hurley 2004b, xxii, xxvi). Similarly, while the following
works are clearly informed by and situated within feminism, feminist theory as a specifically named scholarly endeavor has a shadowy

presence in *The Queer Child* and *A Small Boy and Others,* and its appearance within "The Child Now" is relegated to a footnote (Stockton 2016, 535 n38). Where it does explicitly appear in the outlining of the queer child, perhaps without surprise, are in the special issues on the child within feminist theory journals (*WSQ* and *Feminist Theory*), issues that, while specifically feminist in orientation, include a couple of explorations of the queer child (Burman and Stacey 2010a; Chinn and Duane 2015; Lesnik-Oberstein 2010) but are more interested in the tensions that emerge when thinking gender and childhood together. Other than these texts, however, the queer child and their explication through a queer feminist lens is remarkably absent.

Perhaps this is because feminism itself has had its own ambivalent relationship to childhood. As Erica Burman and Jackie Stacey argue in their introduction to the special issue of *Feminist Theory* on feminism and childhood, it is important to note the anxiety that making the connection between gender and the child (and particularly between women and children) has produced within feminism (2010b, 228). Indeed, the colloquial "womenandchildren," as Burman puts it in an earlier article of hers, historically "*equates* women and children—to the extent of running them together or combining them such that . . . they are seen as a single entity" (2008, 180). This equating of women and children, as Burman and Stacey argue, has produced a patchy genealogy of ambivalent attention to the child within feminism. They write:

> Feminism's relationship to children and childhood has never been far off the political agenda but its theorization has been slow to follow . . . until recently there has been little explicit discussion of how the child and childhood have been, and more importantly, should be understood within feminist theory and politics. (2010b, 227)

This ambivalent take up of the child, they argue, is a product of the multiple structures that have worked to infantilize women, as well as the ways in which childhood is stretched out onto adult women's subjectivity by linking women's lives with children's (2010b, 228). This connection, then, is not just one of metaphorical similitude. Women, particularly as defined through their naturalized connection to motherhood, have their lives shaped around the well-being of children. "In some ideological constructions," Thorne writes, "women are *likened* to children. In other constructions, women are *closely and unreflectively tied* with children; womanhood has been equated with motherhood in a mixing of identities that simply does not occur for men and fatherhood" (1987, 96). These links between women and children have meant not only that feminists had to (and continue to) argue that "women are *not* 'like children,' and [as such] their subordination is not legitimate" (1987, 96), but also that taking up childhood as an object of analysis within feminist thought could risk the entrenchment of this connection.

My intention here, then, is not to claim that queer theorists are not feminists, or to suggest that avowing a feminist analysis might *resolve* the ambivalence of the child in queer feminist theory. Rather, I am suggesting that because feminism was understood to have an ambivalent relationship with the child, perhaps it was assumed that the only way to embrace the child from a queer position was to drop feminism behind, to bracket it along with all its ambivalence. This relationship to feminism means, as I argue later on in this chapter, that the types of normative positions that the queer child is celebrated in rejecting are unevenly directed at motherly and familial practices and subjectivities, an uneven distribution of queer negativity that places the burden of representing and deconstructing heteronormativity onto women's bodies, relations, and intimate lives. But what would it look like to embrace feminism here, and what children might we encounter? What queerness might we stumble upon along the way?

PALINDROMES

In what remains of this chapter, I want to make what Sedgwick (2003) would hopefully call a reparative move. Concerned with the layers of desire within and for the (queer) child, as well as the centrality of antinormativity and the disappearance of feminism that produces and facilitates the naming of the "queer child" as a queer project, I want to introduce Aviva, my own "queer" "child," and I want to think through some of her issues, promises, and difficulties. I do so in the hope of offering an additional approach to queer(ing) childhood that is in line with Sedgwick's call for us to center our own attachments to our objects of critique (2003, 123–51). My attempt to engage, struggle with, and even fail in embracing Aviva is thus a desire to situate my (admittedly paranoid) reading of other approaches to queer children as stemming from my own attachments to them. Here the reading of Aviva I provide below attempts to further elaborate on, as well as re-orient my own reading of queer theory's approach to the queer child, moving it through and beyond a straightforward skepticism or nega-tivity, and then toward a reading of the child that is more speculative.

"I'M GOING TO BE A MOM!" INTRODUCING AVIVA

Aviva is the main character in Todd Solondz's film *Palindromes* (2004). Solondz is well known for his films' complex and sympathetic portray-als of characters whose nonnormative intimate lives and desires are usually rendered unintelligible or pathologic. Many of Solondz's films, including *Palindromes,* follow continued narratives by returning to the fictional families portrayed in his earlier films; *Palindromes* builds on *Welcome to the Dollhouse* (1995), while the family whose generational re-productions of messy desire is explicated in *Happiness* (1998) returns in *Life during Wartime* (2009). In continuing to follow these familial narratives, *Palindromes* brings us into a world that, while often disqui-eting, is at least familiar. The film itself begins with grainy home-video footage of the funeral of Dawn Wiener, the main character in *Welcome to the Dollhouse.* Dawn, we are told, was a troubled child, a middle child who grew obese, had bad skin, and, after allegedly becoming pregnant from a date rape, committed suicide. It is in this context that we meet Aviva, Dawn's six-year-old cousin, who relays this gossip to her mother in a fit of tears: "Missy told me after the funeral that Dawn was preg-nant from a date-rape, and that that's the real reason she killed herself: she hated the idea of bringing another Dawn into the world!" Trauma-tized by Dawn's early death, and upset that Dawn would even conceive of not wanting a child, Aviva becomes convinced that the best way to make meaning in the world is by producing her own children and lov-ing them unconditionally: "I want to have lots and lots of babies! As many babies as possible," she tells her mother, "Because that way, I'll always have someone to love." The film's narrative takes off "several years later . . ." as we follow thirteen-year-old Aviva over the course of about a year as she works to build relationships that will provide her with the type of sex that will give her a child.

Aviva herself is difficult to describe, not just for the fact that she remains oddly mysterious and mostly silent, but also because Aviva is cast by eight different actors during the course of the film: Emani Sledge, Valerie Shusterov, Hannah Freiman, Rachel Corr, Will Denton, Sharon Wilkins, Shayna Levine, and Jennifer Jason Leigh. These actors are not cast in a way that reflects the temporality of the film; they do not, that is, all look like similar versions of the same person in different moments of her life. Rather, their incongruous bodies (some more harmonious than others) all occupy the screen in various, somewhat random intervals of a narrative that follows Aviva for only a short period of time. Yet never in the film are Aviva's shifts in casting remarked upon. Indeed, when we first meet Aviva, she (Emani Sledge) is a young black girl, even as everyone at Dawn's funeral, and Aviva's own parents, are white: a difference that goes unnamed, even as Aviva's physiques, genders, and ages change.[9] As Berlant, who writes briefly on *Palindromes* in "A Properly Political Concept of Love: Three Approaches in Ten Pages" (2011b), describes them:

> Their genders, races, and degrees of fatness and tallness change, as do their normative attractiveness and class-related comportment: they're graceful yet grotesques [sic], even when they're played by a movie star. But they enact the same style of encountering the world, a dreamy, aleatory longing, and a slightly catlike stealthiness on their way to getting what they want and adjusting when necessary. (2011b, 689)

The film thus follows these actors—whose bodies (if not their affective bearing) vary greatly—as they cyclically replace one another as Aviva struggles with, and then escapes, the monotone drudgery of her parents (Angela Pietropinto and Bill Buell), and seeks to become a parent to castaway children just like herself.

Aviva's first attempt to become a mother gets violently intercepted by her parents. Seven years after Aviva's discussion with her mother about Dawn, she (now Valerie Shusterov, a young, chubby white teenage girl with long curly brown hair) is still determined to have multiple children as soon as she can, and her first opportunity presents itself when her family visits a couple with a teenage son named Judah (Robert Agri), a large, dopey white boy who has no qualms about impregnating her. When Aviva's parents discover her pregnancy (the subsequent morning sickness gives it away), they demand that she (now Hannah Freiman, a skinny young white woman with long, straight red hair) get an abortion. Aviva has no choice in this matter. For Aviva, being a child means that her capacity to make decisions about her body and her sexuality do not belong to her; these are decisions for her parents to make.[10] Without choice, Aviva is driven to the abortion clinic, walked through a cluster of pro-life protestors, and reassured that all will be okay. Unfortunately, however, the procedure has complications that result in the need for a hysterectomy. Aviva, however, awakes from the procedure without this knowledge. Despite forcing her to undergo the abortion, Aviva's parents do not disclose to her that she will no longer be able to become pregnant.

Furious with her parents, Aviva runs away from home and the doctor that stole her child from her, seeking someone else who will give her a baby. Throughout her journey, title shots alternating between pink and blue (with scrapbook-like images of dresses and overalls respectively), punctuate the narrative as each new embodiment of Aviva (listed in the casting as their overlay baby-name) is introduced. Aviva's desire for a child sends her on an *Alice in Wonderland*– like journey on which she meets a bevy of odd characters. Solondz, as Berlant concludes from watching his films, "is not really a fan of humans. He finds them squishy and monstrous and cognitively disabled by their too-intense attachment to their appetites and habits" (2011b, 689), and so the people we encounter on Aviva's journey are all somewhat emblematic of this excessive and perverse humanity that Solondz enjoys.[11] One of the first people Aviva meets is Joe (whose real name is Bob, or possibly Earl), a sweaty and heavy-set truck driver (Stephen Adly Guirgis) who has anal sex with her in a motel room and then abandons her in the morning. Forced to be on her own again, "Huckleberry" Aviva (Will Denton, a skinny teenage white boy with mid-length hair) wanders the highway until she, now

"Mama Sunshine" Aviva (Sharon Wilkins, a large, adult black woman) is brought by a strange, nerdy, lisping, and terminally ill child to the home of Mama Sunshine (Debra Monk). Mama Sunshine, as the name might suggest, is an excessively chipper, larger-than-life mother figure to a gang of children who, one could argue, are "queer" in a multitude of ways. The Sunshine family consists of twelve children, including a blind albino girl, an epileptic boy, a girl whose leukemia is in remission, a boy who is described as having been "born a heathen," and a few characters whose peculiarities go without definition but include varying degrees of nonnormative genders, sizes, and abilities. One of them is a dog. Mirroring Aviva's own shifts in casting, Mama Sunshine's children could be understood as representing for Aviva the type of unconditional loving relationality that stems from having lots and lots of babies (even if they are not one's own). While she only stays in this household for a couple of days, Aviva quickly makes friends, finds Jesus, joins the Sunshine Singers (the Sunshine family's Jesus sing-along-group), and learns how to give a proper burial to (and pray for) all the children lost to the "baby killers" and who have been dumped in the landfill behind the Sunshine home.

Despite believing that she has been accepted into a new queer household, Aviva surreptitiously learns that the Sunshines have a medical exam as a bar for entry. Peering into the basement through open blinds, Aviva looks into a room where the Sunshine family's doctor (Richard Riehle), Joe/Bob/Earl, and Bo Sunshine, the patriarch of the Sunshine household (Walter Bobbie) are having a meeting. As the camera takes up Aviva's gaze, partially obstructed by blinds that the camera, moving up and down, attempts to readjust for, we hear the doctor's news: "That new girl of yours. I don't know how to say this, Bo, but when I examined her yesterday . . . that girl's a child whore. I just think you oughta know that much before you go any further with her becoming a part of the family and all." Overhearing this conversation, Aviva learns that the limit of the embrace of a queer child turns out to be the moment the queer child becomes the sexual child.

Rejected from yet another household, and castigated once again from a family because of her precocious desire to have one of her own, Aviva, now "Bob" Aviva (Shayna Levine, a young, curvy, white woman with long, dark curly hair) decides to take matters into her own hands. She joins forces with Joe/Bob/Earl, who has returned in the narrative because he has been hired as a hitman by Bo to kill the very abortion doctor who performed Aviva's abortion/hysterectomy (the cheekily named Dr. Fleischer). Reunited with the man she hopes will give her a baby, and determined to help him kill the man who took away her first attempt at creating one, Aviva embarks on a *Lolita*-esque drive across the country. After finding and killing Dr. Fleischer (Stephen Singer), and—accidentally—his young daughter, Aviva and Joe/Bob/Earl flee to a hotel room where the clerk, suspicious of their relationship, alerts the authorities to the presence of a pedophile. The police arrive, Joe/Bob/Earl is killed on the spot, and Aviva—now "Mark" Aviva (played by Jennifer Jason Leigh, a skinny, middle-aged white woman with curly blond hair)—is reunited with her parents.

QUEERING MOTHERHOOD

Aviva is not a queer child in the traditional sense. She exhibits no homosexual attractions during her childhood (except, perhaps, in the fifteen fleeting seconds in which, once again cast as "Huckleberry" Aviva, she is having sex with Judah), and she is clearly attached to a vision of the good life that is almost dogmatically reproductive. Indeed, Aviva's desires are exclusively reproductive: not knowing that she cannot produce a child of her own, she never expresses any desire (for food, friendship, or other objects) other than to be a mother. "I'm not going to have any boyfriends. I don't want any boyfriends!" she tells her perplexed mother, who mistakes this declaration of her singular desire for a child (uncoupled from any form of coupling) as her coming out as a lesbian. "What do you mean you don't want any? Are you trying to tell me something? Aviva? It's okay, you can talk to me. Are you a . . ." Frustrated that her mother is missing the point, Aviva interrupts her mother's lingering suggestion with a clear no. But Aviva's refusal to be a queer child must not be mistaken as an easy alignment with heterosexual desire. For even heterosexual sex does not have much of a hold on her. Right before she has sex for the first time with Judah, Aviva asks him if he thinks about sex a lot—a preposterous question given that the walls of Judah's room are plastered with overlapping posters of swimsuit models, and that they have just been discussing his plans to produce a feature-length pornographic film of his own—and yet Aviva confides in him, flatly: "I don't think about it. I just think about having a baby."

Pleasure, it seems, is outside the realm of sex or intimacy for Aviva. For Aviva, sex is what happens to you on the way to acquiring a child. Underneath Judah, and Joe/Bob/Earl, she stares blankly upward, making no attempts at affection and expressing nothing. Aviva's boredom, however, might itself be read queerly. Emphasized in her intimate scene with Joe/Bob/Earl by the film's tepid classical soundtrack and the camera's slow pull back shot exposing the bland motel room, the ennui of copulation perhaps gestures towards Leo Bersani's axiom that, in truth, most people do not actually like sex (Bersani 1987). Refusing the pleasure of a perversely queer sexual identity, and confronting us with her own (and perhaps our) aversion to sex, Aviva forces an analysis of her queerness away from one that emerges out of a queer perverse (homosexual) identity and toward something akin to Cathy Cohen's queer politics.

Cohen argues that "the radical potential of queer politics . . . rests on its ability to advance strategically oriented political identities arising from a more nuanced understanding of power" (2005, 43). This "more nuanced" understanding of power, Cohen writes, while still attending centrally to questions of sexuality, additionally means interrogating the ways in which "multiple systems of oppression are in operation" such that "power and access to dominant resources are distributed across the boundaries of 'het' and 'queer'" (2005, 43). In order to read Aviva queerly, Cohen might argue, our analysis must cross the boundaries of heterosexual and queer, and must look to the specific array of power through which Aviva's sexuality gets into trouble. In the film, this trouble is firmly situated in Aviva's singular desire to be a mother, a desire that is constantly met with intense resistance. From families—her own and the Sunshines'—that define how and when she can be sexual and create her own family, to medical procedures that intervene in her bodily integrity, to the suspicious and regulatory gaze of a public that judges her relationships and calls upon the police to intervene in them, Aviva lives an impossible sexuality that runs up against normative and wished for ways of being in the world, and she experiences rejection, isolation, and abjection for it. Aviva's partner—not to mention her child, or her capacity for reproduction—is killed in an act that violently enforces the impossibility of his and her desires. What makes Aviva such a queer child, then, are the intimacies and relations she inculcates as she seeks to fulfill her singular desire for motherhood. It is a desire for children, that is, that makes Aviva queer.

In order to justify this argument, I want to think about the relationship between the queer child and the queer mother further by returning for a moment to the wider scholarship on the queer child.[12] As I argued in my earlier overview of this scholarship, one of the main strands of antinormativity that emerges almost universally across the queer work that the queer child does is directed at the "normativity" of the family and, more specifically, of motherhood. Motherhood, it appears, is the queer child's worst nightmare. While a number of scholars articulate this point, Bruhm and Hurley make this argument most clearly, and so I unpack their outlining of the queer child's rejection of motherhood here as somewhat paradigmatic of the wider scholarship. In the introduction to *Curiouser,* Bruhm and Hurley's initial example of the queer child is Alice from *Alice's Adventures in Wonderland* (1865). Alice, Bruhm and Hurley argue, is a vivid example of queerness in childhood because, along with her "queer episodes" being "transmogrified" by her sister into pastoral tales, she "rejects the role of motherhood that golden-age Victorian literature sees as inevitable for little girls" (2004b, xi). "One of those queer episodes," Bruhm and Hurley write, "is Alice's adventure in babysitting, during which the infant for whom she is forced to care transforms into a pig" (2004b, xi). Detailing this story, Bruhm and Hurley write:

> Alice releases the pig into the forest with horrifying nonchalance: "It would have made a dreadfully ugly child," she reasons, "but it makes a rather handsome pig, I think." At this moment, Alice rejects the role of motherhood . . . but the rejection is lost on her sister. . . . She [Alice's sister] imagines Alice as a grown woman repeating her adventures to the "other little children" whom "she would gather about her." As the

sister sees Alice's role of storyteller as a particularly *maternal* one, she transposes the queer into the domestic pastoral. (2004b, xi)

According to Bruhm and Hurley, Alice's sister, and her inability to understand the "curiouser and curiouser" quality of Alice's stories, is thus wholly stuck within the realm of the (hetero)normative. Alice, on the other hand, rejecting the gendered expectations of her, and finding pleasure in the strange, figures the queer child. Bruhm and Hurley's use of the word "horrifying" to describe Alice's release of the pig might thus be read not as their own reading; rather, it appears that this is their assessment of a heteronormative reading (that of Alice's sister, to whom this story is told) of this "antimothering" act. Here, a rejection of the necessary assumption of the role of mothering as tied to girlhood is named as a queer refusal, but what are the terms of this naming, and what do they do when mapped onto a queer politics?

On one hand, this account of Alice's adventures in babysitting becomes questionable for whom it assumes the queer child to be. Alice's "queer" rejection of motherhood, we should note, is premised on her blasé adversity to providing care to a child only in the moment that this child transforms into a nonacceptable child form. In the paragraphs just before those that Bruhm and Hurley cite, Alice's "rejection of motherhood" looks and sounds a lot less like a "queer" act, and her infant/pig (rather than Alice herself) appears to be the queer child:

> "Don't grunt," said Alice; "that's not at all a proper way of expressing yourself." The baby grunted again, and Alice looked very anxiously into its face to see what was the matter with it. . . . Alice did not like the look of the thing at all. . . . "If you're going to turn into a pig, my dear," said Alice, seriously, "I'll have nothing more to do with you. Mind now!" . . . This time there could be *no* mistake about it: it was neither more nor less than a pig, and she felt that it would be quite absurd for her to carry it any further. (Carroll [1865] 1977, 59–60)

In this context, wherein the pig, rather than Alice, might figure the queer child, Alice's release of the infant/pig might be understood not as a rejection of mothering per se but rather as a specific refusal to mother a queer child.[13] Whereas a queering of motherhood might rather envision a motherhood that partakes in an embracing love of a child that *is* a pig (handsome or not), in Bruhm and Hurley's reading of motherhood as innately heteronormative, and Alice's (human) body as being the only embodiment that can figure the queer child, motherhood is understood primarily as a sexed *role* rather than an intimate gendered *relation*.

Understanding motherhood as a relation, Sedgwick might remind us, is necessary when working to build a world in which proto-gay kids can grow up queer. In "How to Bring Your Kids up Gay" Sedgwick was concerned with the gendered structures through which proto-gay kids were identified and disciplined, and gendered parental roles played a large part in this: "The reason effeminate boys turn out gay, according to this [psychoanalytic] account, is that other men [specifically their fathers] don't validate them as masculine" (1991, 22). As such, Sedgwick argues, "the one explanation that could never be broached" for the development of the proto-gay child, "is that these mysterious skills of survival, filiation, and resistance could derive from a secure identification with the resource-richness of a mother" (1991, 22–23). In this discourse, Sedgwick writes:

> Mothers, indeed, [are understood to] have nothing to contribute to this process of masculine validation, and women are reduced in the light of its urgency to a null set: any involvement in it by a woman is overinvolvement, any protectiveness is overprotectiveness, and, for instance, mothers "proud of their sons' non-violent qualities" are manifesting unmistakable "family pathology." (1991, 23)

For Sedgwick, then, motherhood is not just a sexed role—one that bears the brunt of gendered policing—additionally, and crucially, it is a source of support, validation, and sexual and gendered pedagogy for proto-gay kids.[14] To see motherhood as merely a role that queer children necessarily refuse (indeed their refusal itself is what makes them queer) is thus to participate in a discourse that simultaneously locates blame unevenly with the mother (motherhood as the site of heteropatriarchy) and refuses to acknowledge the loving, generous, pedagogical, laborious, and relational aspects of motherhood.[15]

Along these lines, Aviva's singular desire for reproductivity makes her a difficult queer child but an intriguing queer mother.[16] For there is a queerness that lingers around Aviva's heterosexuality that I argue we need to take seriously. Precisely because she is a child, Aviva's commitment to hyperbolic, heteronormative, reproductive futurity, and her commitment to the idea of the child "as the emblem of futurity's unquestioned value and purpose" (L. Edelman 2004, 4), incites those around her to respond to her as if her desire for a child were queerness itself. Twisting Edelman's framing of the Child as the figure of reproductive futurity, Aviva's parents argue that *she* is working against her own futurity *as a child* by simultaneously having a child of her own. In the distressed and affectively laden words of Aviva's mother:

> I won't let your life be ruined by this. . . . I know this is difficult, but really you're still just a child. There's so much you have to live for, and experience. You don't want to be tied down by a baby! . . . What if it turns out deformed? If it's missing a leg, or an arm, or a nose, or an eye? If it's brain damaged or mentally retarded? Children of very young mothers often turn out that way, and then what? Then you're stuck! Your life is ruined forever! You end up on food stamps! Alone! (Solondz 2004)

Seemingly perversely responding to Edelman's rhetorical question of: "Who *would,* after all, come out *for* abortion or stand *against* reproduction, *against* futurity, and so against *life*? Who *would* destroy the Child?" (2004, 16), Solondz answers: Aviva's parents.[17]

In this moment Eelman's argument that the "structural position of queerness" as an "identification with the negativity of this drive [the death drive]" (2004, 27) comes into crisis, as Aviva's child is projected as, and figured as, the disabled, poor, racialized subject. As the content and affect of Aviva's mother's statement makes clear, it is *this* child subject (contra Edelman's queer one) that is understood to interrupt Aviva's own childish hold on reproductive futurity.[18] At the same time, as Aviva's white heterosexual mother demonstrates, the subjects who occupy the structural position of the death drive (at least for Aviva) are much more capacious—and certainly more racist, classist, and ableist, let alone heterosexual—than Edelman diagnoses them as being. Espousing racist, classist, ableist, and gendered discourses around "children having children" (Fields 2005) and the figure of the innocent child suggests not only, as José Muñoz has argued, that "[t]he future is only the stuff of some kids . . . [r]acialized kids, queer kids, are not the sovereign princes of futurity" (2009, 95) but also that the coercive investment in procreative futurity is unevenly distributed. Reading reproduction as raced, for example, would demand that a queer analysis of reproductive futurity attend to those populations who are posed as a problem *specifically for their reproductivity;* for their reproduction of a racial futurity in the face of vast regimes that seek their sterilization and their nonexistence.[19] Along these lines, Sharon Holland argues that there is a need to rethink the "place of reproduction" within queer theory such that it is not understood just as "hetero or homo, not as feminist or women's," but is additionally a structure of "biology, race, and belonging" (2012, 74). Theorizing Aviva as a queer child *and* a queer mother demands that the queer approaches to childhood shift towards a different understanding of mothering that attends to sexuality and reproduction as a project of racial belonging and futurity as much as it is one of gendered or intimate pleasure and danger.

Aviva's heterosexual parents, in other words, take up the figural position of the death drive, demanding that Aviva's child be destroyed and arguing that her child signifies the "radical dissolution of the contract, in every sense social and Symbolic" (L. Edelman 2004, 16). Aviva's complicated positioning in this scene thus figures her as the queer-child-*as*-queer-mother (of queer child). And it is precisely these competing layers of reproductivity, futurity, innocence, and queerness that Aviva's childhood holds in tension. Held together, Aviva's queer politics, or the queer politics we require to support Aviva, thus begs that different questions be asked of Edelman's theory of queerness and the death drive.

THE DEATH DRIVE AND THE QUEER ANALYST

Because Aviva begs that new questions be asked of Edelman's theory, I want to resist the urge—so often done in queer theory that one could be forgiven for thinking it is compulsory—to reject his conclusions outright. Rather than refusing Edelman's analysis, what happens if we accept his premise that queerness (as figural) is positioned in a negative relation to the Child (as universal) and we follow his framing of the political along a Lacanian model of the Symbolic order? What interventions and understandings does his argument hold, and how might twisting it, rather than rejecting it, be useful for an analysis of queer motherhood and the desire for childhood? For indeed, one of the ongoing repercussions of the tendency to outright refuse Edelman's polemic is that it has become, for many scholars, the "End of Theory" on the Child. This is unfortunate both for the bevy of critical scholars working on childhood who are told, incorrectly, that the last word on childhood has been said and for Edelman, whose text has (perhaps intentionally) become the very signifier of negativity he is invested in queerness maintaining.

For both Edelman and myself, a queer analysis of childhood begins with an analysis of desire. Drawing upon Lacan's theories of the Symbolic order (Lacan 1977a, 1977b), Edelman calls the coercive universalization of the Child "reproductive futurism," and he argues that its framing of the political operates as a "mirror of desire" (2004, 10):

> Politics . . . names the struggle to effect a fantasmatic order of reality in which the subject's alienation would vanish into the seamlessness of identity. . . . This means not only that politics conforms to the temporality of desire . . . but also that politics is a name for the temporalization of desire. . . . Politics, that is, . . . allegorizes or elaborates sequentially, precisely *as* desire, those over-determinations of libidinal positions and inconsistencies of psychic defenses occasioned by what disarticulates the narrativity of desire: the drives. (8–9)

In order to understand Edelman's argument, it is important to unpack what he means by desire. Using a Lacanian model, Edelman argues that desire is "born of and sustained by a constitutive *lack*" (10). In Lacan's terms, desire is "neither the appetite for satisfaction, nor the demand for love, but the difference that results from the subtraction of the first from the second, the phenomenon of their splitting" (1958, 287). Desire, in other words, can only be maintained by its unfulfillment, for its fulfillment (obtaining the desired object) would bring into being its own end. It is because politics, as Edelman argues, is the narrativization of desire (a narrative that promises a fulfillment of desire's lack, but only by deferring this fulfillment off onto the fantasy of the future, which only politics itself can eventually bring about), that it wraps itself so tightly around the figure of "the Child." Politics relies on the Child, Edelman argues, because the Child is a figure imagined to enjoy "unmediated access to Imaginary wholeness," precisely for its location in the imagined past; it thus embodies for politics the site at which "being and meaning are joined as One" (2004, 10). Promising this figure, or wrapping itself around the promises that this figure makes in relation to our own imagined wholeness, politics thus allows us to refuse to acknowledge the "overdeterminations of libidinal positions and inconsistencies of psychic defenses" (9) that we are necessarily constituted by.

If politics, however, is the mirror of desire, then the death drive, Edelman writes, "names what the queer, in the order of the social, is called forth to figure: the negativity opposed to every form of social viability" (2004, 9). Drives are important to Edelman because they emerge not in relation to lack, but rather "in relation to a constitutive *surplus*" (10). The surplus that the drive, and specifically the death drive, marks, is, Edelman writes, "the excess embedded within the Symbolic through the loss, the Real loss, that the advent of the signifier effects" (9). Articulating this Real loss that the signifier effects, Edelman argues that the signifier is an

> alienating and meaningless token of our Symbolic constitution as subjects . . . this signifier only bestows a sort of *promissory* identity, one with which we can never succeed in fully coinciding because we, as subjects of the signifier, can only be signifiers ourselves, can only every aspire to catch up to whatever it is we might signify by closing the gap that

divides us and, paradoxically, makes us subjects *through that act of division alone.* (8)

If the queer figures the death drive, if it marks the surplus of the Symbolic, then it is the constant and reiterative—for Lacan and Freud the drives are nothing if not repetitive—reminder that the political subject, and hence politics itself, is necessarily constituted by the failure of this promissory identity. This queer signification of Real loss—being made, in other words, to signify the reality that promised wholeness can only exist in fantasy—is absolutely necessary for a queer politics, Edelman argues. Acknowledging this excess, he writes, means "recognizing and refusing the consequences of grounding reality in denial of the drive" (2004, 17). As such, queerness, as the reiterative reminder of the failures and deferrals of politics, must, Edelman argues, remain this reminder; its "efficacy," its "real strategic value, lies in its resistance to a Symbolic reality" (18). In this sense, Edelman's argument is not so much about *the child* as it is about the desires and fantasies that suggest politics can stave off the death drive. Inasmuch as it *is* about the child, it is because the Child is a site for this fantasy's cathexis.

My divergence from Edelman's analysis, however, rests precisely here: where he ends. In taking on the role of the drive, Edelman demands of queerness that it not just refuse to engage with politics on its terms—indeed, that it seeks to unravel politics through a negation of its terms—but also that its relationship to the ego and the ethical is that of a reiterative resistance (the death drive) *internal to the analysand.* Why, I ask, not demand that queerness instead take up the position of the analyst? Taking on a position internal to the analysand and containing the political and the queer within this subject not only limits the possibilities for imagining different subjects who might inhabit these figures, as I argued above, but also refuses to think beyond itself, or to intervene in its own problematic processes. Remaining within the analysand, the queer as "ethical" is bound only for a repetition of its conditions of emergence.

To make this point, I turn not to Edelman or Lacan but rather to Freud. Describing the role of psychoanalysis generally, and the analyst specifically, Freud writes:

> The patient cannot remember all of what is repressed in him, and what he cannot remember may be precisely the essential part of it. Thus he acquires no sense of conviction of the correctness of the construction that has been communicated to him. He is obliged to *repeat* the repressed material as a contemporary experience instead of, as the physician would prefer to see, *remembering* it as something belonging to the past. . . . When things have reached this stage, it may be said that the earlier neurosis is now replaced by a fresh, "transference-neurosi." It has been the physician's endeavour to . . . force as much as possible into the channel of memory and to allow as little as possible to emerge as repetition. ([1920] 1955, 18–19)

In this statement, Freud suggests that the role of the analyst is to interrupt the patient's repeating of a repressed past trauma within current experience by working with the patient to uncover the original trauma. In so doing, the patient might recognize and acknowledge (bring into memory) the repressed event and can begin to consciously process it. The analyst's role, in other words, is to bring into light the underlying instigators of repetitious acts that are engendered by repression such that they might be intervened in.[20] In this sense, if queer theory worked toward cultivating the position of the analyst rather than the death drive internal to the analysand, it might understand its relationship to the social as one that is propelled by the desire for critique, social change, and interruption rather than stubborn reiteration.

Engaging with Edelman's mapping of the political as the narrativization of desire from the position of the analyst rather than the analysand still allows for many of Edelman's critiques to hold, but it repositions what relationship queerness, as a political project and a scholarly one, has to the problematic structures through which queer is constituted, and in which it can intervene. Here, queerness might, rather than say "no" to a Symbolic reality that projects its lack onto the Child, instead become the vessel onto which politics transfers the repressions that structure this problematic relation, and thereby begins to live through them, recollect them, and recognize them. In moving away from merely figuring the death drive, a politics of opposition that locates itself in the figural and active role of the analyst might thus instead engender a relation to its object that appears as something less akin to unending negativity, and more akin to speculative hope.

The Queer Child on Screen

This chapter began with a young queer boy's performance that betrayed the lines of identification and celebration that were bound up with him. It was this betrayal, I noted, that brought me to undertake an analysis of the attachments, demands, and desires placed within the production of the queer child within queer theory. Doing so led me to Aviva and an argument for an incorporation of motherhood and reproductive futurity into queer theory. To conclude, however, I want to offer Aviva as not just an object of analysis for queer theory but additionally as an epistemology. I do so in the hope that it might prompt the speculative movement from internal negativity to analysand by raising questions about desire and identification.

As I have already noted, eight actors were cast for Aviva, "some of whom," Jon Davies writes, "look the part of a thirteen-year-old Jewish girl, while others do not" (2007, 379). Because of this incongruous casting throughout *Palindromes,* Aviva confronts us with her multiplicity, making us reflect on our attachments to and identifications with her different embodiments in various moments. Along these lines, Aviva's circuitous casting makes us ask additional questions that challenge our frames for identifying queer children. Most important of which is, Is she a child? This question leads us to others: Is she having sex because someone is forcing her, or is she having it with consent? And, wait, isn't she too young to consent, or to have a child? Well, maybe not *this* version of Aviva, but certainly *that* version. *That* version is definitely too young. But at what point does Aviva become this or that version, and how long does she stay that way? And are these other versions really just different versions of an "original" Aviva? Maybe there is a particular form of hers that we think, or are supposed to think, most accurately reflects who she really is: perhaps it is one of the ones who "looks the part"? I argue, however, that the very point of this multiple casting is that it is impossible to know. The question that Aviva poses for any of these readings of her then, is not whether Aviva is a queer child, but, rather, what does it mean to locate someone in childhood or in queerness in the first place? What version of them do we hang on to in order to use them as emblems of queer children?

For Berlant, the significance of Aviva's embodiments is a question of casting, and as such it is irrelevant. Or, rather, the question itself (asking after the meaning of casting particular racial and gendered actors) *is* relevant, even if the one eventually cast is irrelevant. Comparing "Dawn" Aviva—the six-year-old Aviva we are first introduced to and who returns to deliver the final line of the film—to her cousin Dawn Weiner, Berlant writes:

> Dawn is white and Aviva is African American, a difference on which there is no comment, because one question of the film is whether "casting" X specific being in the role of the exemplary object really matters when we are talking about love. (2011b, 688)

Here I depart from Berlant's reading. For while the lack of comment may have no bearing on who occupies the position of exemplary object within loving attachments—and yet here too the racialized and gendered histories of impossible, illegal, or disavowed romantic formations might suggest that, indeed, it does matter—in order to understand the work that the "queer" "child" does on the screen, we must situate these various castings within a wider discussion on spectatorship, the gaze, and identification.[21]

Carefully attending to the question of casting means not just thinking about whose bodies appear on screen and whether or not they accurately represent the "original," it also means considering what relationship the act of looking at these bodies has to the forms of pleasure, desire, and identification that Aviva's various embodiments engender. One of the difficulties of doing such a reading of *Palindromes,* however, is that not only, by centering on a young female protagonist, does it depart from the type of film that Laura Mulvey (1975) initially used to elaborate her highly influential theory of the male gaze, it also refuses to sustain a consistent body within the frame. *Palindromes,* which revels in irony, camp, playfulness, and absurdity, is thus at odds with the genre of film Mulvey works with, and yet it is precisely the film's refusal to allow for a straight forward identification with Aviva that I am interested in exploring here.

In the decades since Mulvey's field-defining article, analyses of the pleasure of looking and the ambivalent and multiple lines of identification, desire, and looking relations that constitute cinema have proliferated exponentially. Scholars such as Mary Ann Doane, Teresa de Lauretis, and Jackie Stacey have expanded Mulvey's work by thinking about the different relations of identification and desire as they structure looking relations and spectatorship.[22] Additionally, for bell hooks (1992), Jane Gaines (1990), and others, the structures of identification and desire are not just about sexual difference and sexuality but are also structured through questions of race and class.[23] In this sense, Diana Fuss (1995) argues that identification cannot be theorized outside of its colonial history, and that any recuperative approach to identification needs to situate the potentials and limits of identification within its colonial genealogies. In her reading of Frantz Fanon's *Black Skin White Masks* (1967), cross-racial and cross-gendered identification takes place within Fanon's text in complex ways. Fuss argues that in his articulation of the "Negrophobic" white woman's rape fantasy "a cross-gendered and cross-racial identification" takes place wherein the woman "usurps the position she herself has assigned to the black man and plays the role not only of victim but of aggressor" (1995, 155). Here, cross-racial identification takes place precisely through the fear of and desire for the black man's sexuality. For Kobena Mercer, who theorizes the act of the white spectator looking at the image of the black body through the work of Robert Mapplethorpe, "the image of the black male body presents the [white male] spectator with a source of erotic pleasure" (1994, 436), and this erotic pleasure re-inscribes a "fundamental *ambivalence* of colonial phantasy, oscillating between sexual idealization of the racial other and anxiety in defense of the identity of the white male ego" (438).[24] Here, thinking of the multiple gendered, aged, and raced positionings that Aviva takes on, we could add, Is narrative pleasure only about white pleasure? Is racial identification and the pleasure (or displeasure) one takes in viewing the white (female) body on the screen always restricted to

an identification with (or rejection of) whiteness? How does identification work across generations? And are there ways of reading the
racialized and gendered bodies in the image as multiply signifying,
producing identification and opposition, and speaking to both the
gendered and racialized nature of desire, affiliation, and sexuality?

I return to these founding debates because I argue that reading
them through *Palindromes* provides another way of thinking across
these questions of identification and desire—both as they relate to
scholarship on cinema, and as they facilitate queer theory's broader
desire for the queer child. *Palindromes* is an unconventional film that
relies on absurdity, strangeness, and oddness in order to disturb and
challenge the viewer. In this sense, if Aviva's body is to be read directly,
as straightforwardly engendering a particular identification from
a particular gendered and racialized spectator, then each different
shift in casting facilitates a specific way of reading the scene. Depending on who the spectator is, "Dawn" Aviva would thus facilitate lines
of identification different from "Henrietta" Aviva's, and so on. But
identification does not always work so directly, and the structures
of looking made possible within *Palindromes* do not allow such an
identification at all. Beginning from an approach that prioritizes the
"multiple and coexisting" registers of identification, which "produce
conflicts, convergences, and innovative dissonances within gender"—
and I am tentatively adding racial—"configurations" (Butler 1990,
85–86), Aviva's shifts in casting might be read as all individually
being available for overlapping gendered and racial identifications in
themselves. Additionally, because of the film's oddness and strangeness, and its reliance on the bizarre (both in terms of its diegesis and
its cinematography), *Palindromes* refuses the very potential for a direct
identification. *Palindromes* might, in this sense, be what Halberstam
defines as "queer cinema," a category of film that creates "invitations
to play through numerous identifications within a single sitting" and
allows for a "creative reinvention of ways of seeing" (1998, 180).

Aviva's shifts in casting specifically and intentionally elicit and
proliferate multiple ways of seeing, identifying with, and desiring her.
At the very moment that a straightforward approach to spectatorship
and identification seems to make more sense in relation to Aviva's

particular relationship to the shot, scene, and narrative that she occupies, a new title scene appears and a new Aviva with her. What Aviva thus proposes, with each of her shifts in casting, is that any attempt to secure her in a particular reading can never catch up with her. In this line of analysis, the queer work Aviva does is in getting us to become uncomfortable with the lines of critique we have become accustomed to. We are left unable to place her, or her desires, or what's best for her, because she absolutely refuses to be recognized in such a way. She is simultaneously six, thirteen, in her mid-forties, a teenage white boy, a full-figured black woman, a young Dominican woman, and a couple of emaciated white women of different ages. Perhaps she is also each of the Sunshine family's children. Aviva thus becomes the type of queer child that Ohi elaborates, one who "thwarts a sense of an easy identification" and insists upon the very "impossibility of identification" itself (2004, 104).

However, indicative of queer critique more generally, this invitation for free play requires particular racialized interruptions in, and relations to, the Aviva we see. Interestingly, Solondz himself spoke of this casting technique in such a way that highlighted the substitutability of the actors (and the multiplicities of identification) while at the same time recognized the differences in effect that each of their particular bodies had on the viewer:

> As far as the casting thing goes . . . each one has a different reason. I knew that I needed to begin with a black child to set some things off. Maybe she's adopted because Ellen Barkin is the mom and then you say, "No. She's Latino. She's a redhead. Wait." At a certain point, or first your [sic] disoriented, but then it kicks in, the *connection*. It's like, "Okay, it's the same character, but different actors playing this one character." . . . Then . . . you get to a big black woman, and for me that was my Gulliver, so to speak, with the Lilliputians around her. (Solondz, quoted in Murray, n.d.)

For Solondz, the use of different actors comes from a desire to emphasize their connection and their possible mutuality, but, at the same time, it is precisely the (fetishistic) shock of the black woman's body (and the black child's incongruity with the white family) that interrupts and makes possible the viewer's multiple identifications with Aviva. Here, then, an entirely flexible model for spectatorship and identification cannot sustain itself on its own.[25] As Stacey cautions, "This more flexible model of spectatorship suggests that sexual difference"—and here I am adding racial difference and one's location within childhood—"is so fluid as to have little determining significance in cinematic spectatorship" (1994, 31).

Rather than innocently inviting free play, therefore, Aviva's shifts in casting—and specifically her black adult and child bodies, bodies that I argued in "Disavowing Black Childhood" are rendered incoherent with childhood—interrupt not only the act of identification but also the queer theoretical frames through which multiple, proliferative identifications are assumed to take place. There is, in other words, a normativity lingering within the (queer) child that allows for its playfulness. This normativity—here understood as unmarked whiteness, elsewhere, I argued, conscripted as antifamily and against reproduction—allows, on one hand, a panoply of refusals, encounters and affiliations of nonnormative bodies and communities. At the same time, however, this queer embrace of a particular child and her normative confines as the emblem of queer affiliation becomes stuck within its own terms, refusing to account for the children (and queers) who are tangential to its lines of identification. Rather than highlight the queerness of childhood through an analysis of Aviva's refusals to be securely identified with, a critical queer reading of Aviva's childhood would instead interrogate the terms of desire for the child. It would recognize that particular castings are deemed distinctive enough from childhood to interrupt the act of looking precisely because these children betray the cohesive version of the child that we queerly desire to see.

Aviva's Final Look

At the very end of *Palindromes,* Aviva and a slightly older, taller, and heavier Judah (John Gemberling), have sex once again. In between the thrusts of the young man's awkward and large body, Aviva's various incarnations cycle, as Berlant writes, "in ghostly fashion through the place her body holds in the image" (2011b, 689), while she imagines the possibilities of producing another life via someone else's orgasm. Finally, after Judah finishes, Aviva returns to us as "Dawn" Aviva and breaks the fourth wall. Looking directly into the camera, with a big smile on her face, Aviva declares optimistically: "I have a feeling, though it's just a feeling, that this time, I'm going to be a mom!" Unlike her other shifts in casting, the return of "Dawn" Aviva in this concluding shot comes as a bit of a shock. We have not seen this Aviva since the film opened and a lot has taken place. Too much, perhaps (we hope), for this six-year-old Aviva to have been the Aviva all along. Looking steadfastly into the lens, however, Aviva's statement of "*this time*" demonstrates her awareness of those other times—indeed, it tells us that she has been there with us throughout the film all along. And you—her direct gaze reminds you—you have been watching.

4

Undocumented Dream-Work

Intergenerational Migrant Aesthetics and the Parricidal
Violence of the Border

"Dear DREAMers, Family, Friends, I have a confession to make. After the initial disappointment that came with the vote in December, I awoke from my stupor to realize that the act we were fighting for was an insult" (Mukahhal 2011). So begins a resolute and defiant open letter by Alaa Mukahhal, one of the organizers of the Chicago-based advocacy group Organized Communities Against Deportations. Writing in February 2011 in the wake of the failure of Congress to pass the Development, Relief, and Education for Alien Minors Act (DREAM Act) in a vote on December 18, 2010, Mukahhal was furious. She was not alone. Activists who had been campaigning for years to get Congress to pass the DREAM Act, under the hope that it would at least partially protect undocumented children and young people in the United States, found themselves having to recalibrate their wishes and activist strategies.

In the face of this legislative loss, Mukahhal both mourned and celebrated:

> I will confess dear friends that, lately, I have been relieved and happy. Upon rereading that thing called the DREAM Act, I was hurt, I was insulted, and I felt below human.... The vote failed. But this isn't a setback, it's the beginning of a comeback.... Please do not misunderstand me. I wanted this bill to pass badly. And I know my life and family's lives would be this much easier if it did pass. But in the aftermath of it

all I am able to see what must be done and how much harder we must push. (Mukahhal 2011)

As Mukahhal notes, and as this chapter outlines in further detail, the December 2010 vote on the DREAM Act was a product of over a decade of lobbying, activism, and turmoil. First introduced in the Senate in 2001, the DREAM Act would have allowed undocumented immigrants who met strict criteria, including enrollment in college or enlistment in the military, to be able to apply for conditional residency within the United States.[1] And yet the 2010 defeat was in many senses the act's last hurrah. It failed again in 2011, and it still has not been signed—despite, or perhaps because of, the "success" of the Deferred Action for Child Arrivals (DACA) program, enacted via executive action in 2012 by President Obama and ended by President Trump in 2017.[2]

In her open letter, Mukahhal argues that one of the central issues of the DREAM Act was the fact that the discourses supporting it conscripted undocumented young people into a framing of childhood that had violent consequences for themselves, their parents, and their families. She writes:

We've made so many concessions because the reasoning went, the more we yielded the more likely it will pass. But now we know better. . . . We fought this battle on their terms and arguments. We were constantly on the defense. Every time, they yelled "Your parents broke the law. Legalizing you rewards them!", we threw our hands in the air and said "But we were young! We didn't know! It wasn't our choice." (Mukahhal 2011)

Integral to the discourses that propelled the DREAM Act, then, was a child figure that has played a central role across the movements discussed in *Ambivalent Childhoods* thus far. Here the innocent child—more specifically the innocent migrant child—is evoked in the justifications for the DREAM Act's protections of some undocumented children. But its concessionary evocation is simultaneously mobilized to criminalize these very children's parents. Critiquing the ambivalent workings of childhood within and against the DREAMers' antideportation movement, this chapter charts how, after years of organizing for a pathway for undocumented children brought into the United States by their undocumented parents to acquire documentation and partial legality, the 2010 failure of the DREAM Act shifted the tactics of undocumented organizers. This shift reoriented these tactics from a desire for inclusion within citizenship on the grounds of being brought into the United States as innocent children, to a critique of the racist and colonial structures of deportability, innocence, and "crimmigration" politics.[3]

The chapter analyzes this shift in tactics as itself productive of an important challenge to the normative political work that childhood does in relation to belonging and the nation. Over the last three chapters I have critiqued the political and psychic entanglements of childhood with racism, transphobia, and heteronormativity (and queerness). Here I chart out the ways in which "child" and "nation" produce meaning for one another, as well as how undocumented children *and their parents* reworked the terms of this pairing in the wake of the DREAM Act's failure. Indeed, parents play a central role in this chapter's analysis. For it was parents, after all, who were the immediate targets of deportation, and who were criminalized at the expense of their children.[4] I, as do DREAMers, argue that one of the central tactics of the DREAM Act was precisely the severing of parent–child relations and the production of generational rifts in the name of national belonging. In this chapter I name this severing as parricide, and I argue that new analytical and conceptual tools—ones that are based within speculative attempts to enact childhood otherwise—are needed to push back against the role that childhood plays in the parricidal violence of borders and deportation. In making this argument, the chapter's centering of young antideportation activists' refusals to participate in criminalizing discourses of their parents embraces one of the central claims of *Ambivalent Childhoods,* that the workings of childhood are not limited to children.

Severing the mutual hold that "nation" and "child" have over one another was a monumental political task for the DREAMers, particularly given the longstanding purchase these two terms have on each other. The emergence of the modern nation-state and of the modern child in the late eighteenth and early nineteenth centuries, Caroline Levander (2006) argues, relied on and produced one another. "These two ideas work in tandem," she writes, "the child who is increasingly understood to be separate and in need of protection from civic life has historically helped to constitute and buttress the nation" (2006, 6). Indeed, the very term "nation" emerges, Levander reminds us, from the root "natio," meaning "to be born," and as such, "the concept of nation continues to be understood within the founding context that the child provides" (2006, 7). Part of what was at stake, then, in the negotiations of the DREAM Act was not just the legal recognition of a limited cohort of young migrants, it was the very terms under which the nation and the (migrant) child came to signify one another in the early twenty-first century.

While Amanda Armenta (2014, 4) argues that the "American obsession with immigrant 'illegality' is a relatively recent phenomenon," only really coming into prominence in the 1980s and 1990s, Beth Baker-Cristales (2009) traces back the emergence of the term "illegal alien" to the 1930s. As Baker-Cristales argues, the use of the term "illegal alien" facilitated a discursive construction of the criminality of immigrants and was a catalyst for the "unconstitutional deportation of hundreds of thousands of Mexican immigrants and Mexican Americans" (2009, 63). The criminalization of migrants is not, however, limited to Mexican immigrants, or to those from Central and South America more generally. Scholars have pointed to the longstanding and ongoing histories of Chinese exclusion,[5] as well as the ongoing Muslim ban,[6] as just some of the populations stigmatized and criminalized at the border. Across these histories, racism, heteronormativity, and misogyny come together as co-constitutive with exclusion, deportation, and criminality.

Conceptualizing this criminalization, Mae M. Ngai writes that "the illegal immigrant cannot be constituted without deportation—the possibility or threat of deportation, if not the fact" (2004, 58). This framing of the *threat* of deportation, of and beyond the *act* of deportation, is integral to a critical understanding of both the violences of the border and the plight of undocumented children and families who would have benefited from the DREAM Act. It comes from a legal landscape that has produced "state machinery to apprehend and deport" unauthorized migrants and from the "temporal and spatial 'lag'" that exists between entry and apprehension (2004, 58). It is in this regard that Nicholas De Genova (2002, 438) has argued that "it is deportability, and not deportation per se" that must be understood as central to the dynamics of border control and state sovereignty. Deportability, understood as "the protracted possibility of being deported—along with the multiple vulnerabilities that this susceptibility for deportation engenders," De Genova and Nathalie Peutz argue (2010, 14), is the pernicious effect of the legal and discursive landscape of criminalized immigration. And indeed, it is under the dominion of deportability that undocumented children and their families lived and negotiated their partial access to state and local services in the lead up to the DREAM Act.

The condition of deportability has a long history, but it has intensified as a state practice in recent decades. The number of deportations under Obama, who was in office during the 2010 vote on the DREAM Act, was higher than any other previous administration. While this increase was partially due to the effects of the Bush administration's policy change—which ended the practice of so-called voluntary returns (deportations that were not formally recognized)—it coincided with the implementation of stricter guidelines for formal deportations, recorded by Immigration and Customs Enforcement. This policy shift not only increased the *recorded* number of deportations, it also subjected those who were deported to surveillance by border control. It was a policy shift that aligned with and contributed to the wider criminalization of immigration.[7] A number of scholars have described the ways in which deportability, the criminalization of immigration, and the dynamics of racism and "migratism" (Tudor 2018) have been experienced by children and their parents.[8] That said, not many scholars have articulated these dynamics as produced through the idea of childhood itself or through the relation of parent and child.[9]

In parsing out the workings of childhood here, the chapter moves across legal, discursive, narrative, and conceptual framings of undocumented childhood before turning to what I am calling a creative and speculative thought experiment. Following the previous chapters' weaving of cultural critique with a playful psychoanalytic bearing, I make my way from the DREAM Act to the terrain of dreamwork. Inhabiting Freud's account of dream-work as an analytic and as an ethical call, I argue that dream-work, alongside creative and artistic interventions into parricidal violence, will allow for rearticulations of migrant childhood that resolutely intermesh parent and child.

Wishful Thinking

In the years leading up to the introduction of the DREAM Act, DREAMers utilized various narratives and personal stories in order to humanize themselves and to ensure that their demands for belonging and inclusion be recognized by an otherwise racist and anti-immigrant populace. This was, and continues to be, no easy task, particularly given the longstanding discursive and juridical construction of migrants as "illegal" and the conflation of racism, migratism, and deportability. Amid this landscape, DREAMers had to develop, as Walter J. Nicholls argues, "a sophisticated set of arguments to represent themselves and their cause" (2013, 5). Nicholls writes:

> [DREAMers] argued that they were raised in America, they only knew this country, and they were important contributors to its economic, civic, and moral life. They were not a "foreign" threat because they were Americans. They had played by all the rules and they now had a right to live out the American dream, just like anybody else. Denying them the right to live and thrive in the country would be a moral outrage and a profound injustice. (2013, 5–6)

In interviews, news reports, profiles, and media appearances, DREAMers reiterated their essential Americanness. They strategically stressed the fact that for many, they did not even know they were not technically American until they applied—with exceptional GPAs and outstanding extracurricular activities—to college or for financial aid, and were informed they were ineligible. This pairing of innocence and exceptionalism was absolutely central to positioning DREAMers as quintessentially American. It followed a legislative precedent from the Supreme Court, and, in so doing it set a fragile stage upon which a series of tainted claims were made about national belonging.

In response to the criminalization of immigration and amid a backdrop of increasing deportation, DREAMers named their presence in America as being "no fault of their own" and stressed that they had a legitimate claim to American citizenship and the American dream. This narrative of "no fault of their own," which emerged out of the Supreme Court Case *Plyler v. Doe* (1982), was founded on and evocative of a particular deployment of childhood. In *Plyler* the Supreme Court struck down a Texas state statute denying funding for education to undocumented immigrant children in the United States, and it did so by asserting that undocumented children are in the United States through "no fault of their own." This phrasing shaped how, and under what terms, claims to national belonging could be made, and it has thus allowed for a range of avenues to be opened up within activism and legal appeals.[10] At the same time, however, *Plyler* is a complex and ambivalent ruling, one whose mixed terms also open up a series of sticking points that continue to be negotiated and resisted by undocumented and antideportation activists, particularly as they relate to children and their parents.

On one hand, the *Plyler* ruling framed undocumented children as akin to a protected class. Delivering the opinion of the court, Justice William Brennan argued that "the children who are plaintiffs in these cases are special members of this underclass" (Plyler, 219). Being located within the "underclass" meant, Brennan writes, that while "persuasive arguments support the view that a State may withhold its beneficence from those whose very presence within the United States is the product of their own unlawful conduct," these arguments "do not apply with the same force" to the children of "those who elect to enter our territory by stealth and in violation of our law" (219–20). Here undocumented children, in clear distinction to their parents, are enshrined within legal innocence and ignorance, partially protecting them from the "consequences" of their parents' actions. Indeed, Brennan writes that it is "difficult to conceive of a rational justification for penalizing these children for their presence within the United

States" (220). Having defined the undocumented child as innocent, Brennan does not, however, offer them solace. Instead, he establishes a distinction between deportation and deportability, and he defines deportability as the necessary structuring condition of life for undocumented children:

> To be sure, like all persons who have entered the United States unlawfully, these children are subject to deportation. But there is no assurance that a child subject to deportation will ever be deported. An illegal entrant might be granted federal permission to continue to reside in this country, or even to become a citizen. . . . We are [thus] reluctant to impute to Congress the intention to withhold from these children, for so long as they are present in this country through no fault of their own, access to a basic education. (226)

In this key passage from the Court's decision, it is precisely the child's innocent presence within the country that justified the call for their tenuous inclusion within state education. It is, however, important to stress the *tenuousness* of this inclusion, for it is clear that this "innocence" does not protect these children from being subject to deportation. Indeed, innocence is the very grounds upon which the child straddles the fine line between deportability and deportation. The clear implication of Brennan's argument is that, positioned any other way, the undocumented child's hold on life within the "temporal lag" (Ngai 2004) that is the condition of deportability—and indeed the child's hold on the nation—will be violently interrupted by the mechanics of the state.

Knowing that *Plyler* set the legal and discursive grounds upon which tenuous inclusion might be achieved, DREAMers and their allies in various positions of power mobilized around the ruling's language. But this mobilization of *Plyler*'s terms also carried forth the ruling's ambivalences. Speaking to reporters a week before the December 2010 vote, for example, Homeland Security Secretary Janet Napolitano suggested that the DREAM Act would allow her agency to better prioritize its resources:

What doesn't make as much sense [as tracking down "criminal aliens"] is the idea of spending our enforcement resources to prosecute young people who have no criminal records, who were brought here through no fault of their own, so they have no individual culpability, and who now want to go to college or serve in our armed forces. (Napolitano in Naylor 2010)

In this quote, Napolitano not only evokes the innocent, blameless child in language that is clearly citing *Plyler,* she also simultaneously orients this child toward a range of carceral and militarized state projects. The distinction she produces between these innocent children and their criminal parents (and other "criminal aliens") maintains innocence, conscription, and parricide as the terms of inclusion within the nation. Children will only be defended if their presence within the nation does not trouble the adherence criminality has with migration, and if they demonstrate a willingness to serve in the armed forces (a forced conscription that often goes unrecognized). Not all of the evocations of *Plyler* were as explicit as this one in terms of their nationalist fervor, but the logics within them are congruent. In an open letter published on *Politico,* for example, Drew Faust and John Hennessy, presidents of Harvard and Stanford respectively, wrote the following defense of the DREAM Act:

These young people ... were brought to the United States as minors, many as infants and grew up in our neighborhoods [and] communities. They didn't decide to come here, but they have made this their home. .... The DREAM Act would throw a lifeline to thousands of promising students, part of our communities, who, through no fault of their own, face uncertain futures due to their lack of immigration status. (Faust and Hennessy 2010)

Distinguishing "these young people" from "us"—they grew up in *our* neighborhoods—Faust and Hennessy position DREAMers, or at least the ones attending elite institutions, as innocent infants and minors who "already share the American dream" (Faust and Hennessy

2010). The subtlety of the language of *Plyler* here makes its insidiousness no less powerful. Emphasizing that DREAMers "didn't decide to come here" removes any agency from these young people and covertly names ones who *did* decide to come to the United States—their parents, as well as unaccompanied minors—as less deserving of the very lifeline Faust and Hennessy are seemingly defending.

Despite their limitations, statements such as these from people in power only took place after years of action by DREAMers, many of whom risked their safety by outing themselves as undocumented.[11] While countless undocumented young people ended up "coming out of the shadows" in and beyond the decade leading up to the 2010 vote, some of their narratives had a wider reach than others. One of the most well known of these "outings" came from Jose Antonio Vargas, a nationally recognized journalist and documentary film maker who worked for such outlets as the *Washington Post,* the *San Francisco Chronicle,* and the *Huffington Post.* In feature articles for the *New York Times Magazine* (Vargas 2011) as well as *TIME Magazine* (Vargas 2012), Vargas came out as undocumented.[12] In both of these accounts, one of the central moments in his narrative was when he learned that he was undocumented:

> My mother sent me to live with my grandparents in the U.S. when I was 12. When I was 16 and applied for a driver's permit, I found out that my green card—my main form of legal identification—was fake. My grandparents, both naturalized citizens, hadn't told me. It was disorienting, first discovering my precarious status, then realizing that when I had been pledging allegiance to the flag, the republic for which it stands didn't have room for me. (Vargas 2012)

Like many other undocumented children and young people, Vargas's undocumented status was withheld from him, only to be discovered at the moment of attempting to access state services or higher education. After being told by his grandparents to never show his fake green card to anyone, Vargas writes that he "decided then" that he would "never give anyone reason to doubt [he] was an American" (Vargas 2011). Narratives like this, which begin with a moment of surprising and disorienting discovery, tend to juxtapose this dissonance with a recounting of the young person's affection for America and a stated commitment to achieving the American Dream. While not explicitly utilizing the language of *Plyler,* this narrative still relies on the innocent child to garner its readers' empathies. As a trained journalist well versed in weaving together personal narrative with American sentimentality, Vargas, in his retelling of this moment, carefully names his surprising difference from other Americans as administrative rather than affective. It is precisely his "love" for the country and his pledge of allegiance to it as a child that is named as incommensurate with his undocumented status. How could he not be an American, he asks, given his unwavering and lifelong patriotism?

Narratives like these are used because they envelop the undocumented child with American sentimentality. In some cases they work to provide at least momentary protection for a young person and their family. In July 2007, for example, immigration officials who had detained an undocumented family in Florida, and were preparing to deport them, were confronted by friends of Juan Gomez, one of the children in the family. Reporting on this act of solidarity, Julia Preston, a journalist from the *New York Times* who did much of their reporting on the DREAM Act, recounts: "Immigration officials delayed the [family's] deportation on Wednesday after a group of Mr. Gomez's high school friends roused support in South Florida and then flew to Washington to pound on doors. The friends pointed to Mr. Gomez's academic record—a near-perfect 3.96 grade-point average—and top scores on 11 Advanced Placement exams" (Preston 2007a).

Preston goes on to describe Juan as "an affable teenager" who tutored classmates in European history and biochemistry and was "an exceptional college candidate" (Preston 2007). As both an "exceptional" student and a volunteer at a neighborhood homeless shelter, Juan's narrated innocence, charity, and outstanding moral character were vital to the success of his friends' advocacy campaign. He and his family were released from detention and told that an appeal for them would be made to the White House by one of Florida's Representatives. As should be clear here, there is a stark contrast between how this narrative positions Juan's past, and, pointedly, his future, and the violent and repeated attempts to disavow Trayvon Martin's childhood as discussed in chapter 1. For Juan, and many undocumented young people like him who do not have access to the confines of citizenship—violent and tenuous as they are—being a teenager is inflected with being "affable," a marked distance from the hostile affect of antiblackness described before. To be a teenager in this discursive landscape is to name one's admirable—rather than inappropriate or atemporal—desire to contribute to the nation.

At the same time, this "folding" of undocumented children into the nation's "biopolitical management of life," to draw upon Jasbir Puar's grammar (2007, xii), carried malicious consequences for undocumented people because it was premised on the state's parricidal desire.[13] Framing undocumented young people as "innocent" victims, children, and exceptional proto-citizens was a central trope through which the DREAM Act was defended and justified. This framing works because it produces the undocumented child as within the category of what Lauren Berlant calls "infantile citizenship." As I have already begun to suggest, the framing of undocumented children within the spaces of childhood and adolescence worked differently from the way it did for black youth in the aftermath of Trayvon's murder. There, I argued, adolescence functioned as a specific racialized disavowal of black childhood, one that, under the logics of what I called "adolescent citizenship," aligned with and furthered a longstanding history of antiblackness. Here I am suggesting that undocumented childhood was not discursively or affectively disavowed. Rather, the narratives that positioned undocumented children and young people within childhood, and, to a lesser extent, adolescence, did so with a closer alignment to Berlant's original twinned articulation of infantile citizenship. In this definition, infantile citizenship is both naïve childish patriotism and a figuring of the state as paternalistic adult male protector of a feminized and infantilized citizenry. Along the first lines of infantile citizenship, that of the childlike adoration for the nation, recall Vargas's affectionate memories of pledging allegiance to the flag as a child. Here Vargas is attempting to elicit what Berlant might identify as a "kind of admiration" from "'knowing' adult citizens" who respond to his narrative by remembering "with nostalgia the time that they were 'unknowing' and believed in the capacity of the nation to be practically utopian" (Berlant 1997, 28–29). Positioning himself as infantile, Vargas seeks to adhere the affective stickiness of nostalgic childhood patriotism to his current demand to be recognized as a citizen. Part of the function of this rhetoric is to refute any possibility for other national attachments; the only patriotism that infantile undocumented children have, it is argued, is toward the United States.[14] In mobilizing the discursive framing of innocent childhood, DREAMers and their advocates toiled to entrench undocumented children and young people within the confines of infantile patriotism and citizenship.

One of the effects of demanding to be located within the subject positioning of infantile citizenship is that it comes with a concomitant demand for the state to be affirmed as parental and paternalistic. Here the "image of the citizen as a minor, female, youthful victim," Berlant writes, justifies and produces a state whose "adult citizens, especially adult men" are primarily mobilized around civil protection (1997, 67). Infantile citizenship thus defines citizenship by and for "fetuses, children, real and imaginary migrants—persons that, paradoxically, cannot act yet as citizens" (1997, 5). Because infantile citizenship requires positioning *the state* as the figural parent or guardian of the "real and imaginary" migrant child, it must wrest the migrant child away from their actual parent. To become the "parent" of the child—to be located within relations of power that justify the *state's* role of protector, arbitrator, and supervisor even when and as the state never actually intends to provide these forms of care—the actual relations of kin and familial belonging must be violently negated and interrupted. This violent substitution, which I am calling "parricide," was absolutely central to the narrative positionings of the innocent undocumented child. It structured the terms of advocacy for DREAMers, and it seeped into the psychic life of undocumented childhood.

THE PSYCHIC LIFE OF PARRICIDE

The effects of parricide and the confinement of undocumented young people within the boundaries of childhood was not just a discursive maneuver. As a consequence of the legal landscape that defines citizenship and participation within ritualized acts of American independence and growing up, many undocumented young people felt like they were unable to become adults. In a profile for the *Las Vegas Sun,* Jessica (a pseudonym) is portrayed as living a difficult life at the hands of her liminal status within the country. She is described, on one hand, as being raised in America with "American sensibilities" and, on the other, as struggling, "riddled with shame," not belonging anywhere, and as floundering. Jessica herself describes this limbo status as itself infantilizing her. "I am going to be an eternal child," she tells the reporter: "I can't work. I can't get my own place. I can't drive. I can't get a credit card [or] be independent" (Jessica, quoted in Corbin 2011). The shame that Jessica feels in regard to her liminal status is shared by many undocumented young people, and I want to think through the complex ways in which such shame gets narrated within this article. I do so in an attempt to unpack the psychic life of the undocumented child that I am suggesting emerges under conditions of parricide and deportability.

Jessica's narrative is, like so many others, presented within the strict narrative confines of American sentimentality, and yet it still manages to provide a much more complex and less polished portrayal of undocumented childhood. Here Jessica describes the moment in which the true impact of her undocumented status finally hit her:

> When Jessica was selected as Student of the Year in eighth grade, she should have celebrated this goldest of gold stars. Instead, she slammed doors, bawled her eyes out and let her parents know she would hate them for the rest of her life. What they were doing to her wasn't right. It wasn't fair. She'd been a model student, and now her middle school wanted to reward her by footing half the bill for a trip to Washington, D.C.—home to all the presidents whose birthdays and middle names she'd memorized. Her parents wouldn't let her go. (Corbin 2011)

Jessica's parents, it turns out, were forbidding her to go because she was undocumented, and they were worried that traveling to Washington, D.C. would flag her and her parents to Immigration and Customs Enforcement. Retelling this moment as a twenty-two year old to the

Las Vegas Sun, Jessica explains that she has since come to another understanding of it:

> Up until then I realized there was this issue with other people, but in my mind it wasn't me. . . . I knew we'd traveled here, but we couldn't possibly be illegal or doing anything wrong. When you're at that age, it's like, "My mom and dad are awesome; they would never do anything bad." (Jessica, quoted in Corbin 2011)

The shame being felt here appears to be not just about Jessica's own liminal status. Mired in a discursive landscape that criminalizes migrants and casts aside undocumented parents in favor of their "blameless" children, Jessica is here perhaps reconciling with the shame that comes from recognizing that her parents—within the violent discourse of the state—*did* do something "bad." Indeed, in the narration of the story itself, this renouncing of her parents is structural to the grammar. Jessica's understanding of her parents' innocence is what is rendered childish here. It is only "where you're at that age," Jessica explains, that you are able to ignore or overlook the "faults" of your parents. In this complex scene of infantile citizenship, then, one produced not by a person in power but rather by a young person grappling in complex ways with the violences of national borders, the consequences of naïve nostalgia become even more ambivalent. On one hand, Jessica's adoration of all the American presidents and of Washington, D.C., as a particular site of wish fulfillment and wonder aligns her with a childish patriotism that is so vital to the workings of infantile citizenship. But at the same time her naivety is not limited to an idolizing of the nation. It is also inclusive of a romanticized adoration of her parents. Under the joint conditions of deportability and parricide, however, this romanticized adoration cannot be sustained. As a form of interpersonal attachment—one that might garner a radical political commitment—it is antithetical to the conditions under which she lives, and it is thus transformed into shame.

Given the extent to which parricide inflected the rhetoric of the advocacy *for* the DREAM Act—which can only give an indication of the affective hostility of the narratives against it—it is no surprise that undocumented children and young people like Jessica would narrate their parent-child relation through shame. We can get a sense of the weight of this discursive landscape in the following selection of narratives from people working to defend DREAMers and the DREAM Act:

> Supporters, who called the measure the Dream Act, said it could pass the Senate because it is intended to benefit young people who grow up in the United States and are illegal immigrants as a result of decisions by their parents. (Preston 2007b)

> The Dream Act tacitly poses important questions to society as a whole. Is the United States ready to provide a modicum of opportunity for those who are well under way to making a positive impact on society? What are the limits of the country's animosity toward undocumented immigrants? Will this country make the children of immigrants pay for the "sins" of their fathers? (Sanchez 2007)

> Many legislators, including some who opposed the broader bill, see the student measure differently because it would benefit immigrant teenagers who are illegal only because of decisions their parents made when the children were young. "It's unfair to make these young people pay for the sins of their parents," Mr. Durbin said. (Preston 2007a)

> It would be difficult to define a more sympathetic group of potential Americans. They must demonstrate that they are law-abiding and education-oriented. Some seek to defend the country they hope to join. . . . Critics counter that the law would be a reward for illegal behavior and an incentive for future lawbreaking. But these immigrants, categorized as illegal, have done nothing illegal. They are condemned to a shadow existence entirely by the actions of their parents. (Gerson 2010)

The above quotes present four different yet aligned moments in which, in the very act of defending the importance of the DREAM Act and the need for its passage, undocumented parents are named "sinners," they are engaging in "law breaking" behavior, are portrayed as making bad decisions, and being legally, and morally, to blame for their child's limited opportunities. While deportability is the condition of life for undocumented children, deportation, in contrast, is the only reality for undocumented parents. This narrative framing, one that discarded and criminalized the parent in order to allegedly "protect" and recognize the innocence of the child, was used over and over again in and beyond the decade that the DREAM Act was being debated within congress. In a speech at American University in July of 2010, for example, President Obama utilized this language, arguing that "We should stop punishing innocent young people for the actions of their parents" (Office of the Press Secretary 2010). Here, as elsewhere, founding the innocence of the undocumented child was dependent on establishing the guilt of their parents. The co-constitution of childhood deportability and parental deportation was a means of eschewing the undocumented child's actual parents in order to install the state as the only legitimate parental figure. Wishing that the innocent child that *Plyler* had so clearly set forth as a stepping-stone for undocumented children to receive state recognition and accommodation would also bring to fruition the passage of the DREAM Act, the dream at the heart of the act was broken not just by legislative loss but by the parricidal violence that structured this very child from the start.

Undocumented Dreams

Part of what I am suggesting here is that while DREAMers knew, of course, that these were dangerous terms to be reliant upon, they (or at least those advocating on their behalf) persisted nonetheless because they were convinced that the specter of childhood would, as it was imagined to have done in the past for other communities, enable the DREAM Act's necessary yet limited legislative change to be made. Undergirding this assumption was the tacit knowledge that, as I have argued throughout *Ambivalent Childhoods*, the category of childhood is unevenly applied to individuals and populations, and that this uneven deployment—particularly within the context of social movements—is a dense site for negotiating the hopes, fears, and contradictions inherent to contestations over belonging. The deployment of childhood within DREAMers' rhetoric, then, operated as a wish fulfillment: as *fantasmatically* providing, through its application to undocumented children and young people, the very terms of state recognition that were being prohibited by the state itself. The evocation of childhood was assumed to, almost in and of itself, bring about the passage of the DREAM Act in advance.

As I have shown throughout *Ambivalent Childhoods,* however, childhood often betrays the desires that are invested within it. It is, in other words, a quisling object, one whose allegiances cannot be relied upon. And yet, rather than completely eschewing or ignoring the wish-fulfillment character of childhood and seeking out untainted or "innocent" political demands in response—as if this were itself possible—I want to sit with the ambivalence of wish fulfillment here and follow it to its multiple registers. Doing so means thinking through the psychic life of undocumented childhood from within a speculative approach. What might it engender, I ask, to think with wish fulfillment, and, centrally, to think within the *oneiric* register of the psychic where wishes are most readily manifest? Might sticking with the wish allow for alternative articulations of childhood, ones that enable different forms of national belonging? Attending to these questions throughout the remainder of this chapter, my speculative approach moves, with hope and trepidation, from the legislative to the psychoanalytic life of dreams.

For Freud, one of the main avenues through which wishes are fulfilled is within dreams. Indeed, Freud initially describes dreams as "the fulfilment of a wish" ([1900] 1954, 121).[15] By this he means that dreams allow for something that is prohibited, either materially or psychically, to be enacted and brought into fruition. In his earlier accounts of dreams as wish fulfillments, Freud speaks, for example, of waking up desperately in need of a drink after having dreamed that he was "swallowing down water in great gulps, [which] ha[d] the delicious taste that nothing can equal" (123). Here, Freud suggests that his thirst during the night produced a wish for a glass of water, a wish that was prohibited by his simultaneous desire to keep sleeping. In place of this prohibition and these competing desires, his dream showed him the wish fulfilled and allowed him to continue sleeping a little while longer (123–24). Similarly, upon being told that a friend's wife had dreamed of having her period, Freud writes:

> The fact that this young married woman dreamt that she was having her period meant that she had missed her period. I could well believe that she would have been glad to go on enjoying her freedom a little longer before shouldering the burden of motherhood. It was a neat way of announcing her first pregnancy. (126)

In both of these scenarios, Freud articulates a methodology for interpreting dreams. Rather than assess dreams as prophecies of the future or as the replaying of simple memories, Freud suggests that interpretation must work to unravel the prohibitions and desires that motivate, in a complex and seemingly incongruous fashion, the manifest content of the dream.

These types of straightforward prohibition dreams, Edwin H. Elias (2016) details, are common for undocumented young people. Undertaking an in-depth study of how the criminalization of immigration and the wider context of deportability influenced the mental health of young people who were recipients of DACA, Elias, a sociologist, provides a glimpse into the dreamscape of a few of his participants. One of the themes of these dreams, Elias writes, is unencumbered travel. Students who were prohibited from leaving the country due to not having documentation that would allow them to return, told Elias about dreams of going overseas (2016, 308). These travel dreams, Elias notes, took both pleasurable and distressing forms. While some of these dreams were premised on fulfilling the wish for freedom to travel, others revolved around nightmare scenarios in which students mistook their DACA status for a visa and left the country, only to find themselves unable to return, or otherwise realized within the dream that they had unwittingly self-deported (2016, 308–12). For Elias, these anxious nightmares are read sociologically as indications that the experience of living as undocumented under conditions of deportability, racism, and anti-immigration produce "everlasting imprints on the individual" in the form of psychological traumas, and "mental health problems" (2016, 322–23). While Elias does not use the language of prohibition or the unconscious in his analysis, I would argue that these nightmare scenarios are indicating the psychic strength of the violences that young people internalize; the prohibition against freedom to travel is so strong that the unconscious has established a defense against the wish, forbidding the dream to fully fulfill it. Undocumented dreams, in this formation, then, align an analysis of wish fulfillment with a critique of deportability. They suggest, as Anna Ríos-Rojas and Mark Stern argue, that "dreams are both immigrants' domain and methodology" (2018, 93); dreams are, they write, "prickly things overwhelmed with hopeful longing and desire that move us to feel that this world, this present, is no longer enough—they are, in some ways, a refutation to the present as such" (2018, 92). For even in the moments in which they take on the form of nightmares, undocumented young people are producing unconscious (as well as conscious) analyses of the prohibitions inherent to contemporary bordering and are imagining, perhaps prefiguring, a world in which borders do not materialize restrictions of travel and freedom of movement.

Yet there are other ways to read the relationship between prohibition and wish fulfillment within undocumented dreams. When the dream provides the thing that is wished for—the thing wanted or needed but prohibited—we might alternatively read wish fulfillment pessimistically as it relates to the DREAM Act as a form of cruel optimism (Berlant 2011a).[16] Here, the dream only *fantasmatically*, rather than materially, provides the fulfillment of the need. As such, while I am invested in understanding this fantasmatic fulfillment as engendering a standpoint-like analysis and critique of bordering and deportability, I am cautious about the structures of attachment that wish fulfillment more generally might reify. Here I do not just mean in the moment that the dreamer (or DREAMer) awakes—Elias, for example, recounts one of his participants as arising from a dream of freedom of movement only to find himself again realizing that in his waking reality he cannot travel after all (2016, 308)—but also in the wider, cultural and discursive life that dreams and dreaming have within national imaginaries of citizenship and national belonging. For the undocumented child wrapped up in a context of deportability—a context of temporal lag, suspension, and perhaps somnambulism—dream life is the terrain upon which quotidian struggles and pleasures, as well as political demands, are anchored. In this sense, dreams and their fantasy life need to be carefully attended to.

What does it mean, then, to think through the gap between fantasmatic fulfillment and material absence? One way of answering this question in relation to the DREAM Act is by disentangling the workings of wish fulfillment within the narrative production of the patriotic infantile migrant child. Indeed, a careful critique of wish fulfillment helps unpack the infantile citizen's problematic enmeshment with the American dream. As a fantasy of equal national opportunity, and as a structure of desire, the American dream—a "dream" whose confined narrative structure constricted the very terms under which DREAMers were able to articulate their demand for recognition— functions precisely by *substituting* the lack of material provision with the excess of fantasmatic fulfillment. What one cannot have, and indeed is structurally prohibited from obtaining, is fulfilled in the lavish wish that is the American dream. This argument, that the wish at the center of the American dream is prohibited by the very structures of American inequality, is not a new one. David Eng and Shinhee Han (2000), for example, make this argument in relationship to the psychic violences of unachievable normative whiteness and ambivalent assimilation endured by Asian Americans across generations. They argue that the discourse of the American dream and of model minority status locates Asian Americans within the "stereotyped dream of material success" at the cost of prohibiting any other form of political or cultural inclusion within the nation (2000, 677–78). And yet, despite the reiterated critique of this "dream," it was this very narrative of the American dream that so many scholars, activists, politicians, and journalists utilized to stake the DREAMers' rightful claims to legal recognition and state protection. To state the obvious, the very nomenclature of "DREAMers" itself intentionally ties the DREAMers to the wish that is the American dream.[17] In this sense, while the analysis of dreams as fulfillments of a wish might allow for a particular critique of the mobilization of childhood within social movements, dreams themselves do not seem, in this light, to offer much as a form of prefiguration akin to the work of speculation that I have sketched out across the other chapters. Perhaps this is why there is not much scholarship that takes seriously the psychic character of dreams for producing an analysis of the DREAMers.

Ríos-Rojas and Stern are the exception to this scholarly lacuna. As they argue, scholars seeking to interrogate the "present manifestation of colonialist legacies of white supremacy and racial capitalism" need to examine the depths to which these structures of power have constrained imaginations, "molding visions for what counts as freedom, justice, and human life" (2018, 93). They suggest that, in regards to the DREAMers, dreams—by which they mean imaginations, aspirations, and prefigurations—have been assimilated within the neoliberalism of the American dream: "the *kinds* of dreams power coerces matter to the degree to which they become acceptable or assimilate into the larger realm of the national imaginary: *DREAMers are dreamed to dream about the (neoliberal) dream*" (2018, 101). Ríos-Rojas and Stern suggest here that while dreams have potential to disrupt ongoing structures of violent subjectification, they are also readily coopted by dominant discourses. One of their central arguments—which aligns with the argument I, following undocumented activists, have been tracing out across this chapter so far—is that the DREAM Act itself is one of those dominant discourses which has constrained undocumented "dreams." While I am partial to their critique of the constraints of the DREAM Act, I am slightly more ambivalent about the fact that they arrive at this analysis through a totalizing characterization of psychoanalysis. In this vein, Ríos-Rojas and Stern argue that the cooptation of "dreams" is enabled, in part, by the problematic power relationship between dreamer and analyst, one in which only the trained analyst has the authority to interpret dreams and uses this position to misinterpret and disempower (2018, 98). "Dreams are being interpreted by power for power," they write, "because power knows what's good for people to dream about" (2018, 98). With this framing of the psychoanalytic encounter, they thus equate analyst and the DREAM Act, arguing that "the DREAM Act is an analyst's (power's) interpretation of 'alien' [undocumented] dreams" (2018, 98). Framing politicians as analysts, Ríos-Rojas and Stern suggest that this cooptation is a willful misinterpretation of DREAMers' "dreams."

Despite their somewhat unforgiving framing of the analyst, I find Ríos-Rojas and Stern's intervention into the cooptation of undocumented dreams to be a helpful articulation of the DREAM Act's normative confines.[18] But are there other ways to think through dreams that do not tie them so specifically to prohibition and wish fulfillment? Ríos-Rojas and Stern tend to speak about dreams as aspirations, rather than as psychic and unconscious processes, and it is within the dream-as-aspiration's conscious life that dreams, they argue, are able to become coopted. While Ríos-Rojas and Stern do not, then, differentiate between dreams-as-aspiration and dreams-as-psychic processes, they do, I would argue, begin to locate the revolutionary potentiality of dreams within the dynamics of the later formulation. Here they argue that while dreams can be shaped by neoliberalism, they are not wholly constrained by it:

> The dream also is excess—at once inside and outside the current neoliberal order of things . . . The dream remains to insist on the other, the errant, the unknowable, the unrepresentable, the unassimilable, the indeterminate, the alien. It is the dream we have yet to dream. The one we are still holding out for. (2018, 102)

Identifying the excess and the unknowable—frames that I suggest might begin to lead us toward an analysis of the unconscious—Ríos-Rojas and Stern suggest that there are "dream[s] we have yet to dream" that might eventually curtail neoliberalism's hold on what is possible to imagine. Their articulation thus begins the work of thinking more carefully about what dreams might do for an antideportation politics, but it is still reliant on a hesitancy to take seriously the multiple registers of dreams. These unassimilable dreams, in other words, seem to be located within the register of consciousness: they emerge from conscious aspirations that cannot be contained by the limits of neoliberalism, rather than emerging from unconscious psychic processes that push at the boundaries of subjectivity and power.[19] Perhaps incorporating another approach to dreams, one that thinks with and beyond their fulfillment of wishes, and one that addresses their shuttling between conscious and unconscious registers, is in order. I work, over the remainder of this chapter, to articulate and explore this approach to dreams, first by turning to the artist Carmen Argote and what I call her work's intergenerational migrant aesthetics, and then by returning to Freud and the DREAMers.

My Father's Side of Home

In 2014 Carmen Argote, a Los Angeles–based artist whose multisited and multimedia work explores how her own migrant family imagined and constructed "home" on both sides of the U.S.–Mexico border, returned to Guadalajara to undertake work in her father's family home. Argote's family had left Guadalajara when she was five years old, and the home was where a few generations of her father's side of the family had lived. Named Mansión Magnolia, the home doubled as the family business, an event space for quinceañeras and weddings. It was, and still is, a sprawling turn-of-the-century stone building designed by the architect Guillermo De Alba in the center of Guadalajara's historical district. Argote was drawn to it because of its beauty, and also because it was a special place for her father. Having lived in Los Angeles for all of her adult life, Argote had heard numerous stories about this home and the space it created for her family. These stories were told, not just because the space the home created for her family was so important at the time, but also because her immediate family's migration to the United States was fraught with ambivalences. Argote's father, who had studied architecture in Mexico and had brought a beautiful hand-drawn portfolio of houses that he dreamed of building with him, was told that the Los Angeles offices he was applying to work with had shifted from drawings to AutoCAD, leaving him working a series of odd jobs. Despite having to work as a crossing guard or truck driver, he always kept a drafting table in their house, and he produced numerous architectural drawings, clearly longing for a life in which he could use his talents to bring houses and homes into the world.

Argote's father's feelings of not fitting in, and his exasperation at the disjuncture between his aspirations and his experiences of migrant life resonated with Argote and her own experiences of growing up in Los Angeles as a child. In an interview with Víctor Albarracín for *Terremoto* in 2017 Argote explains that her interest in homes and places began as she experienced different parts of Los Angeles as a child. Attending kindergarten at an underserved public school whose students were predominantly Korean and Latino, Argote felt connected to her peers, but her teacher suggested to her mother that she apply for a magnet program that would bring her to a school in a further, more wealthy neighborhood:

> That chance meant leaving my neighborhood every day on a school bus and heading west. Crossing the neighborhood and taking Interstate 10 to Brentwood. Even though it was a public school too, it was drastically different. These are two very different economies and two ways of inhabiting the city. (Argote in Albarracín and Argote 2017)

Navigating these two different economies and versions of the city—one white and middle class, the other multiracial, migrant, and under-funded—Argote recalls, made her feel disconnected from both. Experiencing racism in Brentwood and feeling vulnerable to gang violence in her neighborhood, Argote struggled to feel at home. But these feelings of dislocation and of not belonging were not limited to just these two parts of Los Angeles. "On top of all that," Argote says, "there were these ideas about what Mexico was, and what Guadalajara was, that came out of the stories my parents would tell, especially my dad, in which everything I wanted—a pool or a nice house—was available and waiting" (Argote in Albarracín and Argote 2017). As a migrant child struggling to fit in, Argote's fantasies of the good life were oriented by her father not towards the American dream, but rather toward a Mexican one. This, coupled with her father's obsession with architecture and houses, meant that Argote's experiences of movement and not fitting in fostered a longstanding interest in the complexities of migrant belonging.

When Argote was seventeen, her father left her and her family in Los Angeles. Frustrated by the stagnation that migration brought his career, he returned to Guadalajara to take over the operations of La Magnolia from his aunts. His dream, he said, was to design and build a contemporary home for himself and his family in Guadalajara that they could all live in together. Argote's mother, however, had no desire to move to Mexico. She had family in Los Angeles and wanted to keep their kids attending schools in the United States. Her father thus ended up leaving on his own, and his difficult separation from her mother, sister, and her strained their relationships. Argote thus talks about the work she has done in and about her father's home as a reparative project, one that helps her understand his leaving in ways that connect it to migrant experiences more generally.

While in Guadalajara, Argote undertook a number of different projects under the name *My Father's Side of Home.* Describing her father's longing—for home, work, connection and family—as the impetus for her work, Argote stages the project through a series of intergenerational questions:

> What does it mean to leave a place and come to another place, and also to have lived in that place and have memories of it, like my father? And what does it mean for him to be over here . . . wanting that, and then going back and seeing that the city's changed without him? And for me to be growing up with all these narratives, what does that do to my ideas of Guadalajara, how do I see the city differently, or do I even know the city? Where do I fit in or not outside of these narratives? (Argote quoted in Lee, n.d.)

Answering these questions through her art, Argote undertook a series of works at the house over the years—including *Ínsula* (2014), *Inhabiting as Process* (2014), *Mansión Magnolia* (2016), *Las Tías* (2016), and *Mantas* (2014)—the latter two of which I want to think through here. I approach these works as indicative of an intergenerational migrant aesthetics that I am arguing helps rearticulate the complexities and importance of parent–child relationships. This articulation, I argue, pushes back against the parricidal violence of the border that I have been outlining and intervening in across this chapter.

Las Tías is a series of photographs that Argote took in the house as a way of attempting to represent the histories of women who inhabited it before her. Taken in different parts of the house, the photographs share an aesthetic but range in their representation of their subject: Argote's figure. Layering blurred images of her nude body on top of one another in a wash of movement, Argote's photos transgress the boundary between self-portrait and portrait. One, in which Argote's blurry image is barely able to be registered as a figure, features a transparent fleshy cloud in the center of the image, only slightly obscuring what appears to be a hand-painted tile floor. The sienna, black, and ivory tiles, repeating an intricate pattern, are seemingly captured from just below standing height, and the camera's perspective elongates the space, making it appear endless. The only interruptions to the repeated patterning of the stretched-out floor are the effects of a long exposure: an undefined blur in the middle of the frame, hovering above its shadow. Here Argote haunts the image: she is simultaneously present and absent, and her body is less distinctive than a figure would be. There is no definitive sign of *body* here, but we are not in the realm of the flesh as Hortense Spillers (1987) conceives it.[20] The ghostly blur is more substantial within the frame than would indicate it representing the presence of a single being. We feel her presence, but this placing of Argote, or those whom Argote has become, is more affective—haptic perhaps—than visibly discernable.[21] The image is suggestive of intimacy and proximity, of sharing a space with another even though that neighboring is not coeval. As the long exposure captures Argote *across* time rather than fixed within it, the mechanics of the image suggest that the image is about bodies—rather than a body—inhabiting the space over time. It is, in other words, a representation of the inhabiting of the past within the present.

In another image, a body at the base of a stairway is caught mid-descent. Here more of a figure is discernable. While we cannot quite see the top half of the person, her closed, protective posture appears to suggest she is wary of the camera and its gaze. Trailing behind this half-figure is a blur of her bodily motion. We get a sense of a rush of motion, and in this layering of moving figure(s) floating down the wooden staircase we can imagine that this singular, elongated foggy figure might indeed be the mark left by multiple people. As with the image of the figure hovering on the tile floor, Argote here is working to represent the repeated movements of inhabitants across time. Speaking to the significance of this project, Argote writes: "I have developed a series of photographs that express the idea of women housed within each other's presence. I become the house and I become the past inhabitants while simultaneously discovering and interacting with the space. These blurred nudes express the process of layering histories of women" (Argote, n.d.a).

Argote's images here forcefully connect her to her past. She simultaneously is herself and her aunts and grandmothers, as well as the other women who lived and worked within the house. Argote, in both of these images, is and is not herself. She is seeking to represent, through a process of photographic condensation, the histories of intergenerational belonging that are always present within the house.

These images, as examples of what I am calling Argote's intergenerational migrant aesthetics, evoke a certain strain of haunting. Haunting, Avery Gordon writes, "describes how that which appears to be not there is often a seething presence, acting on and often meddling with taken-for-granted realities" (1997, 8). For Gordon, investigating a haunting, ghostly presence will "lead to that dense site where history and subjectivity make social life" (1997, 8). In this sense, following the trail of the haunting presence entails being affectively drawn into "the structure of feeling of a reality we come to experience, not as cold knowledge, but as a transformative recognition" (1997, 8). Haunting presences thus gesture towards alternative, suppressed forms of knowledge and social life that, when taken seriously, interrupt the normative operations of power. For Argote, the ghostly presence that haunts her images are not singular figures, they are condensed unities that, despite inhabiting the space across time, are always present within the now. Here Argote's images in *Las Tías* evoke a haunting presence to underline a form of connection, a representational act that is dreamlike. Dreams, Freud writes, "take into account in a general way the connection which undeniably exists between all the portions of the dream-thoughts by combining the whole material into a single situation or event" ([1900] 1954, 314). Like dreams, Argote's blurred figures denote connection—Argote's connection to her family home and all the women who inhabited it over the years—by representing the ever presence of intergenerational migrant intimacy and proximity through "*simultaneity in time*" (314). Existing simultaneously with her past, as well as the pasts of those whom she may never have known yet whose proximity is integral to her sense of home and belonging, and embodying other figures who cannot be extracted from her form, Argote's work renders any attempt at severing intergenerational ties facile. In *Las Tías,* Argote's intergenerational migrant aesthetics provide a series of visual refusals of the attempts at violently rupturing child from parent. You cannot extract me from my past and my family, Argote seems to be saying with these images, as they are made present within me.

The second series of works by Argote that I am interested in here also emerged from Argote's stay in Mansión Magnolia, but this body of work shifts in form and production from photographs to textiles and installations. Titled *Mantas,* Argote used thin muslin fabric (*mantas*) as her canvas. The use of muslin was important to Argote because, as she describes it, the fabric is "a material that moves through economic classes in Mexico, artisanal and working class" (Argote, n.d.b). Working in the room that was her father's office and had become her bedroom during her stay at La Magnolia, she draped the walls and floor with the muslin and traced every object that touched them: the bed, picture frames, a lamp, a bedside table, and a wardrobe. Giving surface to the mantas, she created a rubbing of the room's texture. The tiles on the floor, the moldings of the door frames, and the grain of the walls were all present on the large panes of muslin. After tracing out the room's texture, she painted each of the walls, as well as the floor, with a single color of acrylic in shades of mustard, moss, and coral, leaving the spaces where the objects touched the fabric unpainted. These objects and their shadows thus cast a white silhouette onto the color-blocked, wall-sized fabrics. Their presence made visible through the absence of paint, the original muslin remained unadulterated.

Working in this way, Argote was seeking to replicate, on a grander scale, some of the architectural drawings that her father had made over the years. These drawings, Argote explains, were simple watercolors showing buildings painted in large color blocks, lines, and geometric patterns, and she wanted her Mantas series to evoke these beautiful, yet slightly elementary evocations of space. But the act of painting on such a scale, and with a watercolor-like technique, meant that when the paintings were complete, something surprising happened. Reacting to the paint, the mantas themselves shrank as they dried, contorting their shape in response to the presence and absence of the objects whose silhouettes marked the canvases. Contemplating this unexpected change in the fabric, Argote came into a different understanding of what the work meant: "I painted the fabric and it shrank. The shrinkage revealed to me that the work was about being derived from something but no longer fitting it, it visually captured my father's experience of wanting to return to Mexico, doing so, and no longer fitting in" (Argote, n.d.b).

Here, Argote describes the shrinkage as reproducing her father's migrant experience, but it might also be understood as representing her own confrontation with the complexities of her desire for homeland. Taking seriously Argote's claim, that the work itself *revealed* this to her, suggests that Argote is conceptualizing this making process in a similar vein to the dynamic between dreams, the unconscious, and analysis. The wish that generated the work—as with the wishes that generate dreams—became both disguised and, upon interpreting from within a migrant standpoint, revealed as the mantas were painted, and then dried. Argote's return to Guadalajara, inhabiting her father's family home, and making artwork inspired by the connection he felt with that space revealed to her that his own sense of belonging was a partial and ambivalent one. It also revealed how central longing is to both his and her experiences of migrant life, yet how difficult it is to resolve. Her wish, that migrant belonging might be resolved in the inhabiting of "home" was thus both revealed and interrupted in the work, but this interruption was itself necessary for her new understanding.

Asking the deceptively straightforward question "Where is home?" Brah contemplates the difficulties and pleasures of belonging for diasporic subjects, and her scholarship helps articulate what it is Argote's work and its unexpected alterations mean. "Home," Brah writes, putting the word in inverted commas, "is a mythic place of desire in the diasporic imagination. In this sense, it is a place of no return, even if it is possible to visit the geographical territory that is seen as the place of 'origin'" (1996, 192). In this light, both Argote and her father returned to something they imagined to be "home," but this home, they discovered, was less a physical place to inhabit than a psychic one. At the same time, Brah notes, "home" is the series of lived experiences attached to inhabiting a place; it is formed by experiences that are historically specific yet constantly being reassembled and reconfigured by movement, intergenerational longing, quotidian affairs, and the workings of memory. Diaspora, therefore, "places the discourse of 'home' and 'dispersion' in creative tension, *inscribing a homing desire while simultaneously critiquing discourses of fixed origins*" (1996, 192–93). In this sense, what Argote is describing as the "revelation" of the artwork could be understood as the muslin interrupting the idea of origin that had been invested into Argote's desire for "home" by her father and as a product of migrant life. Attempting to literally recreate her father's home by tracing its edges and contours, Argote sought to inhabit that "mythic place of desire" that is the site of creative tension between home and homeland, what Brah calls "homing desire." And yet this interruption, for Argote, was not a violent splitting of her from home or from father. It was a manifestation, a representation, of the connection between her and her father despite their separation.

Intrigued by the muslin's response to her attempts at recreating home, Argote took the large sheets of fabric with her to Human Resources, a gallery in Los Angeles, and hung them in the center of the room, draped so as to form the room within the space. The room within a room, which had housed her father and then her in Guadalajara thus itself became transient. It migrated with her and "housed" a handful of guests in its own new home.[22] Simultaneously a physical location, as well as a psychic container for her and her father's desires for homeland, the "home" these mantas created moved with Argote. They transported the physical residue of home across borders and into the public space of the gallery. Here I conceptualize the transient physicality of these mantas as representing, in part, the *psychic* residue and excess that is constitutive of the unconscious, and perhaps of dreams.[23] In Argote's art work, which embraces the speculative politics of dream-work to which I next turn, the surplus desires that structure everyday life are opened up to creative processes of engagement. Her work suggests that dreams *are* migrants' "domain and methodology" (Ríos-Rojas and Stern 2018), but not just because they are aspirational articulations of freedom and justice. Dreams, as I articulate below, are also those messy, interruptive, complicated productions of the dreamer's negotiations of selfhood, belonging and relation. They are excessive, and disorienting, and they simultaneously expose and push back against our deepest wishes.

Dream-Work

Naming his approach's difference from scholars of dreams prior to him, Freud argues that the problem that others have faced in attempting to understand dreams was in their misplaced focus. Arguing that "every attempt that has hitherto been made to solve the problem of dreams has dealt directly with their *manifest* content as it is presented in our memory," Freud claims that he is alone in taking into consideration the "psychical material between the manifest content of dreams and the conclusions of our enquiry: namely, their *latent* content, or (as we say) the 'dream-thoughts'" ([1900] 1954, 277). In their most basic element, Freud writes, "dreams are nothing other than a particular *form* of thinking. . . . It is the *dream-work* which creates that form" (506 n2). Dream-work, for Freud, is the series of unconscious processes that transform the latent content of the dream (the unconscious wishes, hopes, fears, anxieties) into the manifest content (the images, scenes, figures, themes, and representations). It is dream-work, Freud writes, that is "peculiar to dream-life and characteristic of it" (507). Dream-work thus bears a relation to wish fulfillment, but rather than being the motivator of the dream, dream-work is the series of processes through which the dream itself comes into being. My interest here is in considering the mechanics of this "form of thinking" as a way of expanding the analytical terrain beyond the wish fulfillment character of dreams. Doing so, I am arguing that we need to take dream-work seriously. Because dreams are so important, and because, as Freud argues, "dreams are never concerned with trivialities; we do not allow our sleep to be disturbed by trifles" (182),[24] I want to think through what dream-work offers, not just for a critically engaged psychoanalysis, but also for an intergenerational antideportation movement that actively resists the parricidal logics of border politics.

Parricide, as I have argued, works by severing the parent-child relationship, by naming the child as *separable* from the parent, and by insisting that the parent is substitutable with the state—what Mary Zaborskis calls "orphaning" (2016). It relies on a framing of the subject that is individualistic, ahistorical, and actively disengaged with psychoanalytic understandings of the self. Against parricidal logics, ones vested in wish fulfillments premised on the child, dream-work is a structure of thinking and—upon waking, acknowledging, and revising the dream-thoughts from within an antideportation standpoint—affirming new logics.

Dream-work, Freud tells us, moves us back and forth through time; it produces new configurations of subjects and images; new unities are formed by it through the *condensation* of collective figures and composite structures of narrative. Condensation, as a key characteristic of dream-work, is defined by repetition and the construction of composite figures and unities. Here a figure within a dream becomes, through condensation, simultaneously individual and collective. Freud writes, for example, about how in a dream of Irma, one of his patients, she "appeared with the features which were hers in real life, and thus, in the first instance, represented herself" ([1900] 1954, 292), but was, upon reflection, simultaneously representing another of Freud's patients, as well as his eldest daughter. Here, against separability, dream-work—like the photographic work of Argote's *Las Tías*—privileges conflation, multiple readings of representation, and intersubjectivity. In the production of collective figures, Freud writes, "new unities are formed" (295). Importantly, the production of new unities within dream-work is facilitated by dreams' refusals to recognize contradiction. "The way in which dreams treat the category of contraries and contradictories is highly remarkable," Freud writes. "It is simply disregarded" (318). Dream-work renders the paradoxes of contraries and contradictories inessential, taking liberty to represent anything by its wishful opposite. While waking life or conscious observation may not allow two or more separate people to be one, or to inhabit the same body or time, dream-work rejects this kind of impossibility, sharing "particular preference for combining contraries into a unity or for representing them as one and the same thing" (318). This is true not just for separate figures but also of a single figure (or object) across time. In dreams, the connection one has to the past is represented through coevalness. "The connection which undeniably exists between all the portions of the dream-thoughts" Freud writes, is represented "by combining the whole material into a single situation or event" (314). Dreams operate through overdetermination, and the reproduction of logical connection as simultaneity in time. Through dream-work one can simultaneously be one's present self, as well as one's childhood self, the gap in time overlooked by, or rendered inconsequential for, the dream. Indeed, it should be no surprise that, given Freud's general approach to the unconscious, he argues that "we find the child and the child's impulses still living on in the dream" (191). Dreams, then, are one of the key moments when our childhoods are most clearly understood to be lived within the present.

As an ethical call, or a speculative analytic of engagement, dream-work's refusal to recognize contradiction and its prioritizing of temporalities free from linear chronology set the stage for rejecting the parricidal demand to disavow one's past, one's ambivalent and multiple national attachments, and one's intersubjectivity in favor of a singular attachment to the American dream. If the politics that emerged from dreams-as-aspirations took the grammar of "I wish . . ." or "If only, . . ." the speculative politics of dream-work might sound something like:

> I am inseparable from my past.
> I carry the lives of everyone I have known and loved with me at
>   all times.
> My parents, my family, and I must be understood as a unity.
> Your fantasy of our separability cannot supersede my knowledge of
>   our collectivity.
> We inhabit one another, and our childhoods never end.
> All these truths are connected, and they are all happening now.

DREAM-WORK AS DREAM-WORK

Sitting in the middle of the road on Fifth Avenue outside Trump Tower in midtown Manhattan in 2017, Erica Andiola, a recipient of DACA and an organizer with Our Revolution, engaged in this mode of articulation. About to be arrested for civil disobedience, and holding hands with her coorganizers, Andiola trembled but refused to acquiesce. Anticipating the moment she would be handcuffed, placed into custody, and potentially deported, she spoke to a friend who was livestreaming the protest:

> We're fed up. We're fed up with every single attack that has come our way.... And we're going to continue to fight not just for DREAMers, but for our families. We didn't come to this country alone. We came with our communities. We came with our families. And we're sitting here to let [Trump] know we're not going to throw our parents under the bus. We're going to fight for the 11 million [undocumented people in the United States].... We're going to be undocumented and unafraid. And we're not going to back down. (Our Revolution 2017)

Having learned from her previous activist work for the DREAM Act, and being part of a wider movement that had, since the legislative loss, sought to recalibrate its broken dreams and activist strategies, Andiola spoke in terms that refused the parricidal logics that this chapter has been critiquing. Putting her body on the line, risking her livelihood and her freedom, Andiola, like the other undocumented and unafraid activists that came before her and after her, refused to allow herself to be imagined as separate from her communities and her family. Becoming one and the same as her parents, Andiola articulated *and inhabited* a migrant politics that revels in its intergenerational intersubjectivity, and defiantly refused to back down.

Coda: Parricide Revisited

As I sit at my desk in 2019, finishing this chapter about the parricidal violence that structured the push for, and defeat of, the DREAM Act almost a decade ago, I am constantly reminded, in horror, that the moment in which I write has been defined by an exponential growth of, rather than reduction in, child–parent separation. While exact numbers are difficult to ascertain, it is estimated that thousands of migrant children have been separated from their parents, thrown into so-called tender age shelters—more accurately described as cages—as their parents are detained indefinitely, awaiting deportation, for seeking asylum at the border. Under Trump's "zero tolerance" stance on immigration, a heightened criminalizing of border crossings has led to the incarceration and deportation of thousands of migrants, all of whom are now facing criminal courts and mass incarceration. Trump's policy has led to the detention of so many migrant children that new facilities are rapidly being built to keep up with the influx of detained children. These facilities—which many activists label as detention centers or concentration camps—are simultaneously curtailing the livelihoods of thousands of children, separating them from their parents and family members with whom they have been traveling, while, at the same time, making enormous profits for the individuals and organizations overseeing the construction and guarding of the cages.[25] Reports keep emerging about the physical, psychic, and sexual abuses that structure life in these cages, and yet they proliferate still.[26] As of this writing, at least seven children have died since 2018 while detained at the border.

While parricide was the logic under which the DREAM Act was advocated for and lost, it seems inadequate to describe the forms of violence that these cages wreak on children today. Within these cages, which are filled far beyond capacity, guards hand over the care of younger children to older children. Eight-year-old children are given custody of infants under conditions that can only be described as inhumane:

> Children as young as 7 and 8, many of them wearing clothes caked with snot and tears, are caring for infants they've just met, the lawyers [investigating the centers] said. Toddlers without diapers are relieving themselves in their pants. Teenage mothers are wearing clothes stained with breast milk. Most of the young detainees have not been able to shower or wash their clothes since they arrived at the [detention centers]. They have no access to toothbrushes, toothpaste, or soap. (Dickerson 2019a)

These children, many of whom had been detained for weeks, were infested with lice and sleeping on cold concrete floors. Practically all of them, Warren Binford, one of the lawyers inspecting the facilities, noted, had been separated from their families and placed in this cage. "We met almost no children who came across unaccompanied" Binford told the *New Yorker*. "The United States is taking children away from their family unit and reclassifying them as unaccompanied children. But they were not unaccompanied children. And some of them were separated from their parents" (Binford in Chotiner 2019). In this moment, parricidal violence has intensified through a simultaneous logic of infanticide. The state, in other words, has not only maintained its policies of parent–child separation, it has also abandoned its role— which it only ever *claimed* to fulfill—as substitute parent. Incarcerated migrant children, forcibly separated from their parents, are now the ones providing the most care for other migrant children.

In addition to the children who are locked in cages in isolation from their families, thousands more have been sent to live with "foster parents" across the country. Many of these children have been officially declared as lost to the system, unable to be found or tracked by the government. The youngest of these children (at least as far as we know), is Constantin Mutu, separated from his parents when he was just four months old. Sent to a foster family while his father—a Roma migrant seeking asylum for his family—was detained at the border, Constantin was separated from his family for months. He was only able to return to his family back in Romania after a court case that is paradigmatic of the incredulous administrative normalcy of the increasing parricidal and infanticidal violence of the border. At court, a lawyer for the Department of Homeland Security argued that the government should not pay for Constantin's return, suggesting instead that Constantin should be responsible for making his own way back to Romania as an eight-month-old (Dickerson 2019b). At the time of his eventual reunion with his family, in July 2018, Constantin had spent a majority of his life in the care of a foster family. As a two-year-old who still couldn't talk, or walk unassisted, he experienced this "reunion" as itself another separation. As Caitlin Dickerson, journalist for the *New York Times*, recounts:

> Florentina and Vasile Mutu [Constantin's parents] didn't sleep the night before the reunion. They were standing at baggage claim at the airport

in Bucharest when they finally spotted Constantin, hours behind schedule, bobbing toward them in his foster mother's arms. She handed the baby to his mother, but he screamed and reached back in the other direction, his face crumpling into a knot of terror. (Dickerson 2019b)

Across this chapter, I have been arguing for the importance of inter-subjectivity and the parent-child relation. In this moment—under conditions of parricide and infanticide—this importance bears re-peating.[27] Against the ever-increasing horrors enacted by the border, a renewed critical focus on the dynamics of dependency and care is more vital than ever.

Ambivalence and Loss

Childhood has ended, many times over. For decades, apprehensive sociologists, moralizing social commentators, and concerned parents have repeatedly, and preemptively, foretold the end of childhood. Its disappearance, our loss. Television, the internet, video games, integrated schools, working moms, safe playgrounds, padded bikinis, sexting. Each of these have been at the heart of various and panicked declarations that childhood has ended. More endings, to be sure, are just around the corner. And each of them, as before, shall signal less the end of childhood per se, than a fervent attempt at ensuring that it—or at least the particular version of it that is cathected by these ongoing shifts—remain stagnant. In these moments, the statement *of* loss becomes a means of protecting childhood *from* loss. It ensures that childhood's meanings be shut down at the precise moment that its exclusive contours begin to crack. If a particular change is to bring about the end of childhood—and we always seem to know this in advance—then naming childhood as having (almost) ended is a way of closing down that loss, protecting childhood from being lost by refusing to introduce it, or ourselves, to its new parameters. For even if that change comes about, at least we—and I use this term cautiously—have foreclosed the possibility that our version of childhood, the one we hold most dear, will end on terms that are not our own.

I began this book with a discussion of the ambivalence of the demand for childhood: the wish for it in the face of its purposefully uneven distribution, the hope for inclusion within it despite the curiously fortuitous invention of its end. At the same time, across each chapter I have worked to show that many of the terms through which childhood has been demanded are normatively structured, and that to better advocate for "the child" requires speculating about what childhood could be otherwise. Doing so, however, often requires its own losses: letting go of what childhood has been and opening it up to new futures. In many ways, then, this book has already been about loss: the loss of a child; the loss of access to a public space; losing one's hold on a fantasy of national belonging; finding oneself lost to a memory; and losing out on the promise that childhood cruelly provided. In thinking through these losses, I have articulated childhood as a cathexis, as something made whole and productive through the wishes invested within it. Childhood, I have argued, is something central to political desire and national belonging. It is one of the main structures through which we compensate for, and experience, these losses. In making this argument, the present book has attempted to grapple with the ambivalent, productive, and dangerous investments in childhood—both my own and those of others. One of my main structuring arguments has been precisely about this claim. Childhood, I have reiterated, is not a time of life, nor a stage of becoming; rather, it is an object that gets wished for when the crushing weight of the world seems too much, when the force of opposition feels strong enough that one can only resort to investing in an object that has proven time and again to be up for the task. We invest in this object, I have shown, even when (and sometimes precisely because) it is so dangerous to do so, when doing so brings with it the history of exclusion and intensification that has been central to childhood since its inception. Childhood, in this sense, functions as an object-cathexis upon which a great range of political desires can and do take up residence. It is because of this, however, that when childhood falls apart, when our hopes are dashed or we realize that our idea of childhood cannot possibly do the work we need it to do, we too find ourselves at a loss. But what does it mean to be at a loss with childhood? How might we think differently about this "being-with" such that the "loss" is structured not through preemptive and conservative nostalgia but perhaps speculative hope?

To answer this question, I turn, for a final time, to Freud. Working to differentiate mourning from melancholia, Freud outlines two different ways in which the ego recovers from loss. Noting that "people never willingly abandon a libidinal position" ([1917] 1957, 244), Freud argues that mourning is "carried out bit by bit, at great expense of time and cathectic energy" (245). For the melancholic, however, for whom the loss is not just of a person but is rather one "of a more ideal kind" (245), this process is more complicated. In melancholia, Freud writes, the object-cathexis is brought to an end, but the libidinal energy that produced this object-cathexis is not set free; it is rather withdrawn and redirected into the ego as a form of identification. Object-loss, in other words, becomes a stifling and debilitating ego-loss. Importantly, however, the melancholic loss of an object can be repaired. This repair takes place through a recognition of that object's ambivalence and, in embracing ambivalence, a series of possibilities emerge. "Melancholia," David Eng and David Kazanjian write, "raises the question of what makes a world of new objects, places, and ideals possible" (2003, 4). While Eng and Kazanjian's pairing of melancholia and proliferation may seem counterintuitive, loss, mourning, and melancholia are all processes that for Freud have the potential to open up new relations. This is so because each of these states are productively co-constituted with ambivalence. "The loss of a love-object," Freud elucidates, "is an excellent opportunity for the ambivalence in love-relationships to make itself effective and come into the open" ([1917] 1957, 250–51). While this opening up of ambivalence can, Freud warns, result in harm directed toward one's ego, it can also be the avenue toward repair and letting go:

> In melancholia, accordingly, countless separate struggles are carried on over the object, in which hate and love contend with each other; the one seeks to detach the libido from the object, the other to maintain this position of the libido against the assault. (256)

At the same time as the ego has identified with the loss of the object, then, the object's ambivalence is also identified with. This identification-with-ambivalence, however, is often too much for the

ego to bear, and is thus the catalyst for the ego to lessen its identification with loss. As such, while constitutional ambivalence usually
belongs to the repressed, it emerges in melancholia as a means of deal-
ing with the ego's identification with loss:

> Just as mourning impels the ego to give up the object by declaring the
> object to be dead and offering the ego the inducement of continuing to
> live, so does each single struggle of ambivalence loosen the fixation of
> the libido to the object by disparaging it, denigrating it and even as it
> were killing it. (257)

When identification-with-loss becomes identification-with-
ambivalence, the ego works to preserve itself by denigrating the lost
object, disidentifying with it and allowing it to have a life, or afterlife,
of its own. As with the other psychoanalytic mechanisms I have un-
packed throughout *Ambivalent Childhoods*—disavowal, projection,
desire, and dream-work—loss and the ambivalence that enables one
to emerge from that loss can thus also be understood as social mechanisms for enduring life as our objects become something otherwise.

In my earlier exploration of ambivalence, I argued that not only is
it constitutive of object-cathexes, but also that acknowledging it can
be a productive way of interrupting dangerous relations. Unpacking
Freud's articulation of the object-cathexis and the child's development of the super-ego in the book's Introduction, I argued that
while repressed ambivalence structures the child's investments in
their mother, the recognition (or avowal) of this ambivalence is also
precisely what is required to break the child's lines of identification
and desire, and to open them up to new objects and relations. This is
important enough to be reiterated here one last time: as a cathected
object, childhood can become dangerous, as one of the structuring
conditions of its production as an object-cathexis is our repression
of its constitutional ambivalence. This repression, I have argued, allows childhood to stand in for a vast array of political projects, but it
also limits the capacity of these projects, restricting the terms through
which justice—and children—can be advocated for. Fortunately,
however, not only can ambivalence do reparative work against this

repression, as I have just argued via melancholia, but the reparative itself is also deeply enmeshed with, and productive of, ambivalence. Acknowledging our own ambivalence toward childhood—our racial, gendered, sexual, and national lines of investment in it—as well as its own ambivalence, might similarly allow for a means of being "at a loss" with childhood in productive ways. Along these lines, rather than arguing that loss is a "pathologically bereft and politically reactive" state, Eng and Kazanjian seek out what they call a "counter-intuitive apprehension of loss" that is "full of volatile potentiality and future militancies" (2003, 5). In this call for a turbulent and militant future, Eng and Kazanjian situate their analysis of loss within an insistence that "ruptures of experience, witnessing, history, and truth are, indeed, a starting point for political activism and transformation" (2003, 10). For Eng and Kazanjian, a creative reader of loss will necessarily end up in a revolutionary praxis that begins with a broken world and demands a new one. Here being at a loss does not mean abandoning childhood. Nor does it mean foreclosing its meanings such that it cannot signify otherwise. Rather, like the child in the Oedipal triangle, being at a loss means that in coming to a more nuanced and forgiving understanding of our object, our relationship to it can shift, and can open us up to others.

While the strategically unambivalent demand for childhood may still be required to respond to the ongoing and inevitably forthcoming ruptures of childhood that will be experienced in the moment as most urgently devastating, to do justice to childhood we must recognize that the child requires more complex frames of articulation from us. For surely there will be other moments, other times in which we are confronted with childhood's capacity to take on so much work, moments in which we laden childhood with immense directed political and psychic energy but yet again find ourselves at a loss as it falls apart under the weight of our demand. I hope that in these instances we will be able to sit with childhood's ambivalence and learn that what is necessary in response is opening ourselves up to being at a loss with childhood, and embracing the possibilities for new relations that can subsequently emerge.

Acknowledgments

This is a book about collective struggles for belonging and recognition in the face of systemic, interpersonal, and intersecting violences, and it would not be possible without the movements that it thinks with: Black Lives Matter, transfeminism, queer youth activism, and undocumented DREAMers. In different moments, across almost twenty years, the activist organizations that have sustained me, even if I have not always been adequate to the task of sustaining them, have included the Queer Youth Action Team, the Queer Youth Leadership Awards, the Trevor Project, the Point Foundation, LGBT History Month, Schools OUT!, the Sylvia Rivera Law Project, and Bent Bars. Most of what I've learned about the relationship childhood has to social justice, belonging, and the necessity of imagining a world otherwise has come from the incredible people I have met through these organizations: Gabriel Arkles, Wayne Burnette, Tony Fenwick, Rachel Floyd, Pooja Gehi, Chryssy Hunter, Ron Indra, Sam Lamble, Derrick Miller-Handley, Ezra Berkley Nepon, Paul Patrick, Ravi Singh Rangi, Elana Redfield, Stefanie Rivera, Bonnie Ronzio, Stuart Rosenstein, Sue Sanders, Charles Singer, and Huw Williams. I am forever indebted to Marcia Ochoa for, on top of everything else, training me how to think and write about activism and community building.

Like activism, writing is a collective process, and my thinking within these pages has been shaped by a number of individuals, institutions, and communities. Without the encouragement, insight, and labor of my colleagues, friends, and co-conspirators Clare Hemmings and Sadie Wearing, as well as Clara Bradbury-Rance, Aura Lehtonen, Leticia Sabsay, Emma Spruce, and Alyosxa Tudor, this book simply would not exist. These scholars read and provided feedback on numerous drafts. They shaped my thinking, provided me institutional and personal support over the years, and sustained me throughout all the pains and pleasures of academic life. I am also sustained by conversations with Jules Gill-Peterson, Gabrielle Owen, Annie Sansonetti, and Mary Zaborskis, scholars in the vibrant field of critical, intersectional, queer, and trans childhood studies whose work has shaped my own.

Over the past decade, the community that has nourished me has been the Department of Gender Studies at the London School of Economics and Political Sciences. I am immensely thankful for the insight and support from my colleagues there, past and present. Along with those already mentioned, I am grateful for everything I have learned about pedagogy, institutional politics, generosity, and of course feminist debts from my colleagues Walaa Alqaisiya, Megan Armstrong, Hannah Baumeister, Kimberlé Crenshaw, Sonia Corrêa, Mary Evans, Marsha Henry, Naila Kabeer, Ece Kocabiçak, Daniel Luther, Sumi Madhok, YV Nay, Ilya Parkins, Anouk Patel-Campillo, Diane Perrons, Ania Plomien, Nazanin Shahrokni, Wendy Sigle, and Aisling Swaine. Incalculable gratitude is owed to Hazel Johnstone, Kate Steward, and Lucia Pedrioli. With my colleagues, I have had the pleasure of teaching undergraduate, graduate, and doctoral students across a range of courses who have fundamentally shaped how I understand the complexities of race, gender, sexuality, and belonging. Outside my institutional home, I am grateful for the care, guidance, and generosity of Tina Campt, Anne Cheng, Saidiya Hartman, and Alex Pittman, who were my mentors and teachers at Barnard College and Columbia University in 2015.

Many key people helped bring this book into production, and I want to thank everyone at the University of Minnesota Press for their support, in particular Anne Carter, Dani Kasprzak, Leah Pennywark, and Jason Weidemann. Dani saw promise in my initial proposal and had enough belief in it to advocate for it throughout the initial stages of review. I am honored that *Ambivalent Childhoods* was taken under her wing in her final months at the Press. Thanks are due Rebekah Sheldon and Jules Gill-Peterson for their enthusiasm as initial readers of the manuscript. Jackie Stacey and Amber Jacobs were instrumental in shaping this book's analysis of the psychic life of childhood, and I cannot thank Erica Meiners enough for her generosity. Tomás Ojeda provided critical and insightful support during the final stages of writing, just as the pandemic began to completely reshape our lives.

I had the privilege of receiving feedback from a range of audiences. Earlier versions of chapter 1 were presented in 2016 at the Race, Ethnicity, and Postcolonial Studies Symposium, as well as at the British Sociological Association's "What Next for Childhood Studies?" symposium, organized by Marlies Kustatscher and Kristina Konstantoni. Parts of this chapter also benefited from the engagement of the *American Quarterly* editorial board and two anonymous reviewers. The second chapter was aided by feedback from the attendees of my 2019 talk "Troubling Trans Precocity" for Queer at Kings, and from the participants of GenderX, organized by Alyosxa Tudor and Rahul Rao. Sheila Cavanaugh gave instrumental feedback on an earlier version of this chapter for *Transgender Studies Quarterly*. I had the opportunity to present preliminary drafts of chapter 3 at the University of Warwick's "Constructing Sexual Subjects" series in 2014, thanks to Kathryn Medien, and at "Sexual Cultures: Academia Meets Activism," a conference in 2015 organized by Feona Attwood, Meg John Barker, R. Danielle Egan, and Clarissa Smith. At a seminar convened by Naomi Morgenstern, Cynthia Quarrie, and Jean Wyatt titled "The Child, the Parent: Ethics, Politics, Race" for the American Comparative Literature Association's annual meeting in 2019, I received invaluable feedback on chapter 4. Finally, the book as a whole gained tremendously from conversations in 2018 with participants at "Playing with Childhood in the Twenty-First Century," organized by Jules Gill-Peterson.

Maria Alexopoulos, Raf Benato, Milo Bettocchi, Aaron Breslow, Ilana Eloit, Maddy Rita Faye, Marina Franchi, Jacqui Gibbs, Jeremy Guttman, Billy Holzberg, Christie Joy, Farah Kassam, Chris Lloyd, Sam McBean, Ariel Mellinger, Jessica Miller, Johanna Peace, Daniella Pineda, Julia Po, Sean Michael Rau, Marina Salguero, and Keina

Yoshida, among others, provided much needed friendship, encouragement, and joy.

My own childhood was shaped by the love of my brothers, Aaron Breslow, Simon Breslow Gray, Max Hilton-Gray, and David Whitehead, and my parents, Jordan Breslow, Lorraine Gray, Gary Whitehead, and Lisa Whitehead. Thanks are due as well to Greg Duepner, Kimberley Fiterman Duepner, and Matthew Duepner, for all the care and kindness they have shown me.

At its heart, this is a book about how to sustain demands for belonging and the movements that cultivate them without casting aside all their complexities; it is a speculative project about how desire, investment, and ambivalence must structure our commitments to making a better world. These are things I would not be able to adequately articulate without everything I have learned through sharing a life with Edie Duepner. Thank you, again, for everything you teach me about love.

Notes

1. For an exceptional analysis of Patterson's work, one that incorporates a discussion of the innocent "playroom" aesthetics of the gallery space, see Dyer (2020). Dyer's *The Queer Aesthetics of Childhood* provides an important and critical analysis of childhood innocence as it traverses childhood development frameworks and a contemporary politics that is asymmetrical in its delivery of care to children.

2. For a few histories and analyses of the child within the United States, see Ashby (1997), R. Bernstein (2011), Gill-Peterson (2018), M. Jacobs (2009), W. King (1995), Levander (2006), Rollo (2018), Sánchez-Eppler (2005), Winkler (2012).

3. Robin Bernstein's *Racial Innocence: Performing American Childhood from Slavery to Civil Rights* (2011) argues that innocence needs to be understood not just as absence-of but as deflection or obliviousness: as innocent-of. Here racial innocence is understood, not as being unaware of racism, but as being in "an active state of repelling knowledge" (2011, 6). Innocence, in this vein, is not neutral. Rather, it is a means of perpetuating racism by being willfully oblivious to it.

4. See Crenshaw and Ritchie (2015) for an analysis of the gendered nature of contemporary antiblackness and the mainstream erasure of the violences directed at black girls and women. For an analysis of the ways in which black youth are read as adults rather than children, see Dancy (2014), Goff et al. (2014), Rattan et al. (2012).

5. Barrie Thorne's "Re-Visioning Women and Social Change: Where are the Children?" (1987) should be considered a founding text of childhood studies, as she articulated a complex stance on what it might mean to understand children as autonomous, agentic beings prior to the "new paradigm" of childhood studies (A. James and Prout 1990). While the new paradigm is often understood to be the turn toward children's agency, recognizing Thorne's contribution as a central *feminist* antecedent of childhood studies might help anchor the field in genealogies—like her Marxist-feminist analysis—that had already been attending to the paradoxes of children's agency and voice. For a few early feminist contributions to childhood studies, see also Alanen (1988, 1994); Hardman (1973).

6. My use of the term "populations" frames them in relation to the biopolitical. As Elizabeth Povinelli describes it, "The population is the collective political subject of Western liberal democracies, *not* the people. The population is the living vitality that biopower attempts to govern" (2015, 181).

7. Erica Burman (2016a, 2016b, 2017) has been tracing out the ways in which the child operates in Frantz Fanon's writing. Burman argues that the complexity of Fanon's ambivalent allusions to children across his texts should inform debates on anticolonial analyses of children and childhood. For further analyses of the entanglement of childhood and coloniality, see, among others, Nandy (1984), Sánchez-Eppler (2005), Stoler (1995), K. Wilson (2011), Zaborskis (2016).

8. Throughout her writing on childhood, Shulamith Firestone understands children to be agentic beings deserving of their liberation, and she argues that children's forced economic, physical, and familial dependence, as well as their educational and sexual repression, are key facets of patriarchy. At the same time, her conception of childhood freedom is vested in romanticized and exotified notions of poverty (1971, 114–15). Additionally, Firestone's vision for detaching child-rearing from women relies on what Valerie Polakow Suransky calls a "cybernetic socialism" which eliminates pregnancy through technology and severs the child's dependence on the female body (1982, 10). Suransky's concern is that this model of feminism too quickly denies "human attachment, spontaneity, and love, in favor of a nightmarish rationalism and unremitting social alienation

from the very bonds that cement human relationships" (1982, 10). For other feminist approaches to the elimination of childhood, see Greer (1971); Fuller (1979); S. Lewis (2019); Millet (1970).

9. There are, of course, additional social movements that require analysis for the ways in which children and childhood structure their demands for belonging but that this book does not have the space to attend to. As just one example of this, see the scholarship on disability and childhood, for example, Leiter (2004); Priestley (1998); Sabatello (2013); Tisdall (2012).

10. Many authors who critique the figure of the child recognize that it is important to distance their critique from the "actual" lives of "real" children. Lee Edelman, for example, writes that "the image of the Child" is "not to be confused with the lived experiences of any historical children" (2004, 11). Caroline Levander notes that her book "focuses on the idea of the child as a rich site of cultural meaning and social inscription" (2006, 16), and she defines the child as: "not only a biological fact but a cultural construct that encodes the complex, ever shifting logic of the social worlds that produce it" (2006, 16). Claudia Castañeda (2002) refuses to separate the material and the semiotic aspects of figuration. "A figure," Castañeda writes, "is the simultaneously material and semiotic effect of specific practices" (2002, 3). I am less willing to make such a clarifying statement, as I worry that doing so fixes and essentializes the "real" child in ways that go against the notion that childhood is always contested.

11. Although I follow many of Jo-Ann Wallace's convictions, I am less convinced by her (perhaps ambivalent) desire to have a theory of the "child-subject" that incorporates and speaks from, rather than for, children and childhood. As Castañeda (2001) argues, Wallace's desire for self-representing child-subjects is based on the need for an agentic subject to engage in practices of representation. This desire for authenticity has been critiqued by many within feminist postcolonial studies. See, for example Chow (1994); Spivak (1988).

12. Ishita Pande (2012) tracks the imposition and implementation of birth certificates and the "digits of age" in late-colonial India, arguing that chronological age should be understood as functioning within what she calls a "global governmental numerology" that bears less relation to the realities of child protection and more to how late-colonial and

postcolonial states seek to position themselves on the global stage as modern through the child.

13. That age is more connected to relations of power than inherent traits of childhood can be seen most clearly in the uneven definitions and enforcements of the ages of consent, majority, and culpability. In the United States the age of consent varies between sixteen, seventeen, and eighteen years of age, depending on the state, and while many states have close-in-age exceptions (often referred to as "Romeo and Juliet" laws), these exceptions are somewhat complicated. Delaware, for example, has an age of consent of eighteen, but it also has an exception for minors aged sixteen or seventeen who are in relationships with a partner under the age of thirty. See Meiners (2015) for an account of the heteronormativity of age of consent laws and the sexual offender registry. For a few histories of childhood culpability, see A. James and Jenks (1996); Valentine (1996).

14. Speculative politics has a few antecedents, some of which are more specifically worked through in the text. Beyond these, I draw on scholars who gesture toward a speculative reading but who do not explicate what this means precisely. In *Racial Melancholia, Racial Dissociation,* for example, David Eng and Shinhee Han argue that "a more *speculative* humanities-based approach to psychoanalytic theory might supplement its clinical applications, and vice versa" (2019, 8, emphasis added). Similarly, in the conclusion to *Gender Trouble,* Judith Butler writes that their opening question about whether or not feminist politics required a subject in the category of woman was itself a "speculative" one (1990, 194). See also Haraway (2016).

15. For a few accounts of the importance of partial perspectives, embodied knowledge, and critical approaches to objectivity, see, among many others, Bailey (1998), Bar On (1993), Collins (2000), Haraway (1988), Harding (1991), Hennessy (1993), Kilomba (2008), Rich (1984), Stoetzler and Yuval-Davis (2002).

16. Mark Rifkin's definition of the speculative emerges in his *Fictions of Land and Flesh: Blackness, Indigeneity, Speculation* (2019), in which he reads speculative fictions in order to articulate an ethical and political relation that thinks across black and indigenous political imaginations. For Rifkin, the speculative is not limited to a genre: while he reads

speculative fictions, he also defines the speculative as a "mode" or an "ethics." This ethics is primarily geared toward generating what Rifkin calls an "ontological humility," through which one might "[open] up room for the difficult and potentially fraught dynamics of equivocation that arise in moving among disparate worldings" (2019, 10).

17. My immense gratitude to Clare Hemmings, to whom this insight, as well as many others, are indebted.

18. Across *Ambivalent Childhoods*, I am using "ambivalence" across its (depathologized) psychoanalytic registers, and its more colloquial uses. In *Totem and Taboo*, Freud describes ambivalence as the "simultaneous existence of love and hate towards the same object" and he argues that this emotional ambivalence "lies at the root of many important cultural institutions" ([1913] 1950, 157). This form of ambivalence, I argue, structures people's various attachments to the contemporary contours of identity. But ambivalence is also, Freud writes, something which is constitutive of objects, such that, as I discuss in relationship to object-cathexes below, one forms intense attachments to objects through repressing their ambivalence. I argue that objects like childhood operate within the social as if they were not ambivalent, and that recognizing their (and our) ambivalence might enable different modes of relation to childhood. Here I learn from Clare Hemmings's suggestion in *Considering Emma Goldman* (2018) that ambivalence is constitutive of the political, and of feminist politics in particular, and thus that this ambivalence must be embraced rather than disavowed in order to grapple with the complexities of sexuality, gender, and racism.

19. The archive, Jules Gill-Peterson argues in *Histories of the Transgender Child,* is also structured by transphobia (a transphobia co-produced with racism) such that producing a history of trans childhood requires both reconstructing clinical histories that do not operate under the nomenclature "transgender" and taking an alternative approach to archival work. Writing that the "sheer force of medicine as a domineering form of humanism" has overwhelmed and contested the archives of black trans childhood, Gill-Peterson argues that historians need to "invent better interpretive practices that break from dominant epistemes and ontologies" (2018, 32).

20. Misopedy, Toby Rollo writes, is a form of antichild ageism in which childhood is "viewed as a site of naturalized discipline, violence, and

criminality" (2018, 310). Akin to misogyny, misopedy involves both hostility and objectification.

21. See, for example, A. James and Prout (1990); Jenks (1982, 1996).

22. Philippe Ariès's text is not without critique, most of it debating or outright refuting his use of sources and his methodology, as well as the inferences he makes from his sources, and even the possibilities of paintings (or images and representations more generally) as providing an accurate historical source. See, for example, Beales (1975), Hanawalt (1977), L. Pollock (1983), Stannard (1974), and A. Wilson (1980). While these critiques of Ariès differ in their approach to childhood, they tend to pass over the important argument that Ariès made that the shift in the understanding of "children" as a social category was predicated on and productive of shifts in and reifications of class and gender.

23. In *Society Must Be Defended* ([1975–76] 1997), Foucault outlines disciplinary and biopolitical power. Under disciplinary regimes, power's focus is on the individual body. Technologies of surveillance and organization of individuals are established, creating and enforcing societal norms of how a body should look, feel, speak, and be ([1975–76] 1997, 242). Biopolitical power is more focused on the regularization, production, and valuation of populations. Biopolitics, Foucault writes, "is addressed to a multiplicity of men, . . . a global mass that is affected by overall processes characteristic of birth, death, production, illness" (1997, 242).

24. See, for example, Koffman and Gill (2013) and K. Wilson (2011) for analyses of how the distribution of girlhood, empowerment and girl power are co-opted within developmental projects in ways that simultaneously obscure global dynamics of capital and power, and erase collective actions against global forms of neoliberalism.

25. Despite my proclivities for Freud, my thinking in this book has learned immensely from Naomi Morgenstern (2018) and Rebekah Sheldon (2016), scholars who prioritize non-Oedipal psychoanalysis in their critical approaches to the child. I have also gained insight from conversations with Amber Jacobs, who, in her book *On Matricide: Myth, Psychoanalysis, and the Law of the Mother* (2007), advocates for alternative myths that might enable interrogations of the unconscious that are queer and feminist.

26. For a critique of the long-standing pathologization of women and femininity, specifically within psychology, see Tosh (2016). For a few

challenges to Freud's phallocentrism, see Beauvoir (1949), Britzman (2006), Chodorow (1978), Horney ([1926] 1967), Irigaray (1985a; 1985b), and Klein ([1928] 1986).

27. I want to thank Jules Gill-Peterson, an early advocate for this book, for this particular formulation.

28. Here, one might, I hope, hear some echoes of Robyn Wiegman's *Object Lessons* (2012). Wiegman, interrogating the psychic demands made upon the study of identity, asks: "But what happens if the need is too great for the theory to sufficiently feed it, or if the object that represents the need becomes diminished by the worldly limits in which it is forced to live?" (2012, 10). Across *Ambivalent Childhoods* I learn from Wiegman, in terms of her approaches to investment as well as to identity and social justice. For Wiegman, social justice is a "generic figure of the political destination of identity knowledges," and it goes undefined precisely because she is interested in tracing out the debates over what exactly "justice" does and for whom (2012, 3n4). Following Wiegman, I move between the nomenclatures "social justice movements," "identity-based movements," and "demands for belonging," not to flatten out the differences between these formulations, but rather to open up analyses of how childhood is cathected across these sites.

29. While the girl's love-object is her father, Freud writes that her first object-cathexis "must be her mother," because this relation occurs "in attachment to the satisfaction of the major and simple vital needs" ([1933] 1964, 118).

30. Paul Elliott Johnson, for example, argues that Donald Trump's rhetorical demagoguery relied on and produced his audiences' identification as victims who were "voiceless on the basis of their subjugation to the power of the political establishment" (2017, 231). Claims to white masculine victimhood, Johnson writes, function to enable privileged citizens to "interpret the presence of difference and uncertainty as threatening the subject with unjust marginalization" (2017, 231). Similarly, Juliet Hooker argues that "white grievance, particularly the inability to accept loss (both material and symbolic), continues to be the dominant force shaping contemporary racial politics" (2017, 484). While these structures of feeling are not new, they have certainly been amplified in the past decade, as the growth of global populist far-right parties makes clear.

31. For reflections on children's agency and their participation in research, see, among others, P. H. Christensen (2004), C. Gray and Harcourt (2012), Harcourt, Perry, and Waller (2011), M. Hill (2006), and A. James (2007).

32. As Erica Burman and Jackie Stacey (2010b, 230) write, "While feminists have long critiqued the colonial and classed features of academic claims of 'giving a voice' to marginal subjects . . . childhood researchers have until recently been dogged by the prevailing cultural ethic of children's authentic and iconic status, only recently addressing these problems and often largely within the paradigm of existing models of colonization." This tension within childhood studies would not be resolved by recognizing some of the field's feminist genealogies (as feminism has its own ambivalences regarding agency and silence), but, as I noted earlier, doing so might allow for this ambivalence to be addressed, rather than elided.

33. I want to thank Rebekah Sheldon, an early reader of this book, for her insights and for this particular articulation.

1. DISAVOWING BLACK CHILDHOOD

1. In New York in 2011, while black and Latino men between the ages of fourteen and twenty-four only made up 4.7 percent of the population, they made up 41.6 percent of police stops, and according to the New York Civil Liberties Union, "the number of stops of young black men exceeded the entire city population of young black men" (NYCLU 2011). The "broken windows theory" was put forth by George Keeling and James Wilson (1982), who argued that repeated acts of "low level" crime and public disturbance (such as vandalism and panhandling) snowball into further acts of major crime. This policing tactic disproportionately targets low-income people and communities of color. The "school to prison pipeline" (alternatively called the "school prison nexus") is a description of the effects of the increasing police presence in schools, and the enforcement of zero-tolerance policies. It is a system in which the increasingly harsh disciplinary procedures undertaken in schools are linked to the growing incarceration of young people, particularly low-income students and students of color. For more on the school prison nexus, see Annamma (2017); Krueger (2010); Meiners (2011); Monahan et al. (2014). In

relationship to the cycle of indebtedness that the criminal justice system perpetuates, see, for example, the US Department of Justice report *Investigation of the Ferguson Police Department* (2015).

2. According to the Bureau of Justice Statistics, there were 4,347 black men incarcerated in federal prisons or local jails for every 100,000 US residents in 2010, compared with 1,775 Hispanic/Latino men, and just 678 white men (Glaze 2011, 8). These statistics do not take into account immigration detention, military detention, juvenile detention, civil commitment, or people on probation.

3. For abolitionist, transformative, and critical analyses about the criminalization of young people, see Crawford and Newburn (2003) and Muncie, Hughes, and McLaughlin (2002). See also Davis (2003) for one of the foundational prison abolition texts.

4. My argument that childhood is a legacy of white privilege and inheritance is situated in the historical uses of childhood for racist projects in the United States since slavery. Under slavery, the negotiation of black childhood was so integral to racial domination that it threw into rupture the legal structure of inheritance previously standardized in English common law. In 1662 the Virginia legislature overturned English common law and tied a child's bonded inheritance—and racial status—to the mother (General Assembly of Virginia 1662). Further reiterations of this law enslaved mixed-race children with white mothers and criminalized white women for giving birth to such children. As Autumn Barrett (2014), Anna Mae Duane (2010), and Wilma King (1995) argue, this negotiation was not just about how blackness was distributed to children but also how childhood status—and therefore a slave's potential to progress into rights and freedoms—was allocated or denied. For more on the historical negations of black childhood, see J. Breslow (2019).

5. In marking this distinction between negation and disavowal, I am revising the argument that I made in "Adolescent Citizenship, or Temporality and the Negation of Black Childhood in Two Eras" (2019). There my use of the language of negation enabled me to address the different temporal positionings of black childhood from the antebellum era to the "postracial" era, but it did not open up an interrogation of the psychic life of antiblack racism.

6. See, among others, Evans-Winters and Bethune (2014), Fasching-Varner et al. (2014), J. Gray (2015), D. Johnson, Farrell, and Warren (2015), M. T. Nguyen (2015), Rankine (2015), Yancy and J. Jones (2013).

7. For analyses that link Trayvon's and Emmett's murders, see B. K. Alexander (2015), Harawa (2014), and Wills (2013). While this chapter focuses on the nexus of black masculinity, childhood, innocence, and adolescence, it does so not to prioritize an analysis of men's and boys' experiences over those of women and girls. Indeed, recognizing the gendered nature of this violence should be a catalyst for also addressing the ways in which black girls experience gendered, antiblack violence, as Kimberlé Crenshaw and Andrea Ritchie make clear in *Say Her Name* (2015). See also Méndez (2016).

8. The circumstances around the murders of Emmett Till and Trayvon Martin share small details as well as their more grand implications: both boys were killed by vigilantes, and both, coincidentally, were murdered while out to purchase candy.

9. For more on white fantasies of political abandonment, see Rankine (2019).

10. I am not reproducing these images here because I do not want to facilitate their circulation.

11. For an important analysis of the ways in which adolescence and blackness function within literary representation, see Owen (2019).

12. Erica Meiners pushes back against this line of questioning, writing: "Arguing that children and juveniles are developmentally unique and merit differential treatment from adults fails to analyze who counts as a child or a juvenile in this political moment. Nor do these campaigns excavate the collateral consequences of this tactic, or that arguing for children's innocence seems to require that adults are developmentally static and therefore culpable" (2016, 14).

13. Numerous studies have shown that black children are assumed to be older, more culpable, and less innocent than white children. Studies have shown that black youth are more likely to receive harsher punishment, and adult status by jurors (Rattan et al. 2012), and that they are "prematurely perceived as responsible for their actions during a developmental period where their peers receive the beneficial assumption of childlike innocence" (Goff et al. 2014, 540).

14. Trayvon's parents spoke of his love for planes and told reporters that in the summer of 2009 they enrolled him in a nonprofit program in Florida called "Experience Aviation" that builds science, technology, engineering, and math skills through aviation (Segal 2012).

15. For examples of this "culture of poverty" discourse, see Aldous (1969), Bernard (1966), and Moynihan (1965).

16. See E. Gordon (1997) and Spillers (1987) for critiques of the Moynihan Report and its impacts.

17. Written for President Johnson and published by the U.S. Department of Labor, this deeply "victim-blaming" (W. Ryan 1970), pathologizing report simultaneously declared the success of the Civil Rights Movement, and its "inevitable" failure. Most analyses of the Moynihan Report focus on his indictment of black matriarchy and the black family, but there is much to be said about his analysis of black children, especially as a precursor for the conditions under which Trayvon's murder was justified. Moynihan describes the "failure" of the Civil Rights Movement as emerging from "the tangle of pathology" (1965, 29) that is "the negro family" and argues that poverty within black communities is due to their having too many absent fathers, a matriarchal family structure, increasing rates of illegitimate children, and what he calls "the failure of youth" (1965, 34). These failings, Moynihan argued, were contagious: "The children of middle-class Negroes often as not must grow up in, or next to the slums... They are therefore constantly exposed to the pathology of the disturbed group and constantly in danger of being drawn into it" (1965, 29–30). Blackness, in Moynihan's reasoning, is thus the sign of a deeper pathology, and, understood here perhaps more as pathogen than pathology, it is also the source of its spread. As it related to black children, the connection the Moynihan report made between poverty, delinquency, and crime on one hand, and black culture and values on the other, carried over beyond the debates the report engendered, and into the policies and discourses of the following decades.

18. Paul Gilroy's *Against Race* (2000), for example, articulates a desire to leave behind "race," but not in the sense that he understands racism to be over. Rather, he understands race to be so tarnished by, and implicated in, the forms of inhumanity that underlie not just slavery and segregation but also "numerous episodes in colonial history and ... the genocidal

activities that have proved to be raciology's finest, triumphant hours" (2000, 18) that the idea of "race" has no possible future as a benign description or political tool.

19. The "black victimology narrative" frames black critiques about inequality and discrimination as "well-worn tales, at least passé if not now pointedly false assessments of the main challenges facing blacks in a world largely free of the dismal burdens of overt racial divisions and oppression" (Bobo 2011, 13).

20. For more on the history of "the race card," see Crenshaw (1997) and L. Williams (2001).

21. For further accounts of the adolescent, see G. S. Hall (1905), Palladino (1996), and Savage (2008). For further analyses of youth culture and moral panics, see Giroux (1996, 1997), Hudson (1989), Margarey (1978), McRobbie and Thornton (1995), and Shore (2002).

22. In some of this reporting, the link between Skittles and the night of Trayvon's murder was discussed as if it was damaging to the brand. See, for example, the *New York Times* article "For Skittles, Death Brings Both Profit and Risk" (Severson 2012).

23. Thankfully, there are more abolitionist scholars than can be adequately accounted for here. For a few examples, see CR10 Publications Collective (2008), Davis (1971, 2003), Meiners (2016), Mogul, Ritchie, and Whitlock (2012), Spade (2011), and Stanley and N. Smith (2011).

24. This notion of childhood's transferability comes from Robin Bernstein (2011), who situates it in relationship to the two child characters, Eva and Topsy, of Harriet Beecher Stowe's *Uncle Tom's Cabin; or, Life Among the Lowly* (1852). Within its narrative, *Uncle Tom's Cabin* dramatically brings together several versions of childhood to advocate for the abolition of slavery, and, as Bernstein argues, it produces the child as integral to the abolition of slavery and to a monumental shift in prebellum race-relations. Bernstein details how whiteness, innocence, and childhood are transferred from Eva (who is racially marked as a child) to Topsy (who is racially marked as beyond childhood). Topsy, Bernstein argues, thus required the touch of Eva in order to have her childhood and her innocence validated. Both childhood and innocence, in other words, had to emerge from an embodied white child subject to endow, or to be transferred to, a black one (2011, 45–47).

25. These posts, including the ones cited below, can be found at http://iftheygunnedmedown.tumblr.com.

26. In reading these images through the theoretical framework of the "suture," I am drawing on a body of work on cinema that attends to the production of identification through the cinematic apparatus. The "suture," Kaja Silverman writes, "is the name given to the procedures by means of which cinematic texts confer subjectivity upon their viewers" (1983, 195). In simple terms, wherein the camera's limited field of vision comes to be recognized by the viewer *as* limited (and, in psychoanalytic terms, as lacking, as castration, and thus as unpleasurable), the cinematic narrative itself sutures in the viewer, making them desire the narrative's closure, and thus continue to permit the fictional characters to stand in for themselves. As such, the suture persuades the viewer, Silverman writes, "to accept certain cinematic images as an accurate reflection" of their own subjectivity precisely through the transparency, or the concealment, of the "apparatuses of enunciation" (1983, 215). This concept of transparency is important, particularly when the theory of the suture—in adapted terms—becomes useful as a technique and a discursive tool through which digital assemblages, like those in the #IfTheyGunnedMeDown campaign, can be analyzed. For more on the suture within cinema, see J. A. Miller (1977–78). See also Nicole Fleetwood's (2011) analysis of the use of the "suture," the "cut," and the "wound" in the digital assemblage and contemporary media artwork of Fatimah Tuggar.

27. For another meditation on how to remember and represent the loss of a young, complicated, and nuanced black life amid the oppressive weight of discourses of black criminality, see Cacho (2011).

2. TRANSPHOBIA AS PROJECTION

1. The school claimed that it was not discriminating against Coy based on sex, seeing as she was "a male" and was not being denied access to the boy's restroom (S. Chavez 2013, 5–6). It also argued that *even if it was* discriminating against Coy for not letting her use the girls' restroom, this practice was sanctioned by the Colorado Civil Rights Commission (Dude 2012).

2. Because I am working with and against the school district's logic, I will be intermittently using their phrasing of "male genitalia," but this is not

done to sanction this naming. Across this chapter I cite various sources that misgender trans children and that use their names assigned at birth. I leave these in their original to highlight the pervasive disbelief of trans children's gendered autonomy.

3. My use of the nomenclature "transfeminism" is not to suggest that feminism on its own is in danger of cisgendered myopia, nor do I mean to suggest that feminism on its own is anachronistic and thus in need of the new prefix "trans" in order to be relevant. Rather, aligned with Robyn Wiegman's desire to articulate a coalition between assumedly split political projects and fields of knowledge (and their "separate" objects of analysis), I am attempting to continue the wider project of bringing into being a transfeminism that takes up the tensions deemed inherent in this pairing as a generative project that "share[s] political and theoretical genealogies" (Wiegman 2014, 20 n.1) and finds points of coalition between trans and feminist theories. For more work that articulates transfeminism in important ways, see Ahmed (2016), Bettcher and Garry (2009), Enke (2012), K. M. Green and Bey (2017), Heaney (2016), Koyama (2003), Scott-Dixon (2006), Serano (2007), Stryker and Bettcher (2016), Stryker et al. (2008), Tudor (2019), C. Williams (2016).

4. Coy Mathis was not the first, and will not be the last, trans child to take out legal action against a school. In 2015 Gavin Grimm sued his Virginia school district for violating Title IX and the equal protection clause of the Constitution, as the school prohibited him from accessing the boy's restrooms. The court proceedings, which made their way up to the Supreme Court but were vacated, have taken over four years, and thus by the time the final ruling arrived, Grimm was already attending college. In 2016 the Supreme Court announced that it would not take up Grimm's case, arguing that the Fourth Circuit Court of Appeals needed to reconsider its ruling following the Trump administration's redefinition of "sex" in Title IX. However, in August 2019 the U.S. District Court for the Eastern District of Virginia ruled in Grimm's favor, arguing that discrimination against trans students is in violation of Title IX.

5. For scholarship on the trans bathroom debate, see Cavanagh (2010), Gozlan (2017), and Porta et al. (2017).

6. As the Human Rights Campaign and the Trans People of Color Coalition report, transgender women of color are "facing an epidemic of violence

that occurs at the intersections of racism, sexism and transphobia" (2015, 2). See also Park and Mykhalyshym (2016), Truitt (2016).

7. For a complete list of these bills, see NCTE (n.d.).

8. For an explicit version of this rhetoric, see Campaign for Houston (2015). No campaigns, it should be noted, were concerned with the danger posed to boys, precisely because of the ways that sexual innocence is gendered.

9. The scholarship on trans children and young people has been proliferating in recent years. See Farley (2018), Gill-Peterson (2018), Meadow (2018), Salamon (2018), and Vaughn (2016).

10. In Gayle Salamon's *The Life and Death of Latisha King* (2018), a similar moment of (mis)recognition takes place. Salamon's book is a brilliant and devastating phenomenological ethnography of the court case against Brandon McInerney, a fourteen-year-old white boy who murdered Latisha King, a fifteen-year-old mixed-race trans girl, at their high school in 2008. Giving an account of the various ways in which students and faculty at the school directed gendered hostilities at King, Salamon provides this narrative from Debi Goldstein, a teacher: "I had an epiphany a week before the shooting. I saw this pretty little girl talking with the students. She had short hair and nice earrings and cute jeans and a beautiful little figure and then she turned around and I saw it was a boy" (Goldstein quoted in Salamon 2018, 154.) Describing this (mis)recognition, Salamon writes, "The tableau that initially struck her as unremarkable, innocuous, is now revised, and becomes a problem" (155). Salamon also provides another account of the role of projection in transphobia.

11. Prosser's argument about transsexual autobiographies more generally might be a product of his own particular desire for recognition within an "unambivalent status" of maleness (1998, 1). His reading thus differs from other trans scholars who are interested in the spaces between passing, recognition, and misrecognition. See, for example, Snorton (2009), Tudor (2017).

12. Prosser's argument about narrative is specifically located in relation to transsexual autobiographies, and as such is not directly mapped onto the types of narratives that I am working with here. The narratives which I explore below relate to trans experiences beyond transsexual ones, and they are (for the most part) narratives of trans children, rather than adults. At the time *Second Skins* was published, the biographies and

autobiographies available—including: *Christine Jorgensen* (Jorgensen 1967), *Conundrum* (Morris 1974), *Emergence* (Martino 1977), *Mirror Image* (Hunt 1978), *Second Serve* (R. Richards 1983), *Nine Lives* (Rutherford 1993), and *A Self-Made Man* (Hewitt and Warren 1995)—were all written by and about adults. At that time, there simply was not a prevalence of out and public trans children and young people. Now there is a heavily saturated industry of memoirs written by (or on behalf of) trans children, most of whom are white. See, among others, Andrews (2014), Bertie (2017), Jacques (2015), Jennings (2016), Kuklin (2016), Patterson (2019), Tobia (2019), and Whittington (2015).

13. In Prosser's earlier article "No Place Like Home" (1995), he articulates childhood as a narrative device in a similar manner as I am doing here: "The point to be emphasized is that the desire for a different body (a gendered home) has been there all along, as the narrative of discomforting shame suggests, at least since childhood; the shift is in the literalization of this desire through the body" (1995, 495).

14. The question of "before" is also asked in relation to what comes before the ego and whether or not the signifiers of gender are incorporated before gender is understood within language. For an analysis that weaves a reading of Jacques Lacan's mirror stage (1949) with Hortense Spillers' critique of psychoanalysis (1996) and the Clarks' Doll Tests (1947), in order to ask whether or not race signifies prior to language for children's ego development, see Viego (2007).

15. This passage comes from an *ABC News* profile of Jazz Jennings, a trans girl who, due to her television interview with Barbara Walters in 2007 (when she was six years old), is arguably the most well known trans child in the United States. Since her interview, Jennings has had a documentary made about her, *I Am Jazz: A Family in Transition* (Stocks 2011) for the Oprah Winfrey Network. She has also started her own nonprofit organization, Purple Rainbow Tails; has been named one of the twenty-five most influential teens by *TIME Magazine* in 2014 (*TIME* 2014); had a children's book made about her (Herthel 2015); and, at age sixteen, published a memoir titled *Being Jazz, My Life as a (Transgender) Teen* (Jennings 2016). She is now also the star of a biopic TV series for *TLC* titled "I Am Jazz."

16. This example comes from a *CNN* profile of Ryland Whittington, a deaf trans boy who became famous for the documentary made about his life, *Raising Ryland* (Feeley 2015).

17. This excerpt is from an online guest article for *Bitch Magazine* written by a mother of a trans girl (anonymized as "M."), who runs a blog named *Gendermom*.

18. Luce Irigaray argues that the "first distinction" one makes about another's gender—including this founding interpellation—is one based on a fantasy of knowledge that disavows ambivalence, or the possibility one might be wrong (Irigaray 1985b, 13–14).

19. For more on hegemonic masculinity, see A. D. Christensen and Jensen (2014), Connell (1987, 1995), Connell and Messerschmidt (2005), and Kimmel et al. (2005). For literature on female masculinity, and the blurred gendered boundaries of masculine performativity, see Cooper (2002), Halberstam (1998), Nguyen (2008), Paechter (2006), and Schippers (2007).

20. See, for example, the discussion of one of Patricia Gherovici's patients: "Lou took the phallus as a real object, not just as speculation, but as something directly linked to anatomy. As a child, she thought that one day the 'error' was going to be corrected. Challenged by her father's adamant disagreement on gender issues, she concluded that even if she was not yet a boy, she would become one, unlike her mother, who had chosen to become a woman" (2010, 194).

21. An important challenge to these narratives and the work they do is Halberstam's critique of their desire for finality. Halberstam argues that "there are problems with his [Prosser's] formulation of a transsexual desire for realness and his sense that gender realness is achievable. After all, what actually constitutes the real for Prosser in relation to the transsexual body?" (2005, 50–51).

22. It is thus important to disentangle the linearity within particular trans narratives from the understanding that children, or childhood, is linear, or that narrative itself is linear. For more on narrative's "performative dynamic" and intersubjective structure see: Huffer (2013). For the complexity of children's narratives, see Treacher (2006).

23. Carolyn Steedman (1992) critiques autobiography for producing the fantasmatic evidence upon which its structuring nostalgia is assumed to be best suited to uncover. Steedman argues against "the confirmation that biography offers, that life-stories can be told, that the inchoate experience of living and feeling can be marshaled into a chronology, and that central and unified subjects reach the conclusion of a life, and come into possession of their own story" (1992, 163).

24. Janet Mock (2014) provides a powerful account of trans childhood which resists this "always already" narrative. As Mock writes, "When I say *I always knew I was a girl* with such certainty, I erase all the nuances, the work, the process of self-discovery. . . . I wielded this ever-knowing, all-encompassing certainty to protect my identity. I've since sacrificed it in an effort to stand firmly in the murkiness of my shifting self-truths" (2014: 16, emphasis added). Advocating for a trans narrative that settles in the murkiness of ambiguous and ambivalent selfhood, Mock troubles the use of her own childhood as a narrative device to legitimate a coherent adult selfhood. See also Spade (2006).

25. See also Beauvoir (1949).

26. Because the fantasy of being deprived an object that is not missing is located in fantasy, we could additionally say that this temporality is true, in a sense, for the trans girl. For Geneviève Morel (2000), this is described in relationship to the phallus and the real, wherein the male-to-female transsexual reasons as such: "You see that I have a penis, and you say I have a phallus. But I do not experience that phallic jouissance. Then, cut off my penis and *you will not make the same mistake*" (186, emphasis added, as cited in Gherovici 2010, 164–65).

27. For more on the racialization of trans and cisgender-gendering see Ellison et al. (2017).

28. For other analyses of *Tomboy* (some of which are engaged with directly later in this chapter), see Duchinsky (2016), Farley and Kennedy (2015), Vilchez (2015), and Waldron (2013).

29. Analyzing the cinematography of *Tomboy*, Darren Waldron writes: "A predominance of close-ups and medium shots maintains us in proximity to the child characters. Often, we see only their waists, framed from the knees up and chest down, or their legs or torsos. . . . The adults are mainly forced to bend down to enter the shot, and the image-track barely leaves the children. Laure features in almost every shot, centrally positioned as the camera tracks her actions and movements. . . . Even on the rare occasions when the shot focuses on the adults, their conversation is difficult to hear" (2013, 64).

30. As Robbie Duchinsky argues, a feminist reading of *Tomboy* cannot forget that while Laure's becoming Mikael allows for her own transgression of gender boundaries, Lisa, the girl Laure flirts with, is not granted such

freedom: "Lisa facilitates Mikael's movement to insider status, but is not able to follow" (2016). However, because this reading assumes that transgression only happens across sexed lines, it misses the pleasure and agency that Lisa might have in this facilitation. Duchinsky also assumes that Lisa is cis. And while the film gives no indication otherwise, it also doesn't foreclose the possibility that *she* is the trans character here, perhaps indicated by her lack of desire to "transgress" gender lines, or in her own tentativeness in outing Laure.

31. For feminist analyses of tomboys, see, among others, Halberstam (1998, 2004), Jones (1999), Morgan (1998), Paechter (2010), Reay (2001), and Thorne (1993).

32. This argument about the embodied sites of gendered (mis)recognition is mirrored by Eric Plemons (2017), who argues that for many transwomen, the face, rather than the genitalia, is the most important site of embodied gender.

33. The question of the "reveal" of Laure's sex has already been central to the film, as the other children in her social group force Lisa to check her anatomy. And yet, as Waldron writes: "Although Lisa's look conveys her sense of betrayal, their exchange also implies the continuation of their affective connection. Lisa maintains her gaze at the level of Laure's eyes" (2013, 71).

34. For further scholarship on the feminist and queer implications of the glance and the stare within cinema, see Bradbury-Rance (2019).

35. In arguing that the boys fail to read gender as anything other than anatomical difference, I challenge the notion that tomboy performance, as Duchinsky defines it, "not only does not critique gender norms directly, but in fact is dependent upon them" (2016). This straightforward reading of gender roles leaves no space for the ambivalence of gendered performativities and identifications, and it assumes that in order for gendered subversion or critique to take place, the critique itself must be registered by the boys. Against this I argue that Laure and Lisa's mutual smirk signifies a clear pleasure inherent to their own shared critique, and that this in itself is an important moment for feminist analysis.

36. Most analyses of tomboys situate their social group as otherwise solely male, an arguable overstatement of their separation from other girls, and thus these analyses miss the complex negotiations of gender

transgression and play experienced between girls of varying gendered performativities and identities. Shawn McGuffey and Lindsay Rich, however, argue that girls create "group solidarity in resistance to boys' [assumed and overstated] dominance" (1999, 622). For further analyses of girls' group identities, solidarities, and play practices, see Maccoby and Jacklin (1987), Thorne (1993).

37. Juliet Mitchell describes Klein's understanding of "position" as "an always available state, not something one passes through" (1986, 116).

38. Sedgwick, in my reading, slightly mischaracterizes the "depressive position" as it relates to repair. Sedgwick writes: "the depressive position is an anxiety-mitigating achievement that the infant or adult only sometimes, and often only briefly, succeeds in inhabiting: this is the position from which it is possible in turn to use one's own resources to assemble or 'repair' the murderous part-objects into something like a whole" (2003, 128). She thus conflates the depressive position with the act of repair (as if the depressive is the reparative). For Klein, however, the depressive position is something that needs to be "overcome" in order for the child to develop a "happy relationship to its real mother" ([1935] 1986, 143). It is ambivalence, rather than the depressive position alone, which allows the child to do this work.

39. Writing about Sedgwick's title for her essay on the reparative, Lee Edelman argues that her use of "and" and "or" redoubles "the binary logic of the title itself—or rather, of the ambiguity as to whether it binarizes or unifies" (Berlant and Edelman 2014, 44).

3. DESIRING THE CHILD

1. One example of the ways in which discomfort around childhood sexuality structures and hinders contemporary queer youth activism can be seen in the responses to the drag-kid Desmond is Amazing. Desmond is an award-winning queer youth spokesperson who, at the age of only eleven, has over 170,000 Instagram followers and has been profiled in magazines ranging from *Vogue* (Frank 2018) to *The Cut* (Levy 2018). At the same time, his mother, who runs his social media presence, has had numerous people call Child Protective Services against her, accusing her of child abuse, exploitation, and maltreatment. These accusers claim that

Desmond's shows are akin to stripping and that he is being sexualized by the audiences and his parents. Against these claims, Desmond's mother has had to reiterate that Desmond—who came out at the age of eight and whose motto is "be yourself, always"—is too young for his performances to be read in a sexual manner.

2. For two accounts that trouble this position, see Cobb 2005 and Lesnik-Oberstein and Thompson 2002.

3. Confronted with this insight, I am aware that the story I tell in this chapter might be characterized by this defensive proclamation: "If the queer child cannot do what *I* want it to do, then I'll be sure to show you all the ways in which it cannot do what you want of it either." This is a risk I take. I do so—cautiously—both because I have an investment in exposing some of the founding wishes that have structured queer theory's articulation of the queer child and because I want to perform this mode of critique in order to, in the second half of the chapter, unravel it.

4. For analyses of the queer child beyond those which this chapter directly engages, see Durber (2007), Eng (2001), Kalha (2011), Kryölä (2011), and McCreery (2004).

5. In *Beyond the Pleasure Principle* ([1920] 1955), Sigmund Freud argues a child's game—of repeatedly throwing a toy *fort* (gone), only to quickly retrieve it *da* (there)—is an act of repeating a "distressing experience as a game" ([1920] 1955, 15). Freud thus argues that by repeating an unpleasurable act one can "make oneself master of it . . . as a primary event" (16). In arguing that queer theory has a *fort da* relationship with these questions of identity and definition, I am suggesting that queer scholarship tends to reiterate an assumed primary absence—that of a proper object of queer, defined as, to various extents, not intersectional, critical, "queer," specific, global, etc. enough—in order to have a mastery over this loss. In one iteration of this return, a particular queer genealogy (Butler 1990, 1993b; Sedgwick 1990; de Lauretis 1991; Warner 1993) is understood as emerging out of a break from (a certain branch of) feminism and gay and lesbian studies (cf. Halley 2004; Hemmings 2011; Wiegman 2004, 2012). This prompts debates about the "proper object" of queerness (Eng, Halberstam, and Muñoz 2005; Halley and Parker 2011; Wiegman and E. A. Wilson 2015). In another vein, the work on what E. Patrick Johnson

termed black "quare" studies (R. Ferguson 2004; S. Holland 2012; P. Johnson 2008; P. Johnson and Henderson 2005; Somerville 2000), and the arguments against queer's geopolitical referents (Blackwood 2008; Cruz-Malavé and Manalansan 2002; Vanita 2002), challenge the founding whiteness of this primary absence. This return, however, is complicated by queer's feminist, queer of color, and black and indigenous feminist genealogies (Anzaldúa 1987; Lorde 1978; Moraga and Anzaldúa 1981; Muñoz 1999).

6. My questioning of the need to identify a child as queer, and the assumed work that this might do, follows Kadji Amin (2017). Writing about the designation of kinship as queer, Amin writes: "Why is it that identifying a relational form as 'queer kinship' implicitly dignifies it, redeems it, and invests it with pathos? What are the limits of such a redemption?" (2017, 110). Along these lines, I am interrogating what designating the child as queer does to redeem childhood, and what the limits and consequences of such redemption are.

7. Stockton beget the shift from Sedgwick's "proto-gay child" to the "queer child" through, appropriately, a chapter in *Regarding Sedgwick* (Barber and D. Clark 2002), titled "Eve's Queer Child" (Stockton 2002). This chapter playfully suggests that Sedgwick herself wrote Henry James's "The Pupil" (1891)—or at least the version she passed off to Michael Moon, upon which he based his *A Small Boy and Others* (1998)—and that the pupil in the story, Morgan Moreen, was Sedgwick's and James' queer child. And yet, Moreen, Stockton writes, is not Sedgwick's only queer child; so too are the various "versions" of the queer child that unfold from Sedgwick's "How to Bring Your Kids Up Gay" and find themselves in Stockton's own subsequent articulations.

8. A question that should be asked here is, What figures the "queerness" of eventually-homosexual children in a contemporary moment that is increasingly folding homosexuality into the normative? Learning from those who have critiqued the assumed radicalism of the politics that stick to queer (Butler 2009; Duggan 2002; Puar 2007), we cannot assume that becoming a queer or a homosexual adult will necessarily challenge a problematic understanding of childhood. Along these lines, see: K. Bryant (2008) for an analysis of homonormativity in relation to gay and trans children. See also J. Breslow (2020).

9. Even the family portraits in Aviva's home change to reflect the new Avivas, thus emphasizing the film's desire to see these shifts in casting as consistent with the film's diegesis, rather than interruptive to it.

10. This inability to make decisions about her own reproductive health is, of course, not limited to Aviva. In 2015 thirty-eight states required parental notification, twenty-one of which additionally required at least one parent's consent (Guttmacher Institute 2015a). Additionally, eighteen states allow physicians to notify parents that their children are seeking STI services, and twenty states allow only particular classes of minors to consent to contraceptive services on their own behalf (Guttmacher Institute 2015b).

11. At a roundtable discussion on Todd Solondz's oeuvre at the Cambridge Centre for Film and Screen in 2019, Solondz countered this particular characterization of him as disliking people by saying, "I always think my movies are kinder than real life."

12. For a feminist analysis of motherhood and childhood on film, see Addison, Goodwin-Kelly, and Roth (2009); Byars (1991).

13. Even Lewis Carroll describes the pig through the language of the queer: "Alice caught the baby with some difficulty, as it was a queer-shaped little creature, and held out its arms and legs in all directions" ([1865] 1977, 59).

14. Contra Sedgwick, Jacobs would argue that heterosexual parents cannot provide the right type of pedagogy for their queer children: "what young queers in fact need most is other queers. Heterosexual parents . . . are still unable to familiarize their children with the traditions, habits, social codes, aesthetics, or values of specifically queer communities" (2014, 319). I wonder about this direct connection between sexual orientation and pedagogy, as it assumes too much about the radicalism of queer communities and the normativity of heterosexual ones, let alone their separability.

15. For an analysis of the complexities of motherhood, and its social scapegoating, see Rose (2018).

16. Most scholarship on queer motherhood and queer reproduction centers around lesbians becoming mothers, or various techniques through which queer (gay and lesbian) parents can have a child. See, for example, Agigian (2004), M. Bernstein and Reimann (2001), Mamo (2007).

17. There is, of course, a risk in following this line of argument, one that aligns this "queering" with an antiabortion-antichoice politics. As such,

I should be clear that my challenge is not to Aviva's mother's advocating of abortion tout court. Rather, I am pushing back on the ableist and racist discourse through which she makes this demand. Where Aviva's mother and I agree, however, is in her recognition that Aviva's "baby" is in actuality just a fetus; it is, she tells Aviva "not a baby, not yet."

18. Alison Kafer makes a similar point in *Feminist, Queer, Crip* (2013, 29), arguing that "pregnant women with disabilities and pregnant women whose fetuses have tested 'positive' for various conditions are understood as threats to the future: they have failed to guarantee a better future by bringing the right kind of Child into the present."

19. For more on the racist histories of sterilization, eugenics, and the control of black and poor women's reproductive capacities, see, among others, Collins (1999), Davis (1981), Ginsburg and Rapp (1995), Roberts (1997), and S. Thomas (2011).

20. This argument might find difficulty in a particular understanding of countertransference. Within this notion of countertransference, Freud initially warned that the analyst's occasional inappropriate responses to the patient's transferences may cloud the analyst's evaluation ([1910] 1957, 144–45). Because of this, queer theory's working toward the position of the analyst would not necessarily mean that queer theory would transcend its own repetitions. However, as Neil Aggarwal outlines, this "narrow" view of the countertransference has broadened to one in which they are understood as "an inevitable and necessary vehicle toward understanding the patient" (2001, 547). Here, through a "careful monitoring" of the countertransference, "the analyst could obtain useful insights into what the patient was trying to get the analyst to think or feel" (2001, 547).

21. In Freud's chapter on identification in *Group Psychology and the Analysis of the Ego* ([1921] 1955), he defines identification as "the earliest expression of an emotional tie," and as one of the lines of attachment though which the child initiates the Oedipus complex and becomes a gendered and sexual subject ([1921] 1955, 105). Freud argues that identification is different than desire: identification is "what one would like to *be*," while desire describes "what one would like to *have*" (106). Freud's easy separation between wanting to be and wanting to have, has, however, faced numerous critiques. Along with Jackie Stacey (1994), who argues

for a theory of identification that centers its eroticism (and specifically its homoeroticism), Diana Fuss argues that "identifications are erotic, intellectual, and emotional" (1995, 2). For more on the political life of identification, see, among others, Butler (1990); Muñoz (1999).

22. Mary Ann Doane, for example, challenges Mulvey's inattention to the female spectator and her flattening of female identification to a straightforward masculinization. Doane argues that femininity itself can be "flaunted" in order to destabilize the image and defamiliarize the lines of female iconography (1982, 82). Also critiquing the straightforward alignment of the female spectator with a masculine identification, Teresa de Lauretis argues for an understanding of the "double identification" of the female spectator as both the "desire for the other, and [the] desire to be desired by the other" (1984, 143). Responding to both of these understandings of female spectatorship, Stacey (1994) argues for a theory of spectatorship that is not merely textual (such that it additionally incorporates the space of the cinema, and the actual act of being in an audience with others), and she argues for an expansion of the terms of identification beyond heterosexual desire.

23. bell hooks identifies a black feminist "oppositional gaze" that emerges out of an engaged form of looking that is centered within an awareness of the politics of race and racism (1992, 123). In another vein, Gaines writes: "The very questions that Mulvey did not address have become the most compelling: Is the spectator restricted to viewing the female body on the screen from the male point of view? Is narrative pleasure always about male pleasure?" (1984).

24. Additionally, Kaja Silverman (1989) and Gail Ching-Liang Low (1989) both theorize racial identification in relation to white colonial subjects appropriating the dress of the colonized other, and while for Low "the fantasy of donning native costume, in the context of imperialism . . . expresses another attempt at control of subaltern peoples, another attempt at laying the burden of representation on them" (1989, 98), for Silverman cross-racial identification is both structured through imperial desires and, at the same time, can be the site from which a traitorous identification emerges, inspiring anticolonial resistance.

25. Along these lines, I depart from Davies's analysis of the shifts in casting within *Palindromes*. For rather than arguing that the young black girl at

the beginning and end of the film is, as Davies describes her, a "ghost of Aviva's childhood" that haunts her sexual encounters, "remind[ing] us that every adolescent was once a child and that every child will one day grow up" (2007, 380), we might rather attend to the ways that childhood itself is a racially privileged position that is not so equally inhabited—nor, as I argued in my first chapter, "Disavowing Black Childhood," so evenly lived through.

4. UNDOCUMENTED DREAM-WORK

1. Depending on the version of the DREAM Act, applicants would have had to meet the following criteria in order to be eligible: (1) be younger than eighteen years old (or sixteen, in the 2017 version) on initial arrival to the United States; (2) have proof of residence for four consecutive years; (3) have registered with the Selective Service (if male); (4) be between the ages of twelve and thirty-five when the act was enacted; (5) have graduated from an American high school, have passed the General Education Development test, or been admitted to a higher education institution; and (6) be of good moral character.

2. Unlike the DREAM Act, DACA did not provide those eligible with a pathway to citizenship; instead, it allowed some undocumented children to receive a deferred action from deportation that would be issued in two-year, renewable increments. DACA was implemented by Obama in an executive branch memorandum on June 15, 2012. On September 5, 2017, the Trump administration announced it would end the DACA program, but this is still pending the outcome of several court cases challenging this. In the meantime, new applications for DACA have been effectively suspended.

3. "Crimmigration" is the term coined by Juliet Stumpf (2006) that addresses the increasing conflation—rhetorically and materially—of criminalization and immigration. See also Chacón (2009), de Genova and Peutz (2010), Dingeman et al. (2017), and Rathod (2015).

4. This is not to suggest that all children migrate accompanied by parents but that the rhetoric of deportability tended to only make adjustments for undocumented children when it was justified through the criminalizing of adults, as I argue throughout this chapter. Indeed, one of the

problems of the *Plyler* discourse is that it criminalizes children and young people who do migrate unaccompanied.

5. See, among others, Chan (1994), Cheng (2000), Luibhéid (2002), and Tchen and Yeats (2014).

6. See, among others, Beydoun (2017), Hing (2018), and Randolph (2017).

7. According to official statistics, during the period of 2008 to 2018, Immigration and Customs Enforcement removals, defined as "the compulsory and confirmed movement of an inadmissible or deportable alien out of the United States based on such an order" (ICE 2018, 10), fluctuated between 226,119 to 409,849 per year (ICE 2015; 2018). These numbers do not include Enforcement and Removal Operations "administrative arrests," which totaled 158,581 in 2018 alone. In 2018 approximately 50,000 unaccompanied children were arrested and apprehended at the border, in addition to 107,000 individuals processed under the category of "family unit" (ICE 2018, 12).

8. See, among others, Abramovich, Cernadas and Morlachetti (2011), Bhabha (2011, 2014), Foner (2009), S. M. King (2010), and Suárez-Orozco, Hang, and Kim (2011).

9. Those that do often do so through the particulars of birthright citizenship. See, for example, the discussion of the discourse of "anchor babies" in Leo Chavez's *The Latino Threat* (2008). While the "anchor baby" discourse tinged the debate about the DREAM Act, all children eligible for its protections were not born in the United States. Even for children born in the United States, the claim of citizenship for children born to migrant parents is a tenuous one. Thinking through deportability in relation to the paradoxical relationship between citizenship, parentage, and childhood, for example, Jacqueline Bhabha (2009) inquires into the effects of deporting a citizen child's unauthorized parents. Writing that "the most significant citizen-specific entitlement today is the guarantee of nondeportability," Bhabha argues that children whose parents are deported are de facto deported as well: "If a young child's parents are forced to leave a country, so in effect is the child" (2009, 192). Because childhood places children both subject to and prior to the full effects of American citizenship, children with deported parents, Bhabha elucidates, have "no legally enforceable right, unlike their adult [citizen]

counterparts, to initiate family reunion or resist family separation where a family is divided by national borders" (2009, 201). Migrant childhood, Bhabha makes clear, can only ever partially be understood as bringing into being the child's rights of citizenship if the child is imagined as separate from their parent.

10. For a discussion on the importance of *Plyler,* see Olivas (2012). As just one example of the ways in which *Plyler* has been used to overturn anti-immigrant law, see League of United Latin American Citizens v. Wilson, 908 F. Supp. 755—Dist. Court, CD California 1995. In 1994 California Proposition 187, which sought to criminalize, surveil, and eject all undocumented people in the state, was passed. Numerous lawsuits challenging Proposition 187 were filed, and, thanks in part to *Plyler,* much of the ballot initiative was deemed federally unconstitutional.

11. In the decade leading up to the 2010 vote, numerous activists were arrested and some were subject to deportation proceedings, causing DREAMers to articulate fear about coming out and being removed from their families and communities. After one of the most well known acts of civil disobedience in May 2010, for example, when five students—Mohammad Abdollahi, Raúl Alcaraz, Yahaira Carrillo, Lizbeth Mateo, and Tania Unzueta—staged a sit-in at Senator McCain's office, four of them were arrested and the three of them who were undocumented were subjected to deportation proceedings. At the same time as the Obama administration claimed to be reticent to detain and deport student protestors, then, arrests such as these pointed to the realities of the conditions of deportability that undocumented youth faced.

12. Vargas also came out as gay, and it is important to note the centrality of queer activism and activists within the undocumented movement. This was particularly the case in relationship to the artist and activist Julio Salgado, whose artwork provided a pervasive aesthetic and ethics for undocuqueer resistance. See, for example, Cisneros (2018), Cisneros and Bracho (2019), Cisneros and Guiterrez (2018), and Seif (2014a, 2014b).

13. In Jasbir Puar's *Terrorist Assemblages,* she argues that the "folding of queer and other sexual national subjects into the biopolitical management of life" is propelled by and co-constituted with "the simultaneous folding out of life, out toward death, of queerly racialized 'terrorist populations'" (2007, xii). Following Puar's argument about the consequences

of national recognition of particular subjects, I am arguing that there is a similar process being undertaken in the "folding in" of undocumented children into the language of the DREAM Act. It is important to be clear that this tenuous inclusion within the rhetoric of the state is not to suggest that the state is actually providing care.

14. On this point there have been a series of debates about the prevalence of Mexican flags at antideportation protests and whether or not they provide fodder for anti-immigrant fears that immigrants do not assimilate into "American" values. See, for example, Baker-Cristales (2009) and Pineda and Sowards (2007).

15. Freud goes on to complicate this through the formulation: "A dream is a (disguised) fulfilment of a (suppressed or repressed wish)" ([1900] 1954, 160).

16. Lauren Berlant describes "cruel optimism" as a relation to an object of desire that is "actually an obstacle to your flourishing" (2011a, 1). Berlant argues that these relations only become cruel "when the object that draws your attachment actively impeded the aim that brought you to it initially" (1). For Berlant, any object can be structured by a relation of cruel optimism, but the conditions of cruel optimism are most pervasive under the crushing weight of neoliberalism.

17. Here too the narrative evocation of the American dream, and the wish fulfillment characteristic of dream, must be thought together with their mutual reliance on and construction through childhood. Above, I argued that a particular understanding of childhood as a naïve presocial location was integral to DREAMers' accounts of their rightful naturalization within the confines of American citizenship. In his discussion of dreams, Freud shares this framing of childhood: "The dreams of young children are frequently pure wish fulfilments and are in that case quite uninteresting compared with the dreams of adults. They raise no problems for solution" ([1900] 1954, 127). In *The Interpretation of Dreams,* Freud reiterates this dismissal of children's dreams (and therefore their psychic life) in a way that is contradictory to his renowned insistence that our psychic lives are formed during childhood. And, paradoxically, Freud's famous clinical cases—Dora, Little Hans, the Rat Man—are all, my colleague Tomás Ojeda helpfully reminded me, premised on oneiric material from his patient's childhoods.

18. While I agree with them that one of the most salient dangers of the DREAM Act was its conscription of DREAMers within the confines of neoliberalism, I would add, unsurprisingly, that the ways in which the DREAM Act enables violent notions of childhood and parenthood require intervention.

19. This framing of even the unassimilable dream as emerging from conscious processes rather than unconscious ones is perhaps a consequence of Ríos-Rojas and Stern's reticence against psychoanalysis. Understanding the analyst (and perhaps analysis more generally) as wholly tainted by power, Ríos-Rojas and Stern must avoid the unconscious and stick to dreams that are revolutionary but not in need of interpretation, as doing so would position *them* as analysts of undocumented dreams too.

20. Hortense Spillers (1987) makes a distinction between body and flesh, arguing that it marks the difference between the "captive and [the] liberated subject" such that "before the 'body' there is the 'flesh,' that zero degree of social conceptualization that does not escape concealment under the brush of discourse" (1987, 67). While Argote's image here obfuscates the body (or the bodies), she does not do so to evoke the flesh. Argote is representing the multiplicities of subjectivity, rather than their negation.

21. Tina Campt defines the haptic as "multiple forms of touch, which, when understood as constitutive of the sonic frequencies [of] photos, create alternative modalities for understanding the archival temporalities of images" (2017, 72). See also Delgado Huitrón (2019).

22. They hung there as part of the exhibit *My Father's Side of Home,* for which Argote organized a closing event titled "The 16 Hour Experience." This event was an interactive inhabiting of the gallery—part installation, part performance—where a small group of people stayed overnight in the gallery space.

23. Immense gratitude goes to Naomi Morgenstern, Cynthia Quarrie, and Jean Wyatt, as well as all of the participants of "The Child, the Parent: Ethics, Politics, Race," a stream at the American Comparative Literature Association annual meeting in 2019. These scholars responded to an earlier draft of this chapter and provided me with many insights, including this particular formation of Argote's work being indicative of the psychic residue of the unconscious.

24. As noted above, Freud ([1900] 1954, 182) was reluctant to grant children's dream life much nuance, and, as such it was with one exception— *childhood*—that he argued all dreams emerge from psychically significant dream instigators.

25. One organization, Southwest Key Programs Inc., is set to receive a $458 billion contract to build new detention centers for children of various ages detained by border patrol and Immigration and Customs Enforcement.

26. As the *New York Times* reports, "The federal government received more than 4,500 complaints in four years about the sexual abuse of immigrant children who were being held at government-funded detention facilities, including an increase in complaints while the Trump administration's policy of separating migrant families at the border was in place" (Haag 2019).

27. One of the risks of making this argument is that it might reify the nuclear family as the naturalized unit of care. While I want to stress the importance of maintaining families at the border, this demand does not require this traditional notion of the family. See S. M. King (2010, 510) for an important argument that "functional" families, defined as families "which may not satisfy this narrow [biological] conception of family, but satisfy the care-taking needs of children" be included and foregrounded within U.S. immigration law.

Bibliography

Abramovich, Victor, Pablo Ceriani Cernadas, and Alejandro Morlachetti. 2011. *The Rights of Children, Youth and Women in the Context of Migration: Conceptual Basis and Principles for Effective Policies with a Human Rights and Gender Based Approach.* New York: United Nations Children's Fund.

Addison, Heather, Mary Kate Goodwin-Kelly, and Elaine Roth, eds. 2009. *Motherhood Misconceived: Representing the Maternal in U.S. Films.* New York: State University of New York Press.

Aggarwal, Neil. 2001. "Transference in Psychoanalysis: Classical, Contemporary, and Cultural Contexts." In *International Encyclopedia of the Social and Behavioral Sciences,* edited by James Wright, 545–48. London: Elsevier.

Agigian, Amy. 2004. *Baby Steps: How Lesbian Alternative Insemination Is Changing the World.* Middletown, Conn.: Wesleyan University Press.

Ahmed, Sara. 2006. "Orientations: Toward a Queer Phenomenology." *GLQ: A Journal of Lesbian and Gay Studies* 12(4): 543–74.

———. 2016. "An Affinity of Hammers." *Transgender Studies Quarterly* 3(1–2): 22–34.

Alanen, Leena. 1988. "Rethinking Childhood." *Acta Sociologica* 31(1): 53–67.

———. 1994. "Gender and Generation: Feminism and the 'Child Question.'" In *Childhood Matters: Social Theory, Practice, and Politics,* edited by Jens Qvortrup, Majatta Bardy, Giovanni Sgritta, and Helmut Wintersberger, 27–42. Brookfield, UK: Aldershot.

Albarracín, Victor and Carmen Argote. 2017. "Houses, Mansions and Pyramids." *Terremoto,* December 11. https://terremoto.mx/article/houses-mansions-and-pyramids/.

Alcindor, Yamiche. 2012. "Trayvon Martin: Typical teen or troublemaker?" *USA Today,* December 11. http://www.usatoday.com/story/news/nation/2012/12/11/trayvon-martin-profile/17613737.

Aldous, Joan. 1969. "Wives' Employment Status and Lower-Class Men as Husband-Fathers: Support for the Moynihan Thesis." *Journal of Marriage and the Family* 31(3): 469–76.

Alexander, Bryant Keith. 2015. "Introduction: 'From Emmett Till to Trayvon Martin.'" *Cultural Studies ↔ Critical Methodologies* 15(4): 239–41.

Alexander, Michelle. 2012. *The New Jim Crow: Mass Incarceration in the Age of Colorblindness.* New York: The New Press.

Amin, Kadji. 2017. *Disturbing Attachments: Genet, Modern Pederasty, and Queer History.* Durham, N.C.: Duke University Press.

Andrews, Arin. 2014. *Some Assembly Required: The Not-So-Secret Life of a Transgender Teen.* New York: Simon and Schuster.

Annamma, Subini Ancy. 2017. *The Pedagogy of Pathologization Dis/abled Girls of Color in the School–Prison Nexus.* New York: Routledge.

Anzaldúa, Gloria. 1987. *Borderlands/La Frontera: The New Mestiza.* San Francisco: Aunt Lute Books.

Argote, Carmen. n.d.a. "My Father's Side of Home." http://carmenargote.com/guadalajara/.

———. n.d.b. "Mantas." http://carmenargote.com/series/mantas/.

Ariès, Philippe. 1962. *Centuries of Childhood: A Social History of Family Life.* Translated by Robert Baldick. New York: Vintage Books.

Armenta, Amada. 2014. *Protect, Serve, and Deport: The Rise of Policing as Immigration Enforcement.* Oakland: University of California Press.

Ashby, LeRoy. 1997. *Endangered Children: Dependency, Neglect, and Abuse in American History.* Farmington Hills, Mich.: Twayne Publishers.

Bailey, Alison. 1998. "Locating Traitorous Identities: Toward a View of Privilege-Cognizant White Character." *Hypatia* 13(3): 27–42.

Baker-Cristales, Beth. 2009. "Mediated Resistance: The Construction of Neoliberal Citizenship in the Immigrant Rights Movement." *Latino Studies* 7(1): 60–82.

Bat-Ami, Bar On. 1993. "Marginality and Epistemic Privilege." In *Feminist Epistemologies,* edited by Linda Alcoff and Elizabeth Potter, 83–100. London: Routledge.

Barber, Stephen and David Clark. 2002. *Regarding Sedgwick: Essays on Queer Culture and Critical Theory.* London: Routledge.

Barrett, Autumn. 2014. "Childhood, Colonialism, and Nation-Building: Child Labor in Virginia and New York." In *Tracing Childhood: Bioarchaeological Investigations of Early Lives in Antiquity,* edited by Jennifer Thompson, Marta Alfonso-Durruty, and John Crandall, 159–82. Tallahassee: University Press of Florida.

Barry, Dan, Serge F. Kovaleski, Campbell Robertson, and Lizette Alvarez. 2011. "Race, Tragedy, and Outrage Collide after a Shot in Florida." *New York Times,* April 11. www.nytimes.com/2012/04/02/us/trayvon-martin -shooting-prompts-a-review-of-ideals.html.

Beales, Ross. 1975. "In Search of the Historical Child: Miniature Adulthood and Youth in Colonial New England." *American Quarterly* 27(4): 379–98.

de Beauvoir, Simone. 1949. *The Second Sex.* London: Vintage Classics.

Bendix, Trish. 2011. "Céline Sciamma talks 'Tomboy,' 'Water Lilies' and Why LGBT Film Festivals are Still Necessary." *Afterellen.* November 16. http:// www.afterellen.com/movies/93932-cline-sciamma-talks-tomboy-water -lilies-and-why-lgbt-film-festivals-are-still-necessary.

Benedictus, Leo. 2013. "How Skittles Became a Symbol of Trayvon Martin's Innocence." *Guardian,* July 15. https://www.theguardian.com/world/ shortcuts/2013/jul/15/skittles-trayvon-martin-zimmerman-acquittal.

Berlant, Lauren. 1997. *The Queen of America Goes to Washington City: Essays on Sex and Citizenship.* Durham, N.C.: Duke University Press.

———. 2011a. *Cruel Optimism.* Durham, N.C.: Duke University Press.

———. 2011b. "A Properly Political Concept of Love: Three Approaches in Ten Pages." *Cultural Anthropology* 26(4): 638–91.

Berlant, Lauren, and Lee Edelman. 2014. *Sex, or the Unbearable.* Durham, N.C.: Duke University Press.

Bernard, Jessie. 1966. *Marriage and Family among Negroes.* New Jersey: Prentice Hall.

Bernstein, Mary, and Renate Reimann. 2001. *Queer Families, Queer Politics: Challenging Culture and the State.* New York: Columbia University Press.

Bernstein, Robin. 2011. *Racial Innocence: Performing American Childhood from Slavery to Civil Rights.* New York: New York University Press.

Bersani, Leo. 1987. "Is the Rectum a Grave?" *October* 43: 197–222.

Bertie, Alex. 2017. *Trans Mission: My Quest to a Beard.* London: Wren and Rook.

Bettcher, Talia, and Ann Garry. 2003. "Introduction." *Hypatia* 24(3): 1–10.

Beydoun, Khaled A. 2017. "Muslim Bans and the (Re)Making of Political Islamophobia." *University of Illinois Law Review* 5: 1733–74.

Bhabha, Jacqueline. 2009. "The 'Mere Fortuity of Birth'? Children, Mothers, Borders, and the Meaning of Citizenship." In *Migrations and Mobilities: Citizenship, Borders, and Gender,* edited by Seyla Benhabib and Judith Resnik, 187–227. New York: New York University Press.

———, ed. 2011. *Children Without a State: A Global Human Rights Challenge.* Cambridge, Mass.: MIT Press.

———. 2014. *Child Migration and Human Rights in a Global Age.* Princeton, N.J.: Princeton University Press.

Blackwood, Evelyn. 2008. "Transnational Discourses and Circuits of Queer Knowledge in Indonesia." *GLQ: A Journal of Lesbian and Gay Studies* 14(4): 481–507.

Bobo, Lawrence. 2011. "Somewhere Between Jim Crow and Post-Racialism: Reflections on the Racial Divide in America Today." *Daedalus* 140(2): 11–36.

Bonilla-Silva, Eduardo. 2006. *Racism without Racists: Color-Blind Racism and the Persistence of Racial Inequality in the United States.* Oxford: Rowman and Littlefield Publishers.

Brah, Avtar. 1996. *Cartographies of Diaspora: Contesting Identities.* New York: Routledge.

Bradbury-Rance, Clara. 2019. *Lesbian Cinema after Queer Theory.* Edinburgh: Edinburgh University Press.

Braidotti, Rosi. 1994. *Nomadic Subjects: Embodiment and Sexual Difference in Contemporary Feminist Theory.* New York: Columbia University Press.

Breslow, Aaron S., Melanie Brewster, Brandon L. Velez, Stephanie Wong, Elizabeth Geiger, Blake Soderstrom. 2015. "Resilience and Collective Action: Exploring Buffers Against Minority Stress for Transgender Individuals." *Psychology of Sexual Orientation and Gender Diversity* 2(3): 253–65.

Breslow, Jacob. 2019. "Adolescent Citizenship, or Temporality and the Negation of Black Childhood in Two Eras." *American Quarterly* 71(2): 473–94.

———. 2020. "'Flirting with the Islamic State': Queer Childhood with a Touch of Sexual Politics." *Comparative American Studies.* 17(1): 73–86.

Britzman, Deborah. 2006. "Little Hans, Fritz, and Ludo: On the Curious History of Gender in the Psychoanalytic Archive." *Studies in Gender and Sexuality* 7(2): 113–40.

Brown, Wendy. 2000. "Suffering Rights as Paradoxes." *Constellations* 7(2): 230–41.

Bruhm, Steven, and Natasha Hurley, eds. 2004a. *Curiouser: On the Queerness of Children.* Minneapolis: University of Minnesota Press.

———. 2004b. "Curiouser: On the Queerness of Children." In *Curiouser: On the Queerness of Children,* edited by Steven Bruhm and Natasha Hurley, ix–xxxviii. Minneapolis: University of Minnesota Press.

Bryant, Karl. 2008. "In Defense of Gay Children? 'Progay' Homophobia and the Production of Homonormativity." *Sexualities* 11(4): 455–75.

Burch, Andrea. 2011. "Arrest-Related Deaths, 2003–2009—Statistical Tables." *U.S. Department of Justice Bureau of Justice Statistics.* Washington, DC.

Burman, Erica. 2008. "Beyond 'Women vs. Children' or 'WomenandChildren': Engendering Childhood and Reformulating Motherhood." *International Journal of Children's Rights* 16: 177–94.

———. 2016a. "Fanon and the Child: Pedagogies of Subjectification and Transformation." *Curriculum Inquiry* 46(3): 265–85.

———. 2016b. "Fanon's Lacan and the Traumatogenic Child: Psychoanalytic Reflections on the Dynamics of Colonialism and Racism." *Theory, Culture and Society* 33(4): 77–101.

———. 2017. "Fanon's Other Children: Psychopolitical and Pedagogical Implications." *Race Ethnicity and Education* 20(1): 42–56.

Burman, Erica, and Jackie Stacey, eds. 2010a. "The Child and Childhood." *Feminist Theory* 11(3).

———. 2010b. "The Child and Childhood in Feminist Theory." *Feminist Theory* 11(3): 227–40.

Butler, Judith. 1990. *Gender Trouble: Feminism and the Subversion of Identity.* London: Routledge.

———. 1993a. *Bodies that Matter: On the Discursive Limits of "Sex."* London: Routledge.

———. 1993b. "Critically Queer." *GLQ: A Journal of Lesbian and Gay Studies* 1: 17–32.

———. 1997. *The Psychic Life of Power: Theories in Subjection.* Stanford, CA: Stanford University Press.

———. 2009. "Sexual Politics, Torture, and Secular Time." *British Journal of Sociology* 59(1): 1–23.

Butler-Wall, Karisa. 2015. "Risky Measures: Digital Technologies and the Governance of Child Obesity." *Women's Studies Quarterly* 43(1&2): 228–45.

Byars, Jackie. 1991. *All That Heaven Allows: Re-Reading Gender in 1950s Melodrama.* Chapel Hill: University of North Carolina Press.

Cacho, Lisa Marie. 2000 "'The People of California are Suffering': The Ideology of White Injury in Discourses of Immigration." *Cultural Values* 4(4): 389–418.

———. (2011) "Racialized Hauntings of the Devalued Dead." In *Strange Affinities: The Gender and Sexual Politics of Comparative Racialization,* ed. Grace Kyungwon Hong and Roderick A. Ferguson, 25–52. Durham, NC: Duke University Press.

Campaign for Houston. 2015. "TV Spot 1." *YouTube,* October 13. https://www.youtube.com/watch?v=D7thOvSvC4E.

Campt, Tina. 2012. *Image Matters: Archive, Photography, and the African Diaspora in Europe.* Durham, NC: Duke University Press.

———. 2017. *Listening to Images.* Durham, NC: Duke University Press.

Capehart, Jonathan. 2013. "Playing 'Games' with Trayvon Martin's Image." *Washington Post,* February 6. https://www.washingtonpost.com/blogs/post-partisan/wp/2013/02/06/playing-games-with-trayvon-martins-image/.

Carroll, Lewis. (1865) 1977. *Alice's Adventures in Wonderland.* London: Pan Books.

Castañeda, Claudia. 2002. (2002) *Figurations: Child, Bodies, Worlds.* Durham, NC: Duke University Press.

———. 2014. "Childhood." *Transgender Studies Quarterly* 1(1–2): 59–61.

Cavanagh, Sheila. 2010. *Queering Bathrooms: Gender, Sexuality and the Hygienic Imagination.* Toronto: University of Toronto Press.

Chacón, Jennifer. 2009. "Managing Migration through Crime." *Columbia Law Review Sidebar* 109: 135–48.

Chan, Sucheng, ed. 1994. *Entry Denied: Exclusion and the Chinese Community in America, 1882–1943.* Philadelphia: Temple University Press.

Chavez, Leo. 2008. *The Latino Threat: Constructing Immigrants, Citizens, and the Nation.* Stanford, Calif.: Stanford University Press.

Chavez, Steven. 2013. "Determination." State of Colorado Department of Regulatory Agencies, June 17.

Cheng, Anne. 2000. *The Melancholy of Race: Psychoanalysis, Assimilation, and Hidden Grief.* Oxford: Oxford University Press.

Chinn, Sarah and Anna Mae Duane, eds. 2015. "The Child." *Women's Studies Quarterly* 43(1&2).

Chittum, Ryan. 2012a. "Sourcing Trayvon Martin 'Photos' From Stormfront." *Columbia Journalism Review,* March 26. http://www.cjr.org/the_audit/ sourcing_trayvon_martin_photos.php.

———. 2012b. "Audit Notes: Chart of the Day, Trayvon Martin Sourcing Updates." *Columbia Journalism Review,* March 28. http://www.cjr.org/the_ audit/audit_notes_chart_of_the_day_t.php.

Chodorow, Nancy. 1978. *The Reproduction of Mothering: Psychoanalysis and the Sociology of Gender.* Berkeley: University of California Press.

Chotiner, Isaac. 2019. "Inside a Texas Building Where the Government is Holding Immigrant Children." *The New Yorker,* June 22. https://www .newyorker.com/news/q-and-a/inside-a-texas-building-where-the -government-is-holding-immigrant-children.

Chow, Rey. 1994. "Where Have All the Natives Gone?" In *Displacements: Cultural Identities in Question,* 125–51. Bloomington: Indiana University Press.

Christensen, Ann-Dorte, and Sune Qvortrup Jensen. 2014. "Combining Hegemonic Masculinity and Intersectionality." *NORMA* 9(1): 60–75.

Christensen, Pia Haudrup. 2004. "Children's Participation in Ethnographic Research: Issues of Power and Representation." *Children and Society* 18: 165–76.

Cisneros, Jesus. 2018. "Working with the Complexity and Refusing to Simplify: Undocuqueer Meaning Making at the Intersection of LGBTQ and Immigrant Rights Discourses." *Journal of Homosexuality* 65(11): 1415–34.

Cisneros, Jesus, and Christian Bracho. 2019. "Coming Out of the Shadows and the Closet: Visibility Schemas Among Undocuqueer Immigrants." *Journal of Homosexuality* 66(6): 715–34.

Cisneros, Jesus, and Julia Guiterrez. 2018. "'What Does It Mean to Be Undocuqueer?' Exploring (il)Legibility within the Intersection of Gender, Sexuality, and Immigration Status." *QED: A Journal in GLBTQ Worldmaking* 5(1): 84–102.

City of Sanford, Florida. 2012. "Transcript of George Zimmerman's Call to the Police." *Mother Jones.* http://www.motherjones.com/documents/326700 -full-transcript-zimmerman.

Clark, Kenneth, and Mamie Clark. 1947. "Racial Identification and Preference in Negro Children." In *Readings in Social Psychology,* edited by Eleanor Maccoby, Theodore Newcomb, and Eugene Hartley. New York: Holt, Rinehart and Winston.

Cobb, Michael. 2005. "Childlike: Queer Theory and Its Children." *Criticism* 47(1): 119–30.

Cohen, Cathy. 2005. "Punks, Bulldaggers, and Welfare Queens: The Radical Potential of Queer Politics?" In *Black Queer Studies: A Critical Anthology,* ed. E. Patrick Johnson and Mae G. Henderson, 21–51. Durham, N.C.: Duke University Press.

Cohen, Stanley. 1972. *Folk Devils and Moral Panics: The Creation of the Mods and Rockers.* London: MacGibbon and Kee Ltd.

Collins, Patricia Hill. 1998. "Will the 'Real' Mother Please Stand Up? The Logics of Eugenics and American National Family Planning." In *Revisioning Women, Health and Healing: Feminist, Cultural and Technoscience Perspectives,* edited by Adele E. Clarke and Virginia Olesen, 266–82. London: Routledge.

———. 1999. "It's All in the Family: Intersections of Gender, Race, and Nation." *Hypatia* 13(3): 62–82.

———. 2000. *Black Feminist Thought: Knowledge, Consciousness, and the Politics of Empowerment.* London: Routledge.

Connell, R. W. 1987. "Hegemonic Masculinity and Emphasized Femininity." In *Gender and Power: Society, the Person and Sexual Politics,* 182–90. Cambridge, U.K.: Polity Press.

———. 1995. *Masculinities.* Cambridge, U.K.: Polity Press.

Connell, R. W. and James Messerschmidt. 2005. "Hegemonic Masculinity: Rethinking the Concept." *Gender and Society* 19(6): 829–59.

Cooper, Brenda. 2002. "Boys Don't Cry and Female Masculinity: Reclaiming a Life and Dismantling the Politics of Normative Heterosexuality." *Critical Studies in Media Communication* 19(1): 44–63.

Corbin, April. 2011. "Citizen of Nowhere: The Story of One Undocumented Student." *Las Vegas Sun,* January 3. https://lasvegassun.com/news/2011/jan/03/citizen-nowhere.

Cornell, Drucilla. 1994. *Transformations: Recollective Imagination and Sexual Difference.* New York: Routledge.

Cortez, Jamie. 2004. *Sexile.* Los Angeles: The Institute for Gay Men's Health.

CR10 Publications Collective. 2008. *Abolition Now! Ten Years of Strategy and Struggle Against the Prison Industrial Complex.* Oakland: AK Press.

Crawford, Adam, and Tim Newburn. 2003. *Youth Offending and Restorative Justice: Implementing Reform in Youth Justice.* Cullompton, U.K.: Willan Publishing.

Crawley, Heaven. 2007. "When Is a Child Not a Child? Asylum, Age Disputes, and the Process of Age Assessment." London: Immigration Law Practitioners' Association.

Crenshaw, Kimberlé. 1997. "Color-Blind Dreams and Racial Nightmares: Reconfiguring Racism in the Post-Civil Rights Era." In *Birth of a Nation'hood: Gaze, Script and Spectacle in the O. J. Simpson Case,* edited by Toni Morrison and Claudia Brodsky Lacour, 97–168. London: Vintage.

Crenshaw, Kimberlé, and Andrea J. Ritchie. 2015. *Say Her Name: Resisting Police Brutality Against Black Women.* New York: African American Policy Forum.

Cruz-Malavé, Arnaldo, and Martin F. Manalansan. 2002. *Queer Globalizations: Citizenship and the Afterlife of Colonialism.* New York: New York University Press.

Dancy, T. Elon. 2014. "The Adultification of Black Boys." In *Trayvon Martin, Race, and American Justice: Writing Wrong,* edited by Kenneth J. Fasching-Varner, Rema E. Reynolds, Katrice A. Albert, and Lori L. Martin, 49–55. Rotterdam: Sense Publishers.

Davies, Jon. 2007. "Imagining Intergenerationality: Representation and Rhetoric in the Pedophile Movie." *GLQ: A Journal of Lesbian and Gay Studies* 13(2–3): 369–85.

Davis, Angela. 1971. *If They Come in the Morning: Voices of Resistance.* New York: Third Press.

———. 1981. *Women, Race, and Class.* New York: Random House.

———. 2003. *Are Prisons Obsolete?* New York: Seven Stories Press.

Delgado Huitrón, Cynthia Citlallin. 2019. "Haptic Tactic: Hypertenderness for the [Mexican] State and the Performances of Lia García." *Transgender Studies Quarterly* 6(2): 164–79.

Deutsch, Helene. 1946. *The Psychology of Women: A Psychoanalytic Interpretation.* London: Research Books.

Dickerson, Caitlin. 2019a. "'There Is a Stench': Soiled Clothes and No Baths for Migrant Children at a Texas Center." *New York Times,* June 21.

https://www.nytimes.com/2019/06/21/us/migrant-children-border
-soap.html.

———. 2019b. "The Youngest Child Separated from His Family at the Border Was Four Months Old." *New York Times,* June 16. https://www.nytimes .com/2019/06/16/us/baby-constantine-romania-migrants.html?search ResultPosition=1.

Dilulio, John. 1995. "The Coming of the Super-Predators." *Weekly Standard,* November 27. http://www.weeklystandard.com/the-coming-of-the-super -predators/article/8160.

Dingeman, Katie, Yekaterina Arzhayev, Cristy Ayala, Erika Bermudez, Lauren Padama, and Liliana Tena-Chávez. 2017. "Neglected, Protected, Ejected: Latin American Women Caught by Crimmigration." *Feminist Criminology* 12(3): 293–314.

Doane, Mary Ann. 1982. "Film and the Masquerade: Theorising the Female Spectator." *Screen* 23(3–4): 74–88.

Dougherty, Michael Brendan. 2012. "Why Lots of People Think the Media Is Wrong about the Trayvon Martin Case." *Business Insider,* March 26. http:// www.businessinsider.com/the-media-is-getting-the-trayvon-martin-story -wrong-2012-3?IR=T.

Downing, Lisa. 2011. "On the Fantasy of Childlessness as Death in Psycho-analysis and in Roeg's 'Don't Look Now' and von Trier's 'Antichrist.'" *Lambda Nordica* 2–3: 49–68.

Druber, Dean. 2007. "Still Missing: Daniel Morcombe and the Queer Child." *Continuum* 21(1): 19–31.

Duane, Anna Mae. 2010. *Suffering Childhood in Early America: Violence, Race, and the Making of the Child Victim.* Athens: University of Georgia Press.

Duchinsky, Robbie. 2016. "Schizoid Femininities and Interstitial Spaces: Childhood and Gender in Céline Sciamma's *Tomboy* and P. J. Hogan's *Peter Pan.*" *Diogenes.*

Dude, W. Kelly. 2012. "Re: Coy Mathis/Fountain-Fort Carson School District." *Transgender Legal,* December 28. http://www.transgenderlegal.org/ media/uploads/doc_491.pdf.

Duggan, Lisa. 2002. "The New Homonormativity: The Sexual Politics of Neoliberalism." In *Materializing Democracy: Toward a Revitalized Cultural Politics,* edited by Russ Castronovo and Dana Nelson, 175–94. Durham, N.C.: Duke University Press.

Dyer, Hannah. 2020. *The Queer Aesthetics of Childhood: Asymmetries of Innocence and the Cultural Politics of Child Development.* Newark, N.J.: Rutgers University Press.

Edelman, Lee. 2004. *No Future: Queer Theory and the Death Drive.* Durham, N.C.: Duke University Press.

Edelman, Marian Wright. 2012. "Walking While Black." *Children's Defense Fund,* March 21. http://www.childrensdefense.org/newsroom/child-watch -columns/child-watch-documents/walking-while-black.html.

Edwards-Leeper, Laura, Scott Leibowitz, Varunee Faii, and Sangganianavanich. 2016. "Affirmative Practice with Transgender and Gender Nonconforming Youth: Expanding the Model." *Psychology of Sexual Orientation and Gender Diversity* 3(2): 165–72.

Edwards-Stout, Kergan. 2012. "Mother of Transgender Child Speaks Out." *Kergan Edwards-Stout,* September 11. http://kerganedwards-stout.com/ transgender-child.

Elias, Edwin H. 2016. "New Dreams: The Impact of DACA on Undocumented Youth in Southern California." PhD diss., University of California, Riverside.

Ellison, Treva, Kai M. Green, Matt Richardson, and C. Riley Snorton, eds. 2017. "The Issue of Blackness" *Transgender Studies Quarterly* 4(2).

Eng, David. 2001. "Primal Scenes: Queer Childhood in 'The Shoyu Kid.'" In *Racial Castration: Managing Masculinity in Asian America,* pp. 104–36. Durham, N.C.: Duke University Press.

Eng, David, Judith Halberstam, and José Esteban Muñoz. 2005. "What's Queer about Queer Studies Now?" *Social Text* 23(3–4): 1–17.

Eng, David, and David Kazanjian. 2003. "Introduction: Mourning Remains." In *Loss: The Politics of Mourning,* ed. David Eng and David Kazanjian, 1–25. Berkeley: University of California Press.

Eng, David, and Shinhee Han. 2000. "A Dialogue on Racial Melancholia." *Psychoanalytic Dialogues* 10(4): 667–700.

———. 2019. *Racial Melancholia, Racial Dissociation.* Durham, N.C.: Duke University Press.

Enke, Anne. 2012. *Transfeminist Perspectives in and Beyond Transgender and Gender Studies.* Philadelphia: Temple University Press.

Erdely, Sabrina. 2013. "About a Girl: Coy Mathis' Fight to Change Gender." *Rolling Stone,* October 28. http://www.rollingstone.com/culture/news/ about-a-girl-coy-mathis-fight-to-change-change-gender-20131028.

Evans-Winters, Venus, and Magaela C. Bethune, eds. 2014. *(Re)Teaching Trayvon: Education for Racial Justice and Human Freedom*. Rotterdam: Sense Publishers.

Fanon, Frantz. 1967. *Black Skin, White Masks*. Translated by Charles Lam Markmann. London: Pluto Press.

Farley, Lisa. 2018. *Childhood beyond Pathology: A Psychoanalytic Study of Development and Diagnosis*. Albany: SUNY Press.

Farley, Lisa, and R. M. Kennedy. 2015. "A Sex of One's Own: Childhood and the Embodiment of (Trans)gender." *Psychoanalysis, Culture, and Society* 21(2): 167–83.

Fasching-Varner, Kenneth J., Rema E. Reynolds, Katrice A. Albert, and Lori L. Martin, eds. 2014. *Trayvon Martin, Race, and American Justice: Writing Wrong*. Rotterdam: Sense Publishers.

Faust, Drew, and John Hennessy. 2010. "Deserving of the DREAM." *Politico,* December 8. https://www.politico.com/story/2010/12/deserving-of-the -dream-046124.

Feeley, Sarah. 2015. *Raising Ryland*. Mike Marker Entertainment.

Felsenthal, Julia. 2016. "Ebony G. Patterson Confronts Race and Childhood at the Studio Museum in Harlem." *Vogue,* April 5. https://www.vogue.com/ article/ebony-g-patterson-studio-museum-harlem?verso=true.

Ferguson, Ann Arnett. 2001. *Bad Boys: Public School in the Making of Black Masculinity*. Ann Arbor: University of Michigan Press.

Ferguson, Roderick. 2004. *Aberrations in Black: Toward a Queer of Color Critique*. Minneapolis: University of Minnesota Press.

Fields, Jessica. 2005. "'Children Having Children': Race, Innocence, and Sexuality Education." *Social Problems* 52(4): 549–71.

Firestone, Shulamith. 1971. "Down with Childhood." In *The Dialectic of Sex: The Case for Feminist Revolution,* 73–102. London: Cape.

Fleetwood, Nicole. 2011. *Troubling Vision: Performance, Visuality, and Blackness*. Chicago: University of Chicago Press.

Foner, Nancy, ed. 2009. *Across Generations: Immigrant Families in America*. New York: New York University Press.

Foster, Johanna. 1999. "An Invitation to Dialogue: Clarifying the Position of Feminist Gender Theory in Relation to Sexual Difference Theory." *Gender and Society* 13(4): 431–56.

Foucault, Michel. (1975–76) 1997. *"Society Must be Defended" Lectures at the Collège de France, 1975-1976*, ed. Mauro Bertani and Alessandro Fontana, translated by David Macey. New York: Picador.

———. (1977) 1995. *Discipline and Punish: The Birth of the Prison*, translated by Alan Sheridan. New York: Vintage Books.

———. (1978) 1990. *The History of Sexuality Volume I: An Introduction*, translated by Robert Hurley. New York: Pantheon Books.

Frank, Alex. 2018. "Meet the Ten-Year-Old Drag Prodigy Who Just Stole the Show at Gypsy Sport." *Vogue*, February 12. https://www.vogue.com/article/desmond-amazing-drag-gypsy-sport?verso=true.

Freud, Sigmund. (1900) 1954. *The Interpretation of Dreams*, translated and edited by James Strachey. London: George Allen and Unwin Ltd.

———. (1910) 1957. "The Future Prospects of Psycho-analytic Therapy." In *The Standard Edition of the Complete Works of Sigmund Freud, Volume XI*, translated by James Strachey, 139–51. London: Vintage.

———. (1911) 1958. "On the Mechanism of Paranoia." In *The Standard Edition of the Complete Works of Sigmund Freud, Volume XII*, translated by James Strachey, 59–79. London: Vintage.

———. (1913) 1950. *Totem and Taboo: Some Points of Agreement between the Mental Lives of Savages and Neurotics*, translated by James Strachey. London: Routledge.

———. (1917) 1957. "Mourning and Melancholia." In *The Standard Edition of the Complete Works of Sigmund Freud, Volume XIV*, translated by James Strachey, 243–58. London: Vintage.

———. (1920) 1955. "Beyond the Pleasure Principle." In *The Standard Edition of the Complete Works of Sigmund Freud, Volume XVIII*, translated by James Strachey, 7–64. London: Vintage.

———. (1921) 1955. "Group Psychology and the Analysis of the Ego." In *The Standard Edition of the Complete Works of Sigmund Freud, Volume XVIII*, translated by James Strachey, 69–143. London: Vintage.

———. (1923a) 1961. "The Ego and the Id." In *The Standard Edition of the Complete Works of Sigmund Freud, Volume XIX*, translated by James Strachey, 12–66. London: Vintage.

———. (1923b) 1961. "The Infantile Genital Organization: An Interpolation Into the Theory of Sexuality." In *The Standard Edition of the Complete*

Works of Sigmund Freud, Volume XIX, translated by James Strachey, 141–48. London: Vintage.

———. (1925) 1961. "Negation." In *The Standard Edition of the Complete Works of Sigmund Freud, Volume XIX,* translated by James Strachey, 235–39. London: Vintage.

———. (1933) 1964. "Femininity." In *The Standard Edition of the Complete Works of Sigmund Freud, Volume XXII,* translated by James Strachey, 112–35. London: The Hogarth Press.

Fuller, Peter. 1979. "Uncovering Childhood." In *Changing Childhood,* edited by Martin Hoyles, 71–108. London: Writers and Readers Publishing Collective.

Fuss, Diana. 1995. *Identification Papers.* London: Routledge.

Gaines, Jane. 1984. "Women and Representation: Can We Enjoy Alternative Pleasure?" *Jump Cut* 29: 25–27.

———. 1990. "White Privilege and Looking Relations: Race and Gender in Feminist Film Theory." In *Issues in Feminist Film Criticism,* edited by Patricia Erens, 75–92. Bloomington: Indiana University Press.

Galfrmjerz3. 2012. (Untitled online reader comment, comments since deleted) "George Zimmerman Arrested: How Newspaper Front Pages Covered Story (PHOTOS)." *Huffington Post,* April 13. http://www.huffing tonpost.com/2012/04/12/george-zimmerman-arrested-newspaper-front -pages_n_1420692.html?ref=tw.

Gendermom. 2013. "When I Say My Daughter Is Transgender, Believe Me." *Bitch Magazine,* July 8. http://bitchmagazine.org/post/believe-me—my -daughter-is-transgender.

General Assembly of North Carolina. 2016. *Session Law 2016–3 House Bill 2.*

General Assembly of Virginia. 1662. *Act XII: Negro Womens Children to Serve According to the Condition of the Mother.* In *The Statutes at Large; Being a Collection of All the Laws of Virginia, from the First Session of the Legislature in the Year 1619,* edited by William Waller Hening. New York: R & W & G Bartow.

De Genova, Nicholas P. 2002. "Migrant 'Illegality' and Deportability in Everyday Life." *Annual Review of Anthropology* 31: 419–47.

De Genova, Nicholas P., and Nathalie Peutz, eds. 2010. *The Deportation Regime: Sovereignty, Space, and the Freedom of Movement.* Durham, N.C.: Duke University Press.

George Zimmerman Legal Case. 2013. "A Response to Jonathan Capehart's Editorials in Regards to the Zimmerman Case." *GZLegalCase.com,* February 21. http://web.archive.org/web/20130227030350/http://gzlegalcase .com/index.php/press-releases/98-a-response-to-jonathan-capehart-s -editorials-in-regards-to-the- zimmerman-case.

Gerson, Michael. 2010. "How the Dream Act Transcends Politics." *Washington Post,* December 7. http://www.washingtonpost.com/wp-dyn/content/ article/2010/12/06/AR2010120605406.html.

Gherovici, Patricia. 2010. *Please Select Your Gender: From the Invention of Hysteria to the Democratizing of Transgenderism.* New York: Routledge.

Gill-Peterson, J. 2018. *Histories of the Transgender Child.* Minneapolis: University of Minnesota Press.

Gill-Peterson, J., Rebekah Sheldon, and Kathryn Bond Stockton, eds. 2016. "The Child Now." *GLQ: A Journal of Lesbian and Gay Studies* 22(4).

Gilroy, Paul. 2000. *Against Race: Imagining Political Culture beyond the Color Line.* Cambridge, Mass.: Harvard University Press.

Ginsburg, Faye, and Rayna Rapp, eds. 1995. *Conceiving the New World Order: The Global Politics of Reproduction.* Berkeley: University of California Press.

Giroux, Henry. 1996. "Hollywood, Race, and the Demonization of Youth: The 'Kids' Are Not 'Alright.'" *Educational Researcher* 25(2): 31–35.

———. 1997. "Youth and the Politics of Representation: Response to Thomas Hatch's 'If the 'Kids' Are Not 'Alright,' I'm 'Clueless.'" *Educational Researcher* 26(4): 27–30.

Glaze, Lauren. 2011. "Correctional Populations in the United States, 2010." *U.S. Department of Justice Bureau of Justice Statistics.* Washington, D.C.

Goff, Phillip Atiba, Matthew Christian Jackson, Brooke Allison, Lewis Di Leone, Carmen Marie Culotta, and Natalie Ann DiTomasso. 2014. "The Essence of Innocence: Consequences of Dehumanizing Black Children." *Journal of Personality and Social Psychology* 106(4): 526–45.

Goldberg, Alan, and Joneil Adriano. 2007. "'I'm a Girl'—Understanding Transgender Children." *ABC News,* April 27. http://www.transkidspurple rainbow.org/featured/im-a-girl-understanding-transgender-children.

Gordon, Avery F. 1997. *Ghostly Matters: Haunting and the Sociological Imagination.* Minneapolis: University of Minnesota Press.

Gordon, Edmund. 1997. "Cultural Politics of Black Masculinity." *Transforming Anthropology* 6 (1 and 2): 36–53.

Gossett, Reina, Eric A. Stanley, and Johanna Burton, eds. 2017. *Trap Door: Trans Cultural Production and the Politics of Visibility.* Cambridge, Mass.: MIT Press.

Gozlan, Oren. 2011. "Transsexual Surgery: A Novel Reminder and a Navel Remainder." *International Forum of Psychoanalysis* 20(1): 45–52.

Gray, Colette, and Deborah Harcourt, eds. 2012. "Children's Participatory Research." *International Journal of Early Years Education* 20(3).

Gray, Jonathan, ed. 2015. "Trayvon Martin in Popular Culture: A Roundtable." *Modern Language Studies* 45(1).

Green, Erica, Katie Benner, and Robert Pear. 2018. "'Transgender' Could Be Defined out of Existence under Trump Administration." *New York Times,* October 21. https://www.nytimes.com/2018/10/21/us/politics/trans gender-trump-administration-sex-definition.html.

Green, Kai M., and Marquis Bey. 2017. "Where Black Feminist Thought and Trans* Feminism Meet: A Conversation." *Souls: A Critical Journal of Black Politics, Culture, and Society* 19(4): 438–54.

Greer, Germaine. 1971. *The Female Eunuch.* New York: McGraw-Hill.

Grosz, Elizabeth. 1994. *Volatile Bodies: Toward a Corporeal Feminism.* Bloomington: Indiana University Press.

Guttmacher Institute. 2015a. *State Policies in Brief: Parental Involvement in Minors' Abortions.* Washington, D.C.

———. 2015b. *State Policies in Brief: An Overview of Minors' Consent Law.* Washington, D.C.

Guttman, Matt. 2012. "Trayvon Martin Investigator Wanted Manslaughter Charge." *Good Morning America,* March 27. https://gma.yahoo.com/ trayvon-martin-investigator-wanted-manslaughter-charge-151838720— abc-news-topstories.html.

Haag, Matthew. 2019. "Thousands of Immigrant Children Said They Were Sexually Abused in U.S. Detention Centers, Report Says." *New York Times,* February 27. https://www.nytimes.com/2019/02/27/us/immigrant -children-sexual-abuse.html.

Halberstam, Judith. 1998. *Female Masculinity.* Durham: Duke University Press.

———. 2004. "Oh Bondage Up Yours! Female Masculinity and the Tomboy." In *Curiouser: On the Queerness of Children,* edited by Steven Bruhm and Natasha Hurley, 191–214. Minneapolis: University of Minnesota Press.

———. 2005. *In a Queer Time and Place: Transgender Bodies, Subcultural Lives.* New York: New York University Press.

———. 2012. *Gaga Feminism: Sex, Gender, and the End of Normal.* Boston: Beacon Press.

Hall, Granville Stanley. 1905. *Adolescence: Its Psychology and Its Relations to Physiology, Anthropology, Sociology, Sex, Crime, Religion, and Education.* New York: D. Appleton.

Hall, Stuart. 2017. *Familiar Stranger: A Life between Two Islands,* ed. Bill Schwartz. Durham, N.C.: Duke University Press.

Halley, Ian. 2004. "Queer Theory by Men." *Duke Journal of Gender Law and Policy* 11(7): 7–53.

Halley, Janet, and Andrew Parker, eds. 2011. *After Sex? On Writing since Queer Theory.* Durham, N.C.: Duke University Press.

Hanawalt, Barbara. 1977. "Childrearing among the Lower Classes of Late Medieval England." *Journal of Interdisciplinary History* 8(1): 1–22.

Hanson, Ellis. 2004 "Knowing Children: Desire and Interpretation in *The Exorcist.*" In *Curiouser: On the Queerness of Children,* edited by Steven Bruhm and Natasha Hurley, 107–36. Minneapolis: University of Minnesota Press.

Harawa, Daniel. 2014. "The Black Male: A Dangerous Double-Minority." In *Trayvon Martin, Race, and American Justice: Writing Wrong,* ed. Kenneth Fasching-Varner, Rema Renolds, Katrice Albert, and Lori Martin, 57–60. Rotterdam: Sense Publishers.

Haraway, Donna. 1988. "Situated Knowledges: The Science Question in Feminism and the Privilege of Partial Perspective." *Feminist Studies* 14(3): 581–607.

———. 2016. *Staying with the Trouble: Making Kin in the Chthulucene.* Durham, N.C.: Duke University Press.

Harcourt, Deborah, Bob Perry, and Tim Waller, eds. 2011. *Researching Young Children's Perspectives: Debating the Ethics and Dilemmas of Educational Research with Children.* London: Routledge.

Harding, Sandra. 1991. *Whose Science? Whose Knowledge? Thinking from Women's Lives.* Milton Keynes, U.K.: Open University Press.

Hardman, Charlotte. 1973. "Can There Be an Anthropology of Children?" *Journal of the Anthropological Society of Oxford* 4(3): 85–99.

Hart, William David. 2013. "Dead Black Man, Just Walking." In *Pursuing Trayvon Martin: Historical Context and Contemporary Manifestations of Racial*

Dynamics, edited by George Yancy and Janine Jones, 91–101. New York: Lexington Books.

Hartman, Saidiya. 2007. *Lose Your Mother: A Journey along the Atlantic Slave Route.* New York: Farrar, Straus and Giroux.

———. 2008. "Venus in Two Acts." *Small Axe* 12(2): 1–14.

———. 2019. *Wayward Lives, Beautiful Experiments: Intimate Histories of Social Upheaval.* New York: W. W. Norton and Company.

Heaney, Emma. 2016. "Women-Identified Women: Trans Women in 1970s Lesbian Feminist Organizing." *Transgender Studies Quarterly* 3(1–2): 137–45.

Hemmings, Clare. 2011. *Why Stories Matter: The Political Grammar of Feminist Theory.* Durham, N.C.: Duke University Press.

———. 2018. *Considering Emma Goldman: Feminist Political Ambivalence and the Imaginative Archive.* Durham, N.C.: Duke University Press.

Hennessy, Rosemary. 1993. "Women's Lives/Feminist Knowledge: Feminist Standpoint as Ideology Critique." *Hypatia* 8(1): 14–34.

Hewitt, Paul and Jane Warren. 1996. *A Self-Made Man: The Diary of a Man Born in a Woman's Body.* London: Headline Book Publishing.

Hill, Malcolm. 2006. "Children's Voices on Ways of Having a Voice: Children's and young people's perspectives on methods used in research and consultation." *Childhood* 13(1): 69–89.

Hing, Bill Ong. 2017. "Entering the Trump Ice Age: Contextualizing the New Immigration Enforcement Regime." *Texas A&M L. Review* 5: 253–321.

Holland, Sharon. 2012. *The Erotic Life of Racism.* Durham, N.C.: Duke University Press.

hooks, bell. 1992. *Black Looks: Race and Representation.* New York: Routledge.

Horney, Karen. (1926) 1967. "The Flight from Womanhood: The Masculinity-Complex in Women as Viewed by Men and by Women." In *Feminine Psychology,* 54–70. London: Norton.

Human Rights Campaign and Trans People of Color Coalition. 2015. "Addressing Anti-Transgender Violence: Exploring Realities, Challenges and Solutions for Policymakers and Community Advocates." Washington, D.C.

Hudson, Annie. 1989. "Troublesome Girls." In *Growing Up Good: Policing the Behaviour of Girls in Europe,* edited by Maureen Elizabeth and Maureen Cain, 197–219. London: Sage.

Huffer, Lynne. 2013. *Are the Lips a Grave? A Queer Feminist on the Ethics of Sex.* New York: Columbia University Press.

Hunt, Nancy. 1978. *Mirror Image: The Odyssey of a Male to Female Transsexual.* New York: Holt, Rinehart, and Winston.

Immigration and Customs Enforcement. 2015. "ICE Enforcement and Removal Operations Report: Fiscal Year 2015." Washington, D.C.

———. 2018. "Fiscal Year 2018 ICE Enforcement and Removal Operations Report." Washington, D.C.

Irigaray, Luce. 1985a. *This Sex Which Is Not One,* trans. Catherine Porter and Carolyn Burke. Ithaca, N.Y.: Cornell University Press.

———. 1985b. *Speculum of the Other Woman,* trans. Gillian Gill. Ithaca, N.Y.: Cornell University Press.

———. 1993. *An Ethics of Sexual Difference,* trans. Carolyn Burke and Gillian C. Gill. London: Athlone.

Jacobs, Amber. 2007. *On Matricide: Myth, Psychoanalysis, and the Law of the Mother.* New York: Columbia University Press.

Jacobs, Jason. 2014. "Raising Gays: On Glee, Queer Kids, and the Limits of the Family." *GLQ: A Journal of Lesbian and Gay Studies* 20(3): 319–52.

Jacobs, Margaret. 2009. *White Mother to a Dark Race: Settler-Colonialism, Maternalism, and the Removal of Indigenous Children in the American West and Australia, 1880–1940.* Lincoln: University of Nebraska Press.

Jacques, Julie. 2015. *TRANS: A Memoir.* London: Verso Books.

James, Allison. 2007. "Giving Voice to Children's Voices: Practices and Problems, Pitfalls and Potentials." *American Anthropologist* 109(2): 261–72.

James, Allison, and Chris Jenks. 1996. "Public Perceptions of Childhood Criminality." *British Journal of Sociology* 47(2): 315–31.

James, Allison, and Allan Prout, eds. 1990. *Constructing and Reconstructing Childhood: Contemporary Issues in the Sociology of Childhood.* London: Routledge.

James, Henry. (1891) 1992. "The Pupil." In *The Faber Book of Gay Short Fiction,* edited by Edmund White. Boston: Faber.

Jenks, Chris, ed. 1982. *The Sociology of Childhood: Essential Readings.* London: Batsford.

———. 1996. *Childhood.* London: Routledge.

Jennings, Jazz. 2016. *Being Jazz: My Life as a (Transgender) Teen.* New York: Random House Books for Young Readers.

Johnson, Devon, Amy Farrell, and Patricia Y. Warren, eds. 2015. *Deadly Injustice: Trayvon Martin, Race, and the Criminal Justice System.* New York: New York University Press.

Johnson, Patrick E. 2008. *Sweet Tea: Black Gay Men of the South.* Chapel Hill: University of North Carolina Press.

Johnson, Patrick E. and Mae G. Henderson, eds. 2005. *Black Queer Studies: A Critical Anthology.* Durham, N.C.: Duke University Press.

Johnson, Paul Elliott. 2017. "The Art of Masculine Victimhood: Donald Trump's Demagoguery." *Women's Studies in Communication* 40(3): 229–50.

Jones, Owain. 1999. "Tomboy Takes: The Rural, Nature, and the Gender of Childhood." *Gender, Place and Culture* 6(2): 117–36.

Jorgensen, Christine. 1967. *Christine Jorgensen: A Personal Autobiography.* San Francisco: Cleis Press.

Kafer, Alison. 2013. *Feminist, Queer, Crip.* Bloomington: Indiana University Press.

Kalha, Harri. 2011. "What the Hell Is the Figure of the Child? Figuring Out Figurality in, around, and beyond Lee Edelman." *Lambda Nordica* 2–3: 17–46.

Keeling, George, and James Wilson. 1982. "Broken Windows: The Police and Neighborhood Safety." *Atlantic.* http://www.theatlantic.com/magazine/archive/1982/03/broken-windows/304465/.

Kelley, Robin D. G. 2002. *Freedom Dreams: The Black Radical Imagination.* Boston: Beacon Press.

Kent, Kathryn R. 2004. "'No Trespassing': Girl Scout Camp and the Limits of the Counterpublic Sphere." In *Curiouser: On the Queerness of Children,* ed. Steven Bruhm and Natasha Hurley, 173–89. Minneapolis: University of Minnesota Press.

Khanna, Ranjana. 2003. *Dark Continents: Psychoanalysis and Colonialism.* Durham, N.C.: Duke University Press.

Kilby, Jane. 2010. "Judith Butler, Incest, and the Question of the Child's Love." *Feminist Theory* 11(3): 255–65.

Kilomba, Grada. 2008. *Plantation Memories: Episodes of Everyday Racism.* Münster: Unrast.

Kimmel, Michael, Jeff Hearn, and R. W. Connell, eds. 2005. *Handbook of Studies on Men and Masculinities.* London: Sage.

Kincaid, James. 1998. *Erotic Innocence: The Culture of Child Molesting.* Durham, N.C.: Duke University Press.

King, Shani M. 2009. "U.S. Immigration Law and the Traditional Nuclear Conception of Family: Toward a Functional Definition of Family That Protects Children's Fundamental Human Rights." *Columbia Human Rights Law Review* 41: 509–67.

King, Wilma. 1995. *Stolen Childhood: Slave Youth in Nineteenth-Century America.* Bloomington: Indiana University Press.

Kirkwood, R. Cort. 2012. "Medical Report Shows Martin Attacked Zimmerman." *New American,* May 17. http://www.thenewamerican.com/usnews/item/11413-medical-report-shows-martin-attacked-zimmerman.

Klein, Melanie. (1928) 1986. "Early Stages of the Oedipus Conflict." In *The Selected Melanie Klein,* ed. Juliet Mitchell, 69–83. Harmondsworth, U.K.: Penguin Books.

———. (1935) 1986. "A Contribution to the Psychogenesis of Manic-Depressive States." In *The Selected Melanie Klein,* edited by Juliet Mitchell, 115–45. Harmondsworth, U.K.: Penguin Books.

———. (1940) 1986. "Mourning and Its Relation to Manic-Depressive States." In *The Selected Melanie Klein,* edited by Juliet Mitchell, 146–74. Harmondsworth, U.K.: Penguin Books.

———. (1946) 1986. "Notes on Some Schizoid Mechanisms." In *The Selected Melanie Klein,* edited by Juliet Mitchell, 175–200. Harmondsworth, U.K.: Penguin Books.

Koffman, Ofra, and Rosalind Gill. 2013. "'The Revolution Will Be Led by a Twelve-Year-Old Girl': Girl Power and Global Biopolitics." *Feminist Review* 105: 83–102.

Kovaleski, Serge. 2012. "Trayvon Martin Case Shadowed by Series of Police Missteps." *New York Times,* May 16. http://www.nytimes.com/2012/05/17/us/trayvon-martin-case-shadowed-by-police-missteps.html.

Koyama, Emi. 2003. "The Transfeminist Manifesto." In *Catching a Wave: Reclaiming Feminism for the Twenty-first Century,* edited by Roy Dicker and Alison Piepmeier, 244–59. Boston: Northeastern University Press.

Krueger, Patricia. 2010. "It's Not Just a Method! The Epistemic and Political Work of Young People's Lifeworlds at the School–Prison Nexus." *Race Ethnicity and Education* 13(3): 383–408.

Kryölä, Katariina. 2011. "Adults Growing Sideways: Feederist Pornography and Fantasies of Infantilism." *Lambda Nordica* 2–3: 128–58.

Kuklin, Susan. 2016. *Beyond Magenta: Transgender Teens Speak Out.* Boston: Candlewick Press.

Lacan, Jacques. (1949) 1977. "The Mirror Stage as Formative of the Function of the I as Revealed in Psychoanalytic Experience." In *Écrits,* translated by Alan Sheridan, 1–7. London: Tavistock Publications.

———. (1958) 1977. "The Signification of the Phallus." In *Écrits,* translated by Alan Sheridan, 281–91. London: Tavistock Publications.

———. 1977a. *Écrits,* trans. Alan Sheridan. London: Tavistock Publications.

———. 1977b. *The Four Fundamental Concepts of Psycho-Analysis,* ed. Jacques-Alain Miller, trans. Alan Sheridan. London: The Hogarth Press.

de Lauretis, Teresa. 1984. *Alice Doesn't: Feminism, Semiotics, Cinema.* Bloomington: Indiana University Press.

———. 1991. "Queer Theory: Lesbian and Gay Sexualities An Introduction." *Differences* 3(2): iii–xvii.

Lawrence, C. J. 2014. "Yes, let's do that: Which photo does the media use if the police shoot me down? #IfTheyGunnedMeDown." *Twitter,* August 10. https://twitter.com/CJLawrenceEsq.

Lee, Lauren. n.d. "Carmen Argote: Color in Los Angeles." *Metal.* https://metalmagazine.eu/en/post/interview/carmen-argote-color-in-los-angeles.

Leiter, Valerie. 2004. "Parental Activism, Professional Dominance, and Early Childhood Disability." *Disability Studies Quarterly* 24(2).

Lesnik-Oberstein, Karín. 2010. "Childhood, Queer Theory, and Feminism." *Feminist Theory* 11(3): 309–21.

Lesnik-Oberstein, Karín, and Stephen Thompson. 2002. "What Is Queer Theory Doing with the Child?" *Parallax* 8(1): 35–46.

Levander, Caroline. 2006. *Cradle of Liberty: Race, the Child, and National Belonging from Thomas Jefferson to W. E. B. Du Bois.* Durham, N.C.: Duke University Press.

Levy, Lauren. 2018. "180 Minutes with Desmond Is Amazing." *The Cut.* https://www.thecut.com/2018/03/desmond-is-amazing-is-cooler-than-you.html.

Lewis, Gail. 2014. "Not by Criticality Alone." *Feminist Theory* 15(1): 31–38.

———. 2017. "Questions of Presence." *Feminist Review* 117: 1–19.

Lewis, Sophie. 2019. *Full Surrogacy Now! Feminism against Family.* London: Verso.

Liston, Barbara. 2012. "Family of Florida Boy Killed by Neighborhood Watch Seeks Arrest." *Reuters,* March 7. http://www.reuters.com/article/ us-crime-florida-neighborhoodwatch-idUSBRE82709M20120308.

Lorde, Audre. (1978) 1984. "Uses of the Erotic: The Erotic as Power." In *The Audre Lorde Compendium: Essays, Speeches, and Journals,* 106–12. Hammersmith, U.K.: HarperCollins.

Low, Gail Ching-Liang. 1989. "White Skins/Black Masks: The Pleasures and Politics of Imperialism." *New Formations* 9: 83–103.

Luibhéid, Eithne. 2002. *Entry Denied: Controlling Sexuality at the Border.* Minneapolis: University of Minnesota Press.

Maccoby, Eleanor, and Carol Nagy Jacklin. 1987. "Gender Segregation in Childhood." *Advances in Child Development and Behavior* 20: 239–87.

Mamo, Laura. 2007. *Queering Reproduction: Achieving Pregnancy in the Age of Technoscience.* Durham, N.C.: Duke University Press.

Mann, Tanveer. 2015. "Toddler Becomes Britain's Youngest Transgender Child after Mum Found Her Trying to Cut Off Her 'Bits.'" *Metro,* December 7. https://metro.co.uk/2015/12/07/boy-6-becomes-britains -youngest-transgender-child-after-mum-found-him-trying-to-cut -off-his-willy-5549667/.

Margarey, Susan. 1978. "The Invention of Juvenile Delinquency in Early Nineteenth-Century England." *Labour History* 34: 11–27.

Martin, Karin. 1996. *Puberty, Sexuality, and the Self: Boys and Girls at Adolescence.* London: Routledge.

Martino, Mario. 1977. *Emergence: A Transsexual Autobiography.* London: Crown Publishers.

Martosko, David. 2012. "The *Daily Caller* Obtains Trayvon Martin's Tweets." *Daily Caller,* March 26. http://dailycaller.com/2012/03/26/the-daily-caller -obtains-trayvon-martins-tweets/.

McCreery, Patrick. 2004. "Innocent Pleasures? Children and Sexual Politics." *GLQ: A Journal of Lesbian and Gay Studies* 10(4): 617–30.

McGuffey, Shawn, and Lindsay Rich. 1999. "Playing in the Gender Transgression Zone: Race, Class, and Hegemonic Masculinity in Middle Childhood." *Gender and Society* 13(5): 608–27.

McRobbie, Angela, and Sarah Thornton. 1995. "Rethinking 'Moral Panic' for Multi-Mediated Social Worlds." *The British Journal of Sociology* 46(4): 559–74.

Meadow, Tey. 2018. *Trans Kids: Being Gendered in the Twenty-first Century*. Oakland: University of California Press.

Meiners, Erica R. 2011. "Ending the School-to-Prison Pipeline/Building Abolition Futures." *The Urban Review* 43(4): 547–65.

———. 2015. "Offending Children, Registering Sex." *Women's Studies Quarterly* 43(1&2): 246–63.

———. 2016. *For the Children? Protecting Innocence in a Carceral State*. Minneapolis: University of Minnesota Press.

Méndez, Xhercis. 2016. "Which Black Lives Matter? Gender, State-Sanctioned Violence, and 'My Brother's Keeper.'" *Radical History Review* 126: 96–105.

Mercer, Kobena. 1994. *Welcome to the Jungle: New Positions in Black Cultural Studies*. New York: Routledge.

Miller, Jacques-Alain. 1977–78. "Suture (Elements of the Logic of the Signifier)." *Screen* 18(4): 24–34.

Millett, Kate. 1970. *Sexual Politics*. Garden City, N.Y.: Doubleday.

Mitchell, Juliet. 1986. "Chapter Six." In *The Selected Melanie Klein*, 115–16. Harmondsworth, U.K.: Penguin Books.

Mock, Janet. 2014. *Redefining Realness: My Path to Womanhood, Identity, Love, and So Much More*. New York: Atria Books.

Mogul, Joey L., Andrea J. Ritchie, and Kay Whitlock. 2011. *Queer (In)Justice: The Criminalization of LGBT People in the United States*. Boston: Beacon Press.

Monahan, Kathryn, Susan VanDerhei, Jordan Bechtold, and Elizabeth Cauffman. 2014. "From the School Yard to the Squad Car: School Discipline, Truancy, and Arrest." *Journal of Youth and Adolescence* 43(7): 1110–22.

Moon, Michael. 1998. *A Small Boy and Others: Imitation and Initiation in American Culture*. Durham, N.C.: Duke University Press.

Moraga, Cherríe, and Gloria Anzaldúa, eds. 1981. *This Bridge Called My Back: Writings by Radical Women of Color*. New York: Kitchen Table and Women of Color Press.

Morel, Geneviève. 2000. *Ambigüedades sexuales: Sexuación y psicosis* (Sexual ambiguities: sexuation and psychosis). Buenos Aires: Manantial.

Morgan, Betsy Levonian. 1998. "A Three Generational Study of Tomboy Behavior." *Sex Roles* 39(9/10): 787–800.

Morgenstern, Naomi. 2018. *Wild Child: Intensive Parenting and Posthumanist Ethics*. Minneapolis: University of Minnesota Press.

Morris, Jan. 1974. *Conundrum*. London: Faber and Faber.

Moynihan, Daniel P. 1965. "The Negro Family: The Case for National Action." *U.S. Department of Labor*. Washington, D.C.

MSNBC. 2012. "Trayvon Martin Was Suspended Three Times from School." *MSNBC*, March 26. http://usnews.nbcnews.com/_news/2012/03/26/ 10872124-trayvon-martin-was-suspended-three-times-from-school.

Mukahhal, Alaa. 2011. "Because We Are Human and We Demand Nothing Less." *Organized Communities against Deportations*, January 15. http:// organizedcommunities.org/because-we-are-human-and-we-demand -nothing-less/.

Mulvey, Laura. 1975. "Visual Pleasure and Narrative Cinema." *Screen* 16(3): 6–18.

Muncie, John, Gordon Hughes, and Eugene McLaughlin, eds. 2002. *Youth Justice: Critical Readings*. London: Sage.

Muñoz, José Esteban. 1999. *Disidentifications: Queers of Color and the Performance of Politics*. Minneapolis: University of Minnesota Press.

———. 2009. *Cruising Utopia: The Then and There of Queer Futurity*. New York: New York University Press.

Murray, Rebecca. n.d. "Writer/Director Todd Solondz Discusses 'Palindromes': Todd Solondz on the Origin of 'Palindromes' and Casting Ellen Barkin." *About Entertainment*. http://movies.about.com/od/palindromes/a/ palints040605.htm.

Nandy, Ashis. 1984. "Reconstructing Childhood: A Critique of the Ideology of Adulthood." *Alternatives* 10(3): 359–75.

Naylor, Brian. 2010. "Democrats Push DREAM Act; Critics Call It Amnesty." *NPR*, December 6. https://www.npr.org/2010/12/06/131796206/ democrats-push-dream-act-critics-call-it-amnesty.

Ngai, Mae M. 2014. *Impossible Subjects: Illegal Aliens and the Making of Modern America*. Princeton, N.J.: Princeton University Press.

Nguyen, Athena. 2008. "Patriarchy, Power, and Female Masculinity." *Journal of Homosexuality* 55(4): 665–83.

Nguyen, Mimi Thi. 2015. "The Hoodie as Sign, Screen, Expectation, and Force." *Signs* 40(4): 791–816.

Nicholls, Walter J. 2013. *The DREAMers: How the Undocumented Youth Movement Transformed the Immigrant Rights Debate*. Stanford, Calif.: Stanford University Press.

Noble, Safiya Umoja. 2014. "Teaching Trayvon: Race, Media, and the Politics of Spectacle." *The Black Scholar* 44(1): 12–29.

New York Civil Liberties Union. 2011. *Stop and Frisk: Report on 2011 Findings.* New York: NYCLU.

Office of the Press Secretary. 2010. "Remarks by the President on Comprehensive Immigration Reform." The White House, July 1. Washington D.C. https://obamawhitehouse.archives.gov/realitycheck/the-press-office/remarks-president-comprehensive-immigration-reform.

Office of the Press Secretary. 2013. "Remarks by the President on Trayvon Martin." The White House, July 19. Washington, D.C. https://www.whitehouse.gov/the-press-office/2013/07/19/remarks-president-trayvon-martin.

Ohi, Kevin. 2004. "Narrating the Child's Queerness in *What Maisie Knew.*" In *Curiouser: On the Queerness of Children,* ed. Steven Bruhm and Natasha Hurley, 81–106. Minneapolis: University of Minnesota Press.

Olivas, Michael A. 2012. *No Undocumented Child Left Behind:* Plyler v. Doe *and the Education of Undocumented Schoolchildren.* New York: New York University Press.

Our Revolution. 2017. "Two OurRev staff with DACA were arrested today outside of Trump Tower in civil disobedience: 'We're not going to back down.' #DefendDACA." *Twitter.* https://twitter.com/OurRevolution/status/905152644855029761.

Owen, Gabrielle. 2019. "Adolescence, Blackness, and the Politics of Respectability in *Monster* and *The Hate U Give.*" *The Lion and the Unicorn* 43(2): 236–60.

Paechter, Carrie. 2006. "Masculine Femininities/Feminine Masculinities: Power, Identities, and Gender." *Gender and Education* 18(3): 253–63.

———. 2010. "Tomboys and Girly-Girls: Embodied Femininities in Primary Schools." *Discourse* 31(2): 221–35.

Palladino, Grace. 1996. *Teenagers: An American History.* New York: Basic Books.

Pande, Ishita. 2012. "Coming of Age: Law, Sex, and Childhood in Late Colonial India." *Gender and History* 24(1): 205–30.

Park, Haeyoun, and Iaryna Mykhalyshym. 2016. "LGBT People Are More Likely to Be Targets of Hate Crimes Than Any Other Minority Group." *New York Times,* June 16. https://www.nytimes.com/interactive/2016/06/16/us/hate-crimes-against-lgbt.html.

Patterson, Jodie. 2019. *The Bold World: A Memoir of Family and Transformation*. New York: Ballantine Books.

Payne, Ed, and Ashley Fantz. 2013. "Parents of Transgender First-Grader File Discrimination Complaint." *CNN*, February 28. http://edition.cnn .com/2013/02/27/us/colorado-transgender-girl-school/index.html.

Pew Research. 2012a. "How Blogs, Twitter, and Mainstream Media Have Handled the Trayvon Martin Case." *Pew Research Center*, March 30. https:// www.journalism.org/2012/03/30/special-report-how-blogs-twitter-and -mainstream-media-have-handled-trayvon-m/.

———. 2012b. "News about Trayvon Martin Case Still Top Story." *Pew Research Center*, April 24. http://www.people-press.org/2012/04/24/news -about-trayvon-martin-case-still-top-story/.

Pineda, Richard D., and Stacey K. Sowards. 2007. "Flag Waving as Visual Argument: 2006 Immigration Demonstrations and Cultural Citizenship." *Argumentation and Advocacy* 43(3–4): 164–74.

Plemons, Eric. 2017. *The Look of a Woman: Facial Feminization Surgery and the Aims of Trans-Medicine*. Durham, N.C.: Duke University Press.

Plyler v. Doe. 1982. 457 U.S. 202.

Pollock, Linda. 1983. *Forgotten Children: Parent–Child Relations from 1500 to 1900*. Cambridge: Cambridge University Press.

Porta, Carolyn M., Amy L. Gower, Christopher J. Mehus, Xiaohui Yu, Elizabeth M. Saewyc, and Marla E. Eisenberg. 2017. "'Kicked Out': LGBTQ Youths' Bathroom Experiences and Preferences." *Journal of Adolescence* 56: 107–12.

Povinelli, Elizabeth. 2015. "Transgender Creeks and the Three Figures of Power in Late Liberalism." *Differences* 26(1): 168–87.

Preston, Julia. 2007a. "In Increments, Senate Revisits Immigration Bill." *New York Times*, August 3. https://www.nytimes.com/2007/08/03/ washington/03immig.html.

———. 2007b. "Measure Would Offer Legal Status to Illegal Immigrant Students." *New York Times*, September 20. https://www.nytimes.com/2007/ 09/20/us/20immig.html.

Priestley, Mark. 1998. "Childhood Disability and Disabled Childhoods: Agendas for Research." *Childhood* 5(2): 207–23.

Probyn, Elspeth. 1995. "Suspended Beginnings: Of Childhood and Nostalgia." *GLQ: A Journal of Lesbian and Gay Studies* 2: 439–65.

Prosser, Jay. 1995. "No Place like Home: The Transgendered Narrative of Leslie Feinberg's *Stone Butch Blues*." *Modern Fiction Studies* 41(3): 483–514.

———. 1998. *Second Skins: The Body Narratives of Transsexuality*. New York: Columbia University Press.

Puar, Jasbir. 2007. *Terrorist Assemblages: Homonationalism in Queer Times*. Durham, N.C.: Duke University Press.

Randolph, Kaila C. 2017. "Executive Order 13769 and America's Longstanding Practice of Institutionalized Racial Discrimination towards Refugees and Asylum Seekers." *Stetson Law Review* 47: 1–43.

Rankine, Claudia. 2015. *Citizen: An American Lyric*. Harmondsworth, U.K.: Penguin.

———. 2019. "I Wanted to Know What White Men Thought about Their Privilege. So I Asked." *New York Times*, July 17. https://www.nytimes.com/2019/07/17/magazine/white-men-privilege.html.

Rathod, Jayesh. 2015. "Crimmigration Creep: Reframing Executive Action on Immigration." *Washburn Law Journal* 55: 173–88.

Rattan, Aneeta, Cynthia Levine, Carol Dweck, and Jennifer Eberhardt. 2012. "Race and the Fragility of the Legal Distinction between Juveniles and Adults." *PLoS ONE* 7(5): 1–5.

Reay, Diane. 2001. "'Spice Girls,' 'Nice Girls,' 'Girlies,' and 'Tomboys': Gender Discourses, Girls' Cultures, and Femininities in the Primary Classroom." *Gender and Education* 13(2): 153–66.

Rich, Adrienne. 1984. "Notes towards a Politics of Location." In *Blood, Bread, and Poetry: Selected Prose 1979–1985*. London: Little Brown and Company.

Richards, Renee. 1983. *Second Serve: The Renee Richards Story*. New York: Random House.

Rider, G. Nicole, Barbara J. McMorris, Amy L. Gower, Eli Coleman, and Marla E. Eisenberg. 2018. "Health and Care Utilization of Transgender and Gender Nonconforming Youth: A Population-Based Study." *Pediatrics* 141(3): e20171683.

Rifkin, Mark. 2019. *Fictions of Land and Flesh: Blackness, Indigeneity, Speculation*. Durham, N.C.: Duke University Press.

Ríos-Rojas, Anne, and Mark Stern. 2018. "Do 'Undocumented Aliens' Dream of Neoliberal Sheep? Conditional DREAMing and Decolonial Imaginaries." *Equity and Excellence in Education* 51(1): 92–106.

Roberts, Dorothy. 1997. *Killing the Black Body: Race, Reproduction, and the Meaning of Liberty*. New York: Pantheon Books.

Robles, Frances. 2012. "Multiple Suspensions Paint Complicated Portrait of Trayvon Martin." *Miami Herald,* March 26. http://www.palmbeachpost .com/news/news/state-regional/multiple-suspensions-paint-complicated -portrait—1/nLhx2/.

Rollo, Toby. 2018. "The Color of Childhood: The Role of the Child/Human Binary in the Production of Anti-Black Racism." *Journal of Black Studies* 49(4): 307–29.

Rose, Jacqueline. 1982. "Introduction—II." In *Feminine Sexuality: Jacques Lacan and the École Freudienne,* ed. Juliet Mitchell and Jacqueline Rose, trans. Jacqueline Rose, 27–57. Houndmills, U.K.: Macmillan Press.

———. 1984. *The Case of Peter Pan or the Impossibility of Children's Fiction*. London: Macmillan.

———. 2018. *Mothers: An Essay on Love and Cruelty*. London: Faber and Faber.

Rose, Jacqueline, and Catherine Malabou. 2016. "Sexual Difference and the Symbolic: What Future?" Audio podcast. Birkbeck Institute for the Humanities, London, June 14. Backdoor Broadcasting Company. backdoorbroadcasting.net/2016/06/sexual-difference-and-the-symbolic -what-future/.

Rubin, Gayle. 1975. "The Traffic in Women: Notes on the 'Political Economy' of Sex." In *Toward an Anthropology of Women,* ed. Rayna Reiter. New York: Monthly Review Press.

Rutherford, Erica. 1993. *Nine Lives: The Autobiography of Erica Rutherford*. Charlottetown, P.E.I.: Ragweed Press.

Ryan, William. 1970. *Blaming the Victim*. New York: Knopf Doubleday Publishing Group.

Sabatello, Maya. 2013. "Children with Disabilities: A Critical Appraisal." *The International Journal of Children's Rights* 21(3): 464–87.

Salamon, Gayle. 2018. *The Life and Death of Latisha King: A Critical Phenomenology of Transphobia*. New York: New York University Press.

Sanchez, Marcela. 2007. "Betwixt and Between the Dream." *Washington Post,* October 5. http://www.washingtonpost.com/wp-dyn/content/article/ 2007/10/04/AR2007100401181.html.

Sánchez-Eppler, Karen. 2005. *Dependent States: The Child's Part in Nineteenth-Century American Culture*. Chicago: University of Chicago Press.

Sanders, Katie. 2012. "A Real Photo of Trayvon Martin? Chain Email Makes False Claim." *PolitiFact,* July 17. http://www.politifact.com/florida/statements/2012/jul/17/chain-email/real-photo-trayvon-martin-chain-email-says-so/.

Savage, Jon. 2008. *Teenage: The Creation of Youth 1875–1945.* London: Pimlico.

Schippers, Mimi. 2007. "Recovering the Feminine Other: Masculinity, Femininity, and Gender Hegemony." *Theory and Society* 36(1): 85–102.

Sciamma, Céline. 2011. *Tomboy.* Hold Up Films.

———. 2007. *Water Lilies.* Balthazar Productions.

———. 2014. *Girlhood.* Hold Up Films.

Scott-Dixon, Krista, ed. 2006. *Trans/Forming Feminisms: Trans-Feminist Voices Speak Out.* Toronto: Sumach Press.

Sedgwick, Eve Kosofsky. 1990. *Between Men: English Literature and Male Homosocial Desire.* New York: Columbia University Press.

———. 1991. "How to Bring Your Kids Up Gay." *Social Text* 29: 18–27.

———. 2003. *Touching Feeling: Affect, Pedagogy, Performativity.* Durham, N.C.: Duke University Press.

Segal, Kim. 2012. "Protesters Declare 'I Am Trayvon Martin,' but Who Was He?" CNN, March 30. http://edition.cnn.com/2012/03/30/us/trayvon-martin-profile/index.html.

Seif, Hinda. 2014a. "'Layers of Humanity': Interview with Undocuqueer Artivist Julio Salgado." *Latino Studies* 12(2): 300–309.

———. 2014b. "'Coming Out of the Shadows' and 'Undocuqueer': Undocumented Immigrants Transforming Sexuality Discourse and Activism." *Journal of Language and Sexuality* 3(1): 87–120.

Serano, Julia. 2007. *Whipping Girl: A Transsexual Woman on Sexism and the Scapegoating of Femininity.* Berkeley, Calif.: Seal Press.

Severson, Kim. 2012. "For Skittles, Death Brings Both Profit and Risk." *New York Times,* March 28. http://www.nytimes.com/2012/03/29/us/skittles-sales-up-after-trayvon-martin-shooting.html.

Sheldon, Rebekah. 2016. *The Child to Come: Life after the Human Catastrophe.* Minneapolis: University of Minnesota Press.

Shore, Heather. 2002. "Reforming the Juvenile: Gender, Justice and the Child Criminal in Nineteenth-Century England." In *Youth Justice: Critical Readings,* edited by John Munice, Gordon Hughes, and Eugene McLaughlin, 159–72. London: Sage.

Silverman, Kaja. 1983. *The Subject of Semiotics.* Oxford: Oxford University Press.

———. 1989 "White Skin, Brown Masks: The Double Mimesis, or With Lawrence in Arabia." *Differences* 1(2): 3–54.

Smith, Karen. 2014. *The Government of Childhood: Discourse, Power, and Subjectivity.* London: Palgrave Macmillan.

Smith, Rogers, Desmond King, and Phillip Klinkner. 2011. "Challenging History: Barack Obama and American Racial Politics." *Daedalus* 140(2): 121–35.

Snorton, C. Riley. 2009. "'A New Hope': The Psychic Life of Passing." *Hypatia* 24(3): 77–92.

Solomon, Andrew. 2012. *Far from the Tree: Parents, Children, and the Search for Identity.* London: Scribner.

Solondz, Todd. 1995. *Welcome to the Dollhouse.* Suburban Pictures.

———. 1998. *Happiness.* Good Machine.

———. 2004. *Palindromes.* Extra Large Pictures.

———2009. *Life during Wartime.* Werc Werk Works.

Somerville, Siobhan. 2000. *Queering the Color Line: Race and the Invention of Homosexuality in American Culture.* Durham, N.C.: Duke University Press.

Spade, Dean. 2006. "Mutilating Gender." In *The Transgender Studies Reader,* ed. Susan Stryker and Stephen Whittle, 315–32. London: Routledge.

———. 2011. *Normal Life: Administrative Violence, Critical Trans Politics, and the Limits of Law.* Durham, N.C.: Duke University Press.

Spillers, Hortense. 1987. "Mama's Baby, Papa's Maybe: An American Grammar Book." *Diacritics* 17(2): 64–81.

———. 1996. " 'All the Things You Could Be by Now If Sigmund Freud's Wife Was Your Mother': Psychoanalysis and Race." *Critical Inquiry* 22: 710–34.

Spivak, Gayatri Chakravorty. 1988. "Can the Subaltern Speak?" In *Marxism and the Interpretation of Culture,* ed. Cary Nelson and Lawrence Grossberg, 271–313. Basingstoke, U.K.: Macmillan Education.

———. 1993. *Outside in the Teaching Machine.* London: Routledge.

———. 2004. "Righting Wrongs." *South Atlantic Quarterly* 103(2/3): 523–81.

Stacey, Jackie. 1994. *Star Gazing: Hollywood Cinema and Female Spectatorship.* London: Routledge.

Stanley, Eric and Nat Smith, eds. 2011. *Captive Genders: Trans Embodiment and the Prison Industrial Complex.* Oakland, Calif.: AK Press.

Stannard, David. 1974. "Death and the Puritan Child." *American Quarterly* 26: 456–76.

Steedman, Carolyn. 1992. *Past Tenses: Essays on Writing, Autobiography, and History, 1980–90.* London: Rivers Oram Press.

———. 1995. *Strange Dislocations: Childhood and the Idea of Human Interiority 1780–1930.* Cambridge, Mass.: Harvard University Press.

Steinmetz, Katy. 2014. "The Transgender Tipping Point." *TIME*, May 29. http://time.com/135480/transgender-tipping-point/.

Stocks, Jen. 2011. *I Am Jazz: A Family in Transition.* Figure 8 Films.

Stockton, Kathryn Bond. 2002. "Eve's Queer Child." In *Regarding Sedgwick: Essays on Queer Culture and Critical Theory,* ed. Stephen Barber and David Clark, 181–99. London: Routledge.

———. 2009. *The Queer Child, Or Growing Sideways in the Twentieth Century.* Durham, N.C.: Duke University Press.

———. 2016. "The Queer Child Now and Its Paradoxical Global Effects." *GLQ: A Journal of Lesbian and Gay Studies* 22(4): 505–39.

Stoetzler, Marcel, and Nira Yuval-Davis. 2002. "Standpoint Theory, Situated Knowledge and the Situated Imagination." *Feminist Theory* 3(3): 315–33.

Stoler, Ann Laura. 1995. *Race and the Education of Desire: Foucault's History of Sexuality and the Colonial Order of Things.* Durham, N.C.: Duke University Press.

Stowe, Harriet Beecher. 1852. *Uncle Tom's Cabin, Or, Life among the Lowly.* Bedford, Mass.: Applewood Books.

Stryker, Susan, and Talia M. Bettcher. 2016. "Introduction: Trans/Feminisms." *Transgender Studies Quarterly* 3(1–2): 5–14.

Stryker, Susan, Paisley Currah, and Lisa Jean Moore. 2008. "Introduction: Trans-, Trans, or Transgender?" *Women's Studies Quarterly* 36(3/4): 11–22.

Stumpf, Juliet. 2006. "The Crimmigration Crisis: Immigrants, Crime, and Sovereign Power." *American University Law Review* 56: 367–419.

Suárez-Orozco, Carola, Hee Jin Bang, and Ha Yeon Kim. 2011. "I Felt Like My Heart Was Staying Behind: Psychological Implications of Family Separations and Reunifications for Immigrant Youth." *Journal of Adolescent Research* 26(2): 222–57.

Suransky, Valerie Polakow. 1982. *The Erosion of Childhood.* Chicago and London: University of Chicago Press.

Tchen, John Kuo Wei, and Dylan Yeats, eds. 2014. *Yellow Peril! An Archive of Anti-Asian Fear.* London: Verso.

Texas Senate. 2016. *An Act relating to regulations and policies for entering or using a bathroom or changing facility; authorizing a civil penalty.* SB 6.

Thomas, Susan. 2011. "Race, Gender, and Welfare Reform: The Antinatalist Response." *Journal of Black Studies* 28(4): 419–46.

Thorne, Barrie. 1987. "Re-Visioning Women and Social Change: Where Are the Children?" *Gender and Society* 1(1): 85–109.

———. 1993. *Gender Play: Girls and Boys in School.* Newark, N.J.: Rutgers University Press.

TIME. 2014. "The 25 Most Influential Teens of 2014." *TIME,* October 13. http://time.com/3486048/most-influential-teens-2014/.

Tisdall, E. Kay M. 2012. "The Challenge and Challenging of Childhood Studies? Learning from Disability Studies and Research with Disabled Children." *Children and Society* 26(3): 181–91.

Tobia, Jacob. 2019. *Sissy: A Coming-of-Gender Story.* New York: Penguin Random House.

Tosh, Jemma. 2016. *Psychology and Gender Dysphoria: Feminist and Transgender Perspectives.* New York: Routledge.

Treacher, Amal. 2006. "Children's Imaginings and Narratives: Inhabiting Complexity." *Feminist Review* 82: 96–113.

Truitt, Jos. 2016. "Transgender People Are More Visible Than Ever: So Why Is There More Anti-Trans Legislation Than Ever, Too?" *The Nation,* March 4. https://www.thenation.com/article/transgender-people-are-more-visible-than-ever-so-why-is-there-more-anti-trans-legislation-than-ever-too/.

Tudor, Alyosxa. 2017. "Dimensions of Transnationalism." *Feminist Review* 117: 20–40.

———. 2018. "Cross-Fadings of Racialisation and Migratisation: The Postcolonial Turn in Western European Gender and Migration Studies." *Gender, Place, and Culture* 25(7): 1057–72.

———. 2019. "Im/Possibilities of Refusing and Choosing Gender." *Feminist Theory* 20(4): 361–80.

United States Department of Justice. 2015. *The Ferguson Report: Department of Justice Investigation of the Ferguson Police Department.* New York: The New Press.

Valentine, Gill. 1996. "Angels and Devils: Moral Landscapes of Childhood." *Environment and Planning D: Society and Space* 14(5): 581–99.

Vanita, Ruth, ed. 2002. *Queering India: Same-Sex Love and Eroticism in Indian Culture and Society.* New York: Routledge.

Vänskä, Annamari, ed. 2011a. "Child." *Lambda Nordica* 2–3.

———. 2011b. "Seducing children?" *Lambda Nordica* 2–3: 69–99.

Vargas, Jose Antonio. 2011. "My Life as an Undocumented Immigrant." *New York Times Magazine,* June 22. https://www.nytimes.com/2011/06/26/magazine/my-life-as-an-undocumented-immigrant.html.

———. 2012. "Not Legal Not Leaving." *TIME,* June 25. https://content.time.com/time/subscriber/article/0,33009,2117243-4,00.html.

Vaughn, Shemya, ed. 2016. *Transgender Youth: Perceptions, Media Influences, and Social Challenges.* Hauppauge, N.Y.: Nova Science Publishers.

Viego, Antonio. 2007. *Dead Subjects: Toward a Politics of Loss in Latino Studies.* Durham, N.C.: Duke University Press.

Vilchez, Jennifer. 2015. "The Controversy around Tomboy: The Aversion to Gender Theory in French Education and Culture." *КУЛТУРА / Culture.*

Waldron, Darren. 2013. "Embodying Gender Nonconformity in 'Girls': Céline Sciamma's *Tomboy.*" *L'Esprit Créateur* 53(1): 60–73.

Wallace, Jo-Ann. 1995. "Technologies of 'The Child': Towards a Theory of the Child-Subject." *Textual Practice* 9(2): 285–302.

Wallace, Kelly. 2015. "When Your Young Daughter Says 'I'm a Boy.'" CNN, June 2. http://edition.cnn.com/2015/03/18/living/feat-transgender-child-raising-ryland.

Warner, Michael, ed. 1993. *Fear of a Queer Planet: Queer Politics and Social Theory.* Minneapolis: University of Minnesota Press.

Weintrobe, Sally, ed. 2012. *Engaging with Climate Change: Psychoanalytic and Interdisciplinary Perspectives.* London: Routledge.

Whitelocks, Sadie, and Alex Greig. 2013. "Transgender Child, 6, Wins Civil Rights Case to Use the Girls' Restroom at School in Colorado." *Daily Mail,* June 24. http://www.dailymail.co.uk/news/article-2347149/Coy-Mathis-Transgender-child-6-Colorado-wins-civil-rights-case-use-girls-bathroom-school.html.

Whittington, Hillary. 2015. *Raising R Ryland: Our Story of Parenting a Transgender Child with No Strings Attached.* New York: HarperCollins.

Wiegman, Robyn. 2004. "Dear Ian." *Duke Journal of Gender Law and Policy* 11: 93–120.

———. 2012. *Object Lessons.* Durham, N.C.: Duke University Press.

———. 2014. "The Times We're In: Queer Feminist Criticism and the Reparative 'Turn.'" *Feminist Theory* 15(1): 4–25.

Wiegman, Robyn, and Elizabeth A Wilson, eds. 2015. "Queer Theory without Antinormativity." *Differences* 26(1).

Williams, Christan. 2016. "Radical Inclusion: Recounting the Trans Inclusive History of Radical Feminism." *Transgender Studies Quarterly* 3(1–2): 254–58.

Williams, Linda. 2001. *Playing the Race Card: Melodramas of Black and White from Uncle Tom to O. J. Simpson.* Princeton, N.J.: Princeton University Press.

Wills, Vanessa. 2013. "'What Are You Doing around Here?' Trayvon Martin and the Logic of Black Guilt." In *Pursuing Trayvon Martin: Historical Context and Contemporary Manifestations of Racial Dynamics,* ed. George Yancy and Janine Jones, 225–36. New York: Lexington Books.

Wilson, Adrian. 1980. "Infancy of History of Childhood: An Appraisal of Philippe Ariès." *History and Theory* 19: 132–53.

Wilson, Kalpana. 2011. "'Race,' Gender, and Neoliberalism: Changing Visual Representations in Development." *Third World Quarterly* 32(2): 315–31.

Winkler, Erin. 2012. *Learning Race, Learning Place: Shaping Racial Identities and Ideas in African-American Childhoods.* New Brunswick, N.J.: Rutgers University Press.

Yancy, George, and Janine Jones, eds. 2013. *Pursuing Trayvon Martin: Historical Context and Contemporary Manifestations of Racial Dynamics.* New York: Lexington Books.

Zaborskis, Mary. 2016. "Sexual Orphanings." *GLQ: A Journal of Lesbian and Gay Studies* 22(4): 605–28.

Zinn, Maxine Baca. 1989. "Family, Race, and Poverty in the Eighties." *Signs* 14(4): 856–74.

Index

Jacob Breslow is assistant professor of gender and sexuality at the London School of Economics.